Lost in Transition

Lost in Transition

The Dark Side of Emerging Adulthood

CHRISTIAN SMITH

WITH KARI CHRISTOFFERSEN,
HILARY DAVIDSON,
AND PATRICIA SNELL HERZOG

OXFORD
UNIVERSITY PRESS

OXFORD
UNIVERSITY PRESS

Oxford University Press, Inc., publishes works that further
Oxford University's objective of excellence
in research, scholarship, and education.

Oxford   New York
Auckland   Cape Town   Dar es Salaam   Hong Kong   Karachi
Kuala Lumpur   Madrid   Melbourne   Mexico City   Nairobi
New Delhi   Shanghai   Taipei   Toronto

With offices in
Argentina   Austria   Brazil   Chile   Czech Republic   France   Greece
Guatemala   Hungary   Italy   Japan   Poland   Portugal   Singapore
South Korea   Switzerland   Thailand   Turkey   Ukraine   Vietnam

Copyright © 2011 by Oxford University Press, Inc.

Published by Oxford University Press, Inc.
198 Madison Avenue, New York, NY 10016

www.oup.com

Library of Congress Cataloging-in-Publication Data
Smith, Christian, 1960–
Lost in transition : the dark side of emerging adulthood / Christian Smith ;
with Kari Christoffersen, Hilary Davidson,
and Patricia Snell Herzog.
p. cm.
ISBN 978-0-19-982802-9
1. Young adults—United States—Attitudes.
2. Young adults—United States—Social life and customs—21st century.
3. Young adults—United States—Conduct of life.
I. Christoffersen, Kari Marie. II. Davidson, Hilary.
III. Herzog, Patricia Snell. IV. Title.
HQ799.7.S65   2011
305.2420973′09051—dc22   2010052036

3 5 7 9 8 6 4 2

Printed in the United States of America
on acid-free paper

CONTENTS

Lost in Transition

Introduction

This book is about the lives of 18- to 23-year-old Americans, who we call "emerging adults." We do not pretend to present here a comprehensive view—the complete picture—of emerging adult life. We are focused on the darker side of emerging adulthood.[1]

It is true that there is also a bright side. Some of the lives of emerging adults are full of fun, freedom, new growth, and promising opportunities. There is much good in and about emerging adult life. And many emerging adults we have studied are interesting, creative, and sometimes very impressive people. But the happy part of emerging adulthood is already well documented and only part of the story.[2] There is a dark side as well. We think the dark side deserves more attention. It is of course more enjoyable and reassuring to focus on what is fun and happy and good in life. But at some point that becomes unrealistic, one-dimensional, even fake. If we care to know more of the fullness of the truth about emerging adults, we need to attend also to their mistakes and losses, trials and grief, confusions and misguided living. Those aspects of emerging adult life are what this book is about.

The story of this book points to one conclusion and raises some questions. The conclusion is that—notwithstanding all that is genuinely good in emerging adulthood—emerging adult life in the United States today is beset with real problems, in some cases troubling and even heartbreaking problems. Arriving at that conclusion will involve our describing some key parts of the outlooks, experiences, and practices in emerging adult life today. What we describe comes from what we heard in the course of interviewing hundreds of emerging adults in a national research project on American youth. By our reckoning, much of what we describe damages people, relationships, a sense of a richer purpose in life, a rational social order, and perhaps even the earth's environment. We think these problems are worth describing, pondering, and discussing.

Following the recognition of those problems come these questions: Why those problems? Where do they come from? How do we explain them? What social or cultural forces perpetuate them? Why do or must emerging adults live with them? Answering these questions will shift us from description to explanation, from reporting to analysis. Our answers will not be total or exhaustive. But we hope they will illuminate and spur helpful thought, discussion, and more study.

Our motive for focusing on the dark side of emerging adulthood is not to obsess about the negative for its own sake, nor to sound some kind of alarmist knell of cultural doom. Our aim, rather, is to expand our understanding of emerging adulthood, as a means to help reflect on growing up in the United States today, on life in our society, and on American culture more generally. We think our story will give emerging adults and others who care for and about them reasons to reflect on and talk fruitfully about emerging adult life. Ideally, we hope that what we say here might contribute to the reconsideration of some of our cultural priorities and practices in ways that might enhance the well-being of emerging adults. Before we get there, however, our task is simply to provide some description and analysis of some of the less admirable, more troubling parts of emerging adulthood.

The Sociological Imagination for the Common Good

The reader may already be asking: *what kind of book is this?* Is it scientific sociology or moral or cultural criticism, or something else? The answer is that it is a particular kind of sociology, conducted, we hope, to promote the common good. It is scholarship that employs what our discipline calls "the sociological imagination" to engage in social and cultural criticism and even moral argument. Our purpose is to serve the good of people by educating readers in sociological ways of understanding and encouraging public discussions about problems we see in our own culture and society.

What then is *the sociological imagination*? It is a particular viewpoint, a perspective that teaches us to ask certain kinds of questions and looks for specific types of answers. The sociological imagination is a distinct way of seeing and thinking that takes the influence of human *social* life very seriously, in order to understand and explain the world, our lives, and the lives of others more fully. The sociological imagination seeks to understand the *personal experience of individual people*, on the one hand, and *larger social and cultural trends, forces, and powers*, on the other, by *explaining each in terms of the other*. The larger social world, it recognizes, is constructed and shaped by all of the life activities of its people. That part is not hard to grasp. But the sociological imagination additionally helps us to see that the experiences and outcomes of people's lives are also powerfully shaped by the trends, forces, and powers of larger social institutions and cultural meaning systems.

People, of course, do a lot to shape their own personal lives. But they also always do so in the context of larger social and cultural realities that influence and govern their lives. So, sociology tells us, if we really want to understand and explain people, we need to also understand the larger social and cultural contexts that influence them. Focusing on individual psychology or personalities will not be enough. Understanding and explaining people in this sociological way draws upon a "social logic," or *socio-logic*, that expands our field of vision and increases our power for better comprehending life and the world around us. That is the promise of the sociological imagination.[3] We commend it to readers and hope to demonstrate its payoffs in the chapters that follow.

To be more specific, this book is about better understanding the lives of 18- to 23-year-old Americans. But we do not simply *describe* their lives. We also seek to *understand* and *explain* their lives sociologically, by viewing them in the larger context of the culture and society in which they are lived. We argue that that larger social and cultural context powerfully influences the ideas, experiences, and outcomes of their lives. The following chapters describe the ideas and behaviors of 18- to 23-year-old Americans concerning morality, sex, consumerism, alcohol and drugs, and civic and political engagement. But to better understand and explain those ideas and behaviors, we open up our analysis to look at how different social institutions and forces help generate and promote them. We will examine, for example, the powerful influence of the objective life-course phase known as emerging adulthood on people's personal expectations, beliefs, and behaviors. We will also consider the relationship between America's pervasive mass-consumer economic system and how 18- to 23-year-olds think and act when it comes to seemingly unrelated matters like partying, moral reasoning, and religious faith. How, you may ask, does the economy relate to things like alcohol intoxication? Read on and see. In the chapters ahead we also consider how many other social institutions, cultural trends, and technological developments shape the lives of 18- to 23-year-olds in ways that they are often not even aware of. Included in these are mass public schooling, the digital-communications revolution, colleges and universities, sociocultural pluralism, the mass media, political gridlock, socioeconomic inequality, the sexual revolution, and postmodernism. By helping readers see the connections between these (usually seemingly unrelated) social and cultural forces and the personal, often private, lives of 18- to 23-year-olds, we hope to cultivate in readers the kind of "sociological imagination" described above.

But what about this book being concerned with cultural criticism, moral argument, and people's good? Is that really sociology? The mainstream of American sociology follows one of its founding fathers, Max Weber, by insisting that sociology should be "value free."[4] We understand that approach and affirm much that we consider good in what it tries to accomplish. But ultimately we think it may not really be consistently possible; in any case, we think it need not be the only way to conduct good sociology. In contrast to that "Weberian" view, we take what some have labeled a more "Durkheimian" approach—that is, a view following some of the thinking of another early sociologist, Émile Durkheim.[5] Following numerous other contemporary sociologists of note,[6] we proceed here in the belief that sociological work need not always be value free (even if it perhaps sometimes can be), that it can (and usually does, more or less overtly) take stands on moral issues. We do not assume that our position in what follows will be self-evident and universally shared (what would be the point of publishing that?). But neither do we think that the values and moral arguments that define this book and the probable lack of consensus about them prevent it from being genuine sociology. Think of this book, then, as offering a kind of "critical, public sociology."[7]

Framing the Discussion

Adults in American culture routinely take one of two different attitudes about "kids these days," both of which we think are unhelpful. The first attitude we might call the "Chicken Little" approach. This outlook is essentially one of *fear*—that "the sky is falling," when in fact the sky is probably either not falling or else has been falling for most of human history. People with this attitude are anxious that all that was good in the supposed golden days of yore is now going down the drain. They fear that something decisive has recently happened that is uniquely corrupting youth today. Things are very bad and getting worse. People who are ordinarily called conservatives often tend toward this kind of view.

The second common adult attitude toward "kids these days" we might call the "nothing new under the sun" approach. This outlook is essentially one of *complacency*—a bemused dismissal of any concern about troubles in the lives of youth, when in fact there may well be real troubles, grief, destruction, and waste that deserve addressing. "They'll grow out of it," this attitude says, glibly. "Boys will be boys," it chuckles with a wink and a wave of a hand. "It was no different when I was young" (this last phrase being a baby-boomer favorite). And so on. People who are ordinarily called liberals often tend toward this kind of view.

Adults need to engage emerging adults today with neither fear nor complacency. Both of those reactions spring from outlooks that are simplistic and counterproductive. They usually do more to confirm the political and moral ideologies of the adults who hold them than to take young people seriously on their own terms and consider what might actually be good and bad for them.

The truth is neither that the sky is falling nor that there is nothing to be concerned about in the lives of emerging adults. There are both good things to appreciate and problems to consider in the lives of young people today. On the good side, for example, recent decades have seen declines in the rates of teen pregnancies and abortions.[8] The proportion of youth starting and finishing college has increased over the years.[9] And youth today as a whole are observably less prejudiced against people of other races and ethnicities than were those of earlier generations.[10] We think these things are good and worth recognizing and affirming.

But such positives are only part of the larger, more complex reality. There is, again, also a dark side that shadows the lives of many emerging adults today. That dark side should, in our view, be named and taken seriously. Dismissing it as "nothing new" is, we think, lazy, apathetic, and mindless. That attitude says, "Don't bother me with the troubles, grief, or misguided lives of young people. They either don't matter or there's nothing we can do about it." We disagree.

The better attitude for adults to take toward "kids these days," we think, is something more like "realistic care." This attitude is realistic not in the sense of being jaded or holding low expectations. It is realistic, first, in actually being informed by the facts of empirical reality, rather than personal memories or simplistic, prefabricated, ideological narratives of either conservative or liberal bents which distort reality to fit larger interests. It is also realistic in that it does not expect ordinary human beings to be angels, even though it expects people to try to lead good lives. And it is realistic in acknowledging not only the resilience with which people can often survive and recover from problems in life but also the deep and lasting damage, loss, and suffering that can result from "the way kids are." It is often *not* the case that "they'll just grow out of it." We need to be more realistic than that.

This approach is also "caring." Teenagers and emerging adults desperately need other mature and concerned adults who genuinely care about and for them. Young people need to be loved, to put it as plainly as possible. They need to be engaged, challenged, mentored, and enjoyed. They, like every human being, need to be appropriately cared for, no matter how autonomous and self-sufficient they may think they are. The spirit in which this book is written, then, is not one of fear or complacency but instead what we hope is realistic care.

One other clarification is necessary. In the course of writing this book, one of the sentiments we encountered from others interested in it was something like this: "So emerging adults get drunk and do drugs. Big deal. That's nothing new. Young people today probably get drunk and stoned less than my generation did in our day" (the baby boomers strike again). In case any readers find themselves having similar reactions, let us clarify our position in response. We are less interested here in relative historical change over time than in the reality and meaning of the absolute facts today. We frankly do not ultimately care what former generations did or did not do that might not have been good. We care about emerging adults *today*, what *they* believe, think, and do, and what of significance that may tell us. If something that one thinks is a problem is happening in the present, it may help to put it into historical perspective. But that alone does not put an end to the matter. In the end what matters is whether or not something problematic is happening now and how to respond to it. So we are less interested in questions like "Do emerging adults today have fewer or more problems with intoxication than those in the past?" and more interested in questions like "Why do so many emerging adults today feel such a need to become intoxicated?" Both are legitimate questions. But the second is what interests us here.

More generally, this book is about the fact that very many emerging adults today suffer from what we think are significant problems—troubles they have because of larger problems in the culture and society in which they have been raised. We think we should learn from that. And we think we as a society, as responsible adults, might be able to do something about that. That is our concern.

Naming What's Good

There is no way to write a book like this—or nearly any book, for that matter—without some notion of "the good" informing it one way or another. As noted above, many in the social sciences like to think of themselves as "value neutral." We don't particularly believe in that. We *do* believe that social science should do its best to avoid distorting biases, to prevent ideologies from skewing its findings, in order in the end to describe and explain what is true about what is real in social life. But note that that depends not on "value neutrality" but on its *opposite*: on value *commitments* to truth, scientific integrity, accountability, and so on. Those are nothing if not values driven by beliefs in what is good. Good science is thus always based not on bracketing or setting aside particular human notions of what is good, but rather on an absolute commitment to particular goods, like telling the truth, being willing to be shown to be wrong, etcetera.

So, not only do we in this book not try to hide our ideas about what is good, we unapologetically state them in black and white for all to inspect. We think it can only help social science and American society more broadly to be more straightforward about its beliefs about the good in human life—even if doing so forces us to learn how to argue better about them. So here goes.

We think it is good for people to be able to think coherently about moral beliefs and problems, and to explain why they believe whatever they do believe. We do not think people need to become moral philosophers. But we think it is good for people to be able to understand different moral positions, to consider how different assumptions shape moral beliefs, to think out some of the more obvious logical implications of taking a certain position. We think it is good for people to be able to carry on a basic, constructive discussion about moral differences with other people who disagree. We think these are especially important for people living in a culturally, religiously, and morally pluralistic society like the United States. And almost no emerging adult today is able to do much of that, as we show below. We think that is a problem.

We also think it is good for people to understand and embrace values and purposes in life that transcend the mass-consumerist acquisition of material belongings. There is a lot of good in material prosperity. But we think there are many human values and goods that are not exhausted by materialistic consumption and financial security. Call us old fashioned or part of a new wave. Either way, we think it is good for people to develop and enjoy loving relationships in community, to pursue spiritual truths and values as best as they can understand them, to learn contentment and generosity, to spend themselves in service of the well-being of other people. Many emerging adults are oblivious to these other kinds of human goods, as we also show below, focusing almost exclusively on materialistic consumption and financial security as the guiding stars of their lives. We think that too is a problem.

We think it is good to avoid a lifestyle of routine intoxication. We are not teetotalers. We think it is fine for emerging adults to drink alcohol in safe and healthy ways. We are very open to lowering the legal drinking age in the United States. Most of us are open to the legalization of marijuana. However, we also think that in most cases serious intoxication by alcohol and drugs is bad—especially for those emerging adults who are developmentally immature (which includes very many) and when the intoxication is severe and frequent, not to mention habitual. It is an empirical fact that such intoxication is a key ingredient in the production of many bad outcomes in emerging adult life, from alcohol poisoning to date rape to drunk driving to accidental death. We personally know many people who have victimized themselves and others or who have been hurt or killed by others as a result of their indulging in intoxication. But the issue for us is not merely one of bodily health and safety. One also has to consider the motivational—one might even say "spiritual"—question of *why*? Why do people feel such a need to become intoxicated? What drives that? What is so wrong with nonintoxicated life? And what might that tell us more deeply about the emotional, relational, and psychological condition of emerging adults today? Or about American culture today? We think it is objectively good for people to consume alcohol in moderation. We think many nonprescription drugs—methamphetamines, cocaine, heroin, and so on—should never be consumed by anyone. Many American emerging adults have their "heads screwed on right" about this topic. But many others do not. Intoxications of all sorts are all too common. We find that troubling. We think it too is a problem.

We think that sex is an immensely powerful part of human life—with immense power for benefit or destruction—and so we believe that it is good for sex always to be treated with immense respect and care of a magnitude commensurate to its power. The issue is not about anyone enforcing a regime of sexual repression or prudery. The issue concerns what is truly good in human life and for human persons, what causes human flourishing and not harm, even in areas where that can be difficult to discern.[11] We think it is a matter of empirical fact that it is good for sexual intimacy to be protected within proper boundaries. We think sex that is genuinely good in human life demands relationships of trust and commitment, when it is part and parcel of the fullness of all other aspects of life—however difficult that might be to achieve in real life. We think the human good requires taking all of the possible consequences of sex seriously all along the way. We think it is good for people to protect their physical, mental, and emotional health in intimate relationships. We think the good of sex is ruined by exploitation, coercion, or pure self-gratification. The majority of American emerging adults seem to have little awareness of those understandings of sex and the good. We think that is a problem.

Finally, we think it is good for people to care about the larger social, cultural, institutional, and political world around them. It is of course a good thing to have intimate friends and to sustain a rich private life. But it is also good to spend time in public, to understand oneself as part of a civic order that needs continual regeneration. It is good to care about neighbors, fellow citizens, strangers, maybe even enemies. It is good to be civically involved in some way or other—or at least to wish one were more so. It is good to know one's neighbors, to have some sense of actually belonging in a particular neighborhood or community. It is good to be invested in the public institutions that in various ways serve the common good. It is good to be engaged in political matters, at least to try to be somewhat informed about them from different perspectives. It is good at least to sustain a real hope that the greater public, institutional world has some future worth investing in. But most emerging adults today— contrary to widespread popular perceptions and media reports—have little care about, investment in, or hope for the larger world around them. We think that is a real problem.

That is what we think is good in these areas of life. Therefore, when it comes to contemporary emerging adulthood, because we see significant deficits of the good in these areas, we see them as problems. Readers may of course fundamentally disagree with some or all of our beliefs about the good in human life, in which case, not a lot in this book will make sense to them. We would then think it good to have a good argument with those who disagree about what is good. Engaging our disagreements constructively would, in our view, be part of what is good in human life. But that would require a different focus and format altogether than this book allows. So, for present purposes, we must be content to state our approach, develop the implications, and see what that accomplishes.

It's the *Adult* World, Stupid

Another common attitude that American adults hold about young people—which we reject, just to be clear—is that whatever problems youth have are entirely *their* problems, unrelated to the adults around them. The assumption is that something particular about teenagers or young adults rains problems down on their own heads, problems for which they are entirely responsible, which older adults simply cannot comprehend or explain. The something may be "raging hormones." It might be their not yet properly wired brains. Or it could be simple immaturity, rebelliousness, or stupidity. Whatever the cause, the problem is clearly the young people's fault, this widespread view holds. The adults involved are of course innocent.

Having studied young Americans for a decade, however, we have clearly seen that, contrary to this well-worn cultural script, most of the problems in the lives of youth have their origins in the larger adult world into which the youth are being socialized. It might be the problems of the adults in their immediate lives—their parents, relatives, teachers, family friends, and so on. Or it might be the priorities, values, practices, and institutions of the larger adult world they inhabit—schools, mass media, shopping malls, advertising, and the like. But one way or another, adults and the adult world are almost always complicit in the troubles, suffering, and misguided living of youth, if not the direct source of them. The more adults can recognize and admit that fact, we think, the sooner we will be able to address some of young people's problems more constructively. Meanwhile, none of this book should be read as simply our carping about "emerging-adult problems." The undeniable reality—indeed a key point of this entire book—is that emerging adult problems are ultimately problems of our entire culture and society.

This position has analytical implications. For example, one crucial assumption we make about problems in emerging adult life is that they do not primarily reflect what sociologists call an "age effect." That means we do not think that the characteristics of emerging adulthood observed in the following chapters will dramatically change when emerging adults grow up and settle down into full adulthood. Some "surface" aspects of emerging adult problems will surely change. But we do not believe that the deeper factors behind the problems we address below will be significantly transformed just because 20-year-olds have become 30- and 40-year-olds. Rather, we assume, for what we think are good reasons, that there is more continuity than difference between emerging adult culture and American culture more generally.

This assumption is consistent with one of the major findings of our larger study, namely, that the lives and experiences of youth are great barometers of the condition of the adult world that is socializing them, into which they are being inducted. So if we see problems in emerging adult culture, with some exceptions, we do not expect them to simply change or disappear when those who inherit and sustain that culture settle down, have kids, buy houses, and become "real" adults. Again, we do not expect that emerging adults will somehow magically "grow out of" the kinds of cultural problems we describe in the chapters below and become different sorts of people with a very different kind of culture. If anything, we think that emerging adult life reflects like a mirror onto our larger American culture the true nature of its own controlling values, practices, self-understandings, and commitments.[12]

We actually suspect that this close connection between adult-world problems and evident troubles in the lives of young people—causal links that widely spread fault and responsibility for problems—are partly responsible for the popularity of the "Chicken Little" and "nothing new under the sun" attitudes we observed above. For both of them shift attention and responsibility away from the adults who hold them. In the "sky is falling" attitude, focus and blame are shifted to *someone else*—to liberals, secular humanists, the federal government, "the culture," Hollywood, feminists, the media, and so on. Whether or not there are elements of truth in such claims is not our interest here to judge. Our present point concerns the subtle shifting of blame. Rarely if ever do people warning of the sky falling recognize their *own* complicity or responsibility in helping it to fall. It's usually someone else's fault. If only "they" would stop being so stupid or malicious, then the world could get back to the good way we used to enjoy it. Wouldn't it be nice if it were that simple?

On the other hand, the complacent "nothing new" attitude also shifts responsibility for the problems that young people suffer. Rather than seeing that youth have real problems and then blaming someone else for them, however, this attitude takes the route of self-satisfied denial and simply asks, "So what's the problem? Big deal. There's nothing to fret about. All this is normal for kids. They'll recover. They'll outgrow it. Look at me. I was a typical kid and *I'm okay.*" That's the nub of it. I'm okay. We're okay. Because if we admitted that the problems of youth today are real and serious, then that implicates me and us—it means that *our* own values, priorities, commitments, and lifestyles when we were young and probably still today might have been and are problems. The "nothing new" attitude simply redefines problems out of existence, thereby eliminating the very possibility of any fault, responsibility, or—God forbid!—guilt. Ironically, then, on the surface, the "nothing new" attitude seems brutally honest, "worldly," and "realistic." In reality, insofar as it shifts responsibility as we've described, it depends upon subtle self-deceit, denial, and a forced naiveté about what is really good and bad for people.[13]

Another way to make the larger point: the issues we address in the chapters that follow should concern liberals, moderates, and conservatives alike, for both different and shared reasons. The problems we address do not concern political ideologies or social agendas nearly as much as basic human needs and goods. Our concerns deal with the real-life experiences of young American men and women from all kinds of backgrounds whose lives are far too often confused, disturbed, and sometimes badly damaged by some of the cultural and institutional features of emerging adulthood. The topic at hand is not some distant abstraction. We are talking about our own children, brothers, sisters, friends, neighbors, and maybe even perhaps you yourself. And that is too important to be ideological about.

The Coming of Emerging Adulthood

To get started, we need to understand what "emerging adulthood" is all about. In the last several decades, a number of macrosocial changes have combined to create a new phase in the American life course. Six have been particularly important. First is the dramatic growth of higher education. The GI Bill, changes in the American economy, and government subsidizing of community colleges and state universities led in the second half of the twentieth century to a dramatic rise in the number of high school graduates going on to college and university. More recently, many have felt pressured, in pursuit of the American dream, to add years of graduate-school education on top of their bachelor's degree. As a result, a huge proportion of American youth are no longer stopping school and beginning stable careers at age 18, but are extending their formal schooling well into their 20s. And those who are aiming to join America's professional and knowledge classes—those who most powerfully shape our culture and society—are continuing in graduate- and professional-school programs often up until their 30s.

A second and related social change crucial to the rise of emerging adulthood is the delay of marriage by American youth over the last decades. Between 1950 and 2006, the median age of first marriage for women rose from 20.3 to 25.9 years old. For men during that same time the median age rose from 22.8 to 27.5 years old. The sharpest increase for both took place after 1970.[14] Fifty or sixty years ago, many young people were anxious to get out of high school, marry, settle down, have children, and start a long-term career. But many youth today spend almost a decade between high school graduation and marriage exploring life's many options as singles, in unprecedented freedom.[15]

A third major social transformation contributing to the rise of emerging adulthood as a distinct life phase involves changes in the American and global economy that undermine stable, lifelong careers and replace them instead with careers with lower security, more frequent job changes, and an ongoing need for new training and education. Most young people today know they need to approach their careers with a variety of skills, maximal flexibility, and readiness to retool as needed. That itself pushes youth toward extended schooling, delayed marriage, and, arguably, a general psychological orientation toward maximizing options and postponing commitments. Far from being happy to graduate from high school and take the factory or office job their father or uncle arranged for them—a factory job that likely does not exist anymore—many youth today spend five to ten years experimenting with different job and career options before finally deciding on a long-term career direction.

Fourth, and partly as a response to all of the above, parents of today's youth, aware of the resources it often takes to succeed, seem increasingly willing to extend financial and other support to their children well into their 20s and per-haps early 30s. According to best estimates, American parents spend on their children an average of $38,340 per child in total material assistance (cash, housing, educational expenses, food, etc.) over the 17-year period between ages 18 and 34.[16] These resources help to subsidize emerging adults' freedom to take a good, long time before settling down into full adulthood (which is culturally defined by the end of schooling, a stable career, financial independence, and new family formation).

Fifth, beginning in the 1960s, numerous, mostly reliable technologies of birth control have become widely available and used by married and unmarried people alike. The development and introduction of "the pill" was especially important. Humans have attempted throughout history to control their fertility through various means. But the last five decades have witnessed major changes in the variety, reliability, ease, and accessibility of birth control methods. The cultural effect of this, among others, has been to disconnect sexual intercourse from procreation in the minds of many Americans. Before, having sex meant knowingly taking the risk of becoming a mother or father. After the 1960s, that connection faded, at least in the cultural imagination. Sex then increasingly came to be seen as a normal element of any close or perhaps even casual rela-tionship and had nothing to do with having a baby—serving, for many, as a kind of recreational activity. After the late 1970s and 1980s, sexually trans-mitted diseases such as AIDS and herpes became more widespread concerns. But these diseases focused attention on sexual "health" and "safety," not on the connection between sex and fertility. This effect of widespread birth control technologies has also helped to form the culture of emerging adulthood (and well beyond).

Finally, the 1980s and 1990s saw the widespread diffusion and powerful influence of the theories of poststructuralism and postmodernism in U.S. culture. These began as arcane academic theories among French literary critics, professors of linguistics and literature, and other scholars in the humanities. Soon, however, they spread and were popularized in most of the humanities and some of the social sciences in U.S. colleges and universities. All that belonged to "the modern" was condemned: epistemological foundations, certainty, reason, universalism, the self, authorial voice, the nation state, colonialism, the Word, etc. (and we think, for the better, in some ways). All that was thought to be postmodern was celebrated: uncertainty, difference, fluidity, ambiguity, multivocality, self-construction, changing identities, particularity, historical finitude, localism, audience reception, perspectivalism, and more. For reasons that would require another book to explain, somehow all of this high theory thus became democratized and vulgarized in U.S. culture. Simplified versions of Nietzsche, Foucault, and Derrida were now a driving influence evident on MTV and in high school "world cultures" classes. By the time it reached the American hoi polloi, postmodernism had become a simple-minded ideology presupposing the cultural construction of everything, individualistic subjectivism, soft ontological antirealism, and absolute moral relativism. All of this is very evident in emerging adult culture as well.

These six sociocultural transformations, together with others, have helped to dramatically alter the experience of American life between the ages of 18 and 30. Studies agree that the transition to adulthood today is more complex, disjointed, and confusing than it was in past decades. The steps through schooling, a first real job, marriage, and parenthood are simply less well organized and coherent today than they were in the past. At the same time, these years are marked by a historically unparalleled freedom to roam, experiment, learn, move on, and try again. What has emerged from this new situation has been variously labeled "extended adolescence," "youthhood," "adultolescence," "the twixter years," "young adulthood," the "twenty-somethings," and "emerging adulthood." We find the psychologist Jeffrey Arnett's argument persuasive that, of all of these labels, "emerging adulthood" is the most appropriate.[17] That is because, rather than viewing these years as simply the last hurrah of adolescence or an early stage of real adulthood, it recognizes the very unique characteristics of this new and particular phase of life.

The features marking this stage are intense identity exploration; instability; a focus on self; feelings of being in limbo, in transition, in between; and a sense of possibilities, opportunities, and unparalleled hope. These, of course, are also often accompanied—as we will see in this book—by large doses of transience, confusion, anxiety, self-obsession, melodrama, conflict, disappointment, and sometimes emotional devastation.[18] Many popular television shows of the last few decades—*It's Always Sunny in Philadelphia, Friends, Gossip Girl, Seinfeld*, various MTV "reality shows," and *Dawson's Creek*—reflect through the entertainment industry's lens the character and challenges of this recently developing, in-between stage of life. It all signifies something culturally big and serious.

To grasp the significance of emerging adulthood, it is necessary to realize that life stages are not immutable, natural phases of existence. Rather, they are cultural constructions that interact with biology and material production and are profoundly shaped by the social and institutional conditions that generate and sustain them. Thus, the words "teenager" and "adolescence" as representing a distinct stage of life were very much twentieth-century inventions, brought into existence by changes in mass education, child labor laws, urbanization and sub-urbanization, mass consumerism, and the media. Similarly, a new, distinct, and important stage in life—emerging adulthood, situated between the teenage years and full-fledged adulthood—has appeared in our culture in recent decades—reshaping the meaning of self, youth, relationships, and life commitments, as well as a variety of behaviors and dispositions among the young. As a result, life for many today between roughly 18 and 30 years old has morphed into an entirely different experience than that of previous generations.

A related note on terminology: in the scholarly literature, emerging adulthood refers to 18- to 29-year-olds. The sample of Americans that this book reports on, however, represents only the first half of emerging adulthood, ages 18 to 23. As a consequence, this book's cases, findings, and interpretations do not actually speak for or about all emerging adults in the United States today but rather those emerging adults in the early portion of this life-course stage. However, rather than consistently recognizing this qualification by adding another adjective to the front of every mention of emerging adult—such as "*new* emerging adult," and then perhaps using the clumsy acronym NEA for short—we will instead simply use the term "emerging adult." Readers should keep in mind throughout, however, that this is shorthand for the sake of convenience for just the first half of emerging adulthood. We do not expect that American 24- to 29-year-olds look or sound that much different, though more time and research will reveal whether this is so.[19]

A National Study of the Developing Lives of American Youth

How do we know what we know about emerging adult culture? We and our colleagues have been studying the emerging adults on whom this study is based since 2001, when our sample of youth was 13 to 17 years old. We first conducted a nationally representative telephone survey with a sample of 3,290

13- to 17-year-olds, and then personally interviewed 267 of them in 45 states around the country. In 2005, we conducted a second telephone survey with most of the same teen subjects and reinterviewed 122 of the same interview respondents. Throughout these years we continued systematically to stay in touch with and track as many of our study respondents as was humanly possible, and in 2007 and 2008 we conducted a third wave of survey and interview data collection with the same youth. This book is based primarily on 230 in-depth personal interviews conducted in our third wave of data collection in 2008 all around the United States.

This book examines our sample of youth at the third measured point of their life trajectories, who had by then grown up to be 18 to 23 years old.[20] They had passed beyond the high school era and were entering into emerging adulthood, striking out on their own, and encountering many new challenges and experiences. We want to know here what emerging adult life is like. What are the typical assumptions, beliefs, norms, values, hopes, worries, goals, relationships, patterns of speech, and life experiences that form the character of emerging adult culture? What are the established categories, expectations, explanations, and concerns that structure emerging adult culture and so form the lives of teenagers as they enter the emerging adult life-course phase? Answering such questions well is the central purpose of this book. Because our focus here is on culture, not measurable characteristics distributed in a population, we will draw almost exclusively upon our personal interview data, not our survey data.[21]

This book examines issues that affect the physical and mental health and safety of emerging adults. Some of these issues we say, without exaggeration, are matters of life and death. Readers should realize that the full implications of the issues addressed below are not adequately represented in the evidence presented, because some of the more extreme cases are missing due to death and institutionalization. That is, some of the worst effects of some of the problems examined in this book are not visible in our third-wave interview sample because those who might have told us about those effects have died from accidents and overdoses, committed suicide, or are in prison, residential rehabilitation programs, long-term hospitalization, or mental institutions. Because of the severity of some of the consequences of what we discuss below, we cannot represent the voices of those who, for instance, are in jail for killing other people in automobile accidents while driving drunk. We could not interview those who committed suicide as a result of depression, guilt, confusion, and lack of relational ties to adults who might have helped them. Anyone murdered in drug-related shootings has obviously been dropped from our sample. Those who may have declined to conduct a third interview with us because they do not want to have to talk about their embarrassing sexually transmitted infections and diseases also do not show up in our interview data.[22] Emerging adult alcoholics and addicts living in rehab centers we also could not interview. These represent a minority of our original sample, obviously, but in human terms they are of major signifi-cance.[23] What they represent should not be forgotten as we examine in the fol-lowing chapters the views of emerging adults who are still alive and are clean and healthy enough to continue to participate in our study.

One last thought: sociological analysis often involves analyzing differences in outcomes across race, ethnicity, social class, and gender. That is a valuable approach, one that could be applied to the questions raised in the following chapters. But for the purposes of this book, we focus primarily on emerging adult similarities—the assumptions, beliefs, values, and practices that most emerging adults seem to share in common. So we do not make much of the demographic differences between our interview respondents. We leave to future studies of these and similar data the question of what difference race, ethnicity, social class, gender, or other demographic variables might make when it comes to the matters discussed in this book.

That said, we do not wish to belabor this introduction but to get right into the substantive material of the following chapters. We have sought here simply to set the stage. The next six chapters explore in detail various parts of the life and cul-ture of emerging adulthood. We will develop some analysis and commentary throughout the following chapters and attempt to summarize our argument in the conclusion of this book. But first, the substantive chapters.

‖ 1 ‖

Morality Adrift

Who am I? ... To know who you are is to be oriented in moral space, a space in which questions arise about what is good and bad, what is worth doing and what not, what has meaning and importance to you. ... [Moral] orientation has two aspects; there are two ways that we can fail to have it. I can be ignorant of the lie of the land around me—not knowing the important locations which make it up or how they relate to each other. This ignorance can be cured with a good map. But then I can be lost in another way, if I don't know how to place myself on this map.

—Charles Taylor

We begin our exploration of some of the more unsettling aspects of contemporary emerging adult life by focusing on the question of morality, moral beliefs, and moral reasoning. How do emerging adults think about morality? How do they know what is moral? How do they make moral decisions? Where do they think moral rights and wrongs, goods and bads, even come from? What is the source or basis of morality? And how important is it to emerging adults to choose what is morally good? This chapter examines their answers to these and other questions and then ponders what it all may tell us not only about contemporary emerging adults' own moral imaginations but also about the larger culture and society that has formed them morally.

In our personal, in-depth interviews that we conducted with different kinds of emerging adults around the country, we spent a lot of time talking about morality. The questions we asked approached moral matters in many different ways.[1] We worked hard not to be leading in our questions. Most of our questions were very open-ended. But we also probed a lot and pressed their answers hard, to try to get to the bottom of their moral outlooks and actions. By the time we were done interviewing so many emerging adults, we felt confident that we had solidly grasped what they assume and perceive about moral goods and bads, how they think and feel about right and wrong. We also have some ideas about what it all likely means. The following pages describe what we found and what we make of it.

A Few Preliminaries

Readers should be aware of four important points heading into this chapter. The first is that emerging adult thinking about morality (as with most of the rest of adult Americans) is not particularly consistent, coherent, or articulate. It is not only that not many emerging adults are moral philosophers in the making; everyone knows that. But, in addition, not many of them have previously given much or any thought to many of the kinds of questions about morality that we asked. Thus, much of what they have to say about morality is peppered with uncertain phrases, such as "I don't know," "like," and "I guess."[2] That itself tells us something important. But it should also caution us not to set the bar too high for how much sense we should expect emerging adults to make for us when it comes to morality.

The second point relates to the first. We describe in what follows the approximate proportions of the emerging adults we interviewed (and sometimes surveyed) who expressed different, particular types of moral views. Readers should be aware, however, that in most cases these different views presented are not mutually exclusive. Several of the categories often overlap, so that the percentages do not always add to 100. That means that individual emerging adults can be included in many of the different types of viewpoints discussed below, including some that may not seem to fit together logically. That, again, partly reflects the frequent lack of consistency and coherence in emerging adult thinking about morality.

Third, we do not mean to imply in what follows that the kind of moral problems and issues that emerging adults evidently struggle to sort out are simple, easy, or obvious. They definitely are not. Moral issues can be very complicated. It often takes thoughtful instruction to see the pitfalls of different positions and to learn to work out the possible problematic implications of various moral accounts that may seem at first to make sense. Even then, it can be very tricky to hold convictions along with humility, to balance commitment with complexity, to sustain clarity amid diversity. We ourselves are, of course, not omniscient analysts. We have our own moral uncertainties and disagreements. Our intent in this chapter is simply to describe and help sort out some of what seem to us to be difficult problems besetting emerging adults today when it comes to moral reasoning.

Fourth, and related to the previous point, there are real reasons why emerging adults hold the views about morality that we are about to explore. The problem is not that emerging adults are as a group unintelligent. Neither, we think, is the problem simply that emerging adults are generally out to rationalize immoral behavior. Much of what we find problematic below is, we suspect, the outcome of two other things. The first is emerging adults' well-intentioned attempts to avoid potential problems that they know are real, such as coercive moral absolutism. In this sense, many of the ways that emerging adults often think poorly about moral issues are misguided attempts to achieve some good. That is worth recognizing. Second, we are convinced that most emerging adults have been poorly educated in how to think about moral issues well. The adult world that has socialized emerging adults as they have grown up has provided them with few useful intellectual tools for working on moral questions. As a result, we see in our interviews how unprepared they are for convincing and coherent moral reasoning.

Moral Individualism

The first thing that struck us in conducting interviews about moral issues with emerging adults is how strongly individualistic most of them are when it comes to morality. Six out of ten (60 percent) of the emerging adults we interviewed expressed a highly individualistic approach to morality. They said that morality is a personal choice, entirely a matter of individual decision. Moral rights and wrongs are essentially matters of individual opinion, in their view. Furthermore, the general approach associated with this outlook is not to judge anyone else on moral matters, since they are entitled to their own personal opinions, and not to let oneself be judged by anyone else. "It's personal," they typically say. "It's up to the individual. Who am I to say?"

Consider, for example, the following emerging adult, who explained why she does not cheat at the Ivy League university that she attends, but who also does not judge her peers who she says do cheat. "I don't know," she explains. "I guess that's a decision that everyone is entitled to make for themselves. I'm sort of a proponent of not telling other people what to do." She reports that some of her friends do things that give them unfair advantages in studying, which she considers cheating. "But that's their choice," she observes, "and I'm not going to tell them not to, though it's something that I wouldn't do. I guess it's a good example of like where no one else is hurt by it and you can get away with it." But doesn't that bother her? we ask. And why doesn't she cheat? "I don't know, I guess I want to be proud of my achievements and proud of what happened, and I want to feel like I had full control over the outcome, I think." Everyone for themselves, morally, in other words.

How then, given this moral individualism, do emerging adults explain why different individuals choose their own personal moral codes? Some cite the influence of parents. Some credit friends. Others say religion or the media. But many of those we interviewed who take a strong individualistic approach to morality believe that they have made up their own moral views. For example:

> I don't know. That's something I've asked myself a lot. I have no idea where I ever came up with the idea of like atheism, or where I came up with like just a lot of my views of right and wrong. Because a lot of ideas that I have now [about] right and wrong switch views entirely. I have never heard anybody else that has anything like it [my moral outlook] and I just don't know where it came from. Like just kinda things that I thought up, that I decided was right for me. So I don't know. I honestly don't. It just kinda came outta thin air.

We asked this young woman whether it is okay for a person to break moral rules if they can get away with it, if it works to their advantage. She replied that if the person did not think it was wrong, then they would by definition *not* be breaking a moral rule. It is "not really a moral rule then, is it?" she reasoned. "Because then, yeah, I mean, if you're okay with it morally, as long as you're not getting caught, then it's not really against your morals, is it?" She herself does not think stealing is "okay." But, she observed, "People do dumb stuff all the time. It doesn't make you a bad person per se, but like, yeah, actually, it [stealing] is a dumb thing to do." So morality is defined by each individual's personal standards. Some things are okay, other things are dumb. Whether anything is objectively morally right or wrong is unclear.

One reason some emerging adults appeal to the individual determination of morality seems to be the difficulty, and even impossibility, it appears to them, of trying to sort out difficult moral issues. It is hard enough, it seems, for one person to figure morality out for themselves. The idea of coming up with a moral system that will apply to everyone feels hopeless. Thus, one young man told us this: "Oh my goodness, these questions right now, these questions are really difficult! What makes something right? I mean for me I guess what makes something right is how I feel about it, but different people feel different ways, so I couldn't speak on behalf of anyone else as to what's right and what's wrong." Moral individualism thus relieves the burden of achieving social agreement on moral matters. In the end, moral claims can more easily take this kind of form: "Well, a lot of the times it's personal, it changes from person to person. What you may think is right may not necessarily be right for me, understand? So it's all individual."

A key conceptual confusion on this point revolves around ambiguities in the meaning of the statement that "an individual has to decide for themselves what is moral." We need to distinguish here between (a) moral claims (that are objectively true) being *embraced* subjectively by individuals through a process in which those individuals come to believe them, versus (b) moral claims (that may not be objectively true) taking on a quasi-true *status* for certain individuals as a result of those individuals believing them to be true. The distinction is subtle but crucial. The first, which assumes moral realism, has to do with the personal subjective appropriation of an objective moral fact. The second, which leans toward moral relativism, has to do with the subjective mental construction of what is then *treated* by someone as a moral fact, when it may not be one. An example of the first might be someone saying, "I have come to believe that it is truly wrong for people to cheat on exams." An example of the second might be someone saying, "Personally, for me, it would be wrong to cheat on an exam, that's how I look at it." In both cases, the people have "decided for themselves" what is morally right and wrong. But the two kinds of different decisions mean very different things. To say that "an individual has to decide for themselves what is moral" in the first sense is reasonable but trivial. It essentially says that for someone to believe something they have to believe it. Because emerging adults care about personal authenticity, sometimes this obviously true meaning leaks into their moral reasoning and makes the rhetoric of moral individualism seem sensible. By contrast, to say that "an individual has to decide for themselves what is moral" in the second sense is seriously problematic. It supposes and proposes (1) that no objective moral truths exist (or, if they do exist, humans cannot know them well), and therefore (2) that what people take to be moral truths are only socially constructed, historically and culturally relative ideas about morality, which they may believe are objectively true (and have good reason for doing so). Most of the moral individualism conveyed by emerging adults, we think, ends up expressing this second meaning. But few distinguish between the two meanings. And so the obvious truth of the first tends to make plausible what is in fact a radical, and we think wrong, view of morality suggested by the second meaning.

A strong theme among these moral individualists, as we noted above, is a belief that it is wrong for people to morally judge other people. Each person has to decide for themselves. Nobody else can tell anyone else what to think or do. One emerging adult, for instance, viewed people imposing their moral beliefs on others as actually "sick," observing, "Who am I to judge? is the real question that I would like to ask myself. You know, this person maybe has a different view and I'm essentially trying to not impose my views on other people." Why not? we asked. "I think that definitely, just from my own experience in life, would set me apart from other people. And I don't want to be an ideologue, I don't want to be a Christian missionary." If anything, this emerging adult sees not "immoral" people but people who make moral judgments of others as society's real problem: "You know, some of these people are so firm in their beliefs, I find that that's contributed to a lot of problems that we see today, and maybe not on such a minuscule scale. So maybe [my view is] just a commitment to not imposing your beliefs, or trying to dominate other people, or trying to control people. You know, that's very sick to me." To express one's own moral view is thus synonymous with dominating and controlling others, a kind of pathology that violates other people's dignity and rights.

Even emerging adults who themselves truly believe that other people's behaviors are definitely morally wrong also believe they should keep their views to themselves. When we asked one whether morality is simply whatever people think it is, whether her own moral views are entirely relative, she said, no, she believes in right and wrong. But, she added, "I would probably think in my head that they were wrong, but I wouldn't voice my opinion, because I'm not anyone to be able to judge anyone [else]. I don't really have a say." Why shouldn't anybody judge anybody else, we asked? Why should she not have a say? "I don't know," she answered, "because I just don't think that's right. I don't think it's anyone's place to judge anyone else." In this world of moral individualism, then, anyone can hold their own convictions about morality, but they also must keep those views private. Giving voice to one's own moral views is itself nearly immoral.

Part of what we think is the problem here is driven by ambiguities in meanings of the English word "judge." When it comes to moral matters, many Americans hear the words "to judge" or "judging" in the very negative sense of condemning, castigating, disparaging, or executing. To judge in this sense is to be self-righteously superior, hypercritical, and judgmental. And that itself seems morally wrong—we think it is wrong, in fact. Some may even call to mind the command of Jesus Christ, "Do not judge lest you be judged" (Matthew 7:1). But "to judge," of course, also has other important meanings. It can mean to assess, discern, estimate, appraise, weigh, evaluate, and critique. All of that can be done with great humility, openness, reciprocity, care, and even love for the idea or person being judged. Judging in this sense need not be self-righteous, condemning, triumphalist, or destructive. But making moral judgments in this second sense seems almost inconceivable to most emerging adults today. Here we are critiquing (i.e., judging) many emerging adults' seeming aversion to morally judging anything or anybody. Our critique, however, does not refer to the first meaning of judging above—we do not advocate emerging adults becoming more condemning, castigating, and disparaging of others. However, we *do* believe that emerging adults (and other Americans) need to improve their moral "judging" in the second sense of the word—developing better skills to intelligently assess, evaluate, and critique various moral beliefs and arguments that are claimed in the world. To try to avoid being *judgmental* is good, by our judgment. But to try for morally grounded reasons to avoid all assessment, evaluation, and criticism of every moral belief and behavior is not only ironic, it is impossible and self-defeating. The good we advocate is not to never judge anything or anyone. The good, rather, is to carefully and reasonably judge (weigh, appraise, discern, and perhaps appropriately critique) *all* things in life—*but always with* an awareness of one's own fallibility, openness to learning, care for others, and an interest in all moving closer to truth.[3] The problem is that not only do we hear precious little of that happening among emerging adults, but the very categories and structures of moral reasoning that predominate among them also seem to neutralize the very possibility of that ever happening.

Nonetheless, in the mind of many emerging adults, such a tolerant approach to moral pluralism should lead to a live-and-let-live lifestyle. Consider this case, for instance. When we asked one young woman about the moral difficulties created by moral relativism, she replied, "That's a good question. Yeah, this is where I get caught up. Oh my gosh. I guess I can understand there being rules that people follow." So where, we asked, do those moral rules come from? "I don't know," she said. "I feel like a lot of the rules are made by not just yourself, but influence from other people." But then she observed that different people and countries trying to impose their moral views on others creates conflict and wars. "The West versus the Middle East, our rules and views on life are just so different, so the problem is when you judge too quickly. I definitely know a lot of people who think America is the rule setter for the rest of the world, and I don't quite agree with that. At the same time I don't agree with people in the Middle East trying to say what their rules are." So how should people who disagree work out those differences? we asked. "I guess whatever, oh my gosh, whatever works for an individual is fine with me, as long as it's not affecting me in any way," she answered. "If you wanna make decisions and I might not agree with, that's fine," she continued, "go ahead and do what you need to do. Something that a lot of people might see as wrong, I see it as their choice, [if] I don't see it as something that affects me, I don't personally have a problem with it. But if it's something that's gonna affect me, then I guess it becomes a problem. Does that kinda make sense at all?"

Yet an equally logical outcome of moral individualism turned out to be a live-and-let-*die* lifestyle. That is because another theme in the morally individualistic outlook, especially as applied to possible moral obligations of people to help each other, is a belief that, since each person is responsible to take care of themselves, no person is particularly morally responsible to help other people in need. This exchange illustrates that logic well:

I: Do you think people have any moral responsibility or duty to help others or not?

R: Um, if others are your family and you see someone in danger, yeah. But I don't ever stop when I see somebody on the side of the road, so I guess somewhat sometimes. Maybe if someone is burning in the car, you should try and pull them out, but, no, not really.

I: Are there some other examples of ways we're obligated to help other people?

R: I mean, I really don't donate money, and even if I had money I don't know if I would, so.

I: What about helping people in general? Are we as a society obligated to do something?

R: I really don't think there're any good reasons, nope, nothing.

I: What if someone just wasn't interested in helping others? Would that be a problem or not?

R: No, I don't see why that would be a problem.

I: And why is that?

R: Because I mean is that really our duty, to help others? Is that what we're here for? I mean, they can help [themselves], if they're just getting by, doing what they do by themselves, then do they really need anyone else? So if they don't need help from anyone else, if somebody's asking for some other people all the time then they're not giving in return.

I: So if someone asks for help, we don't have an obligation to them?

R: Yeah, it's up to each individual, of course.

The major first point to understand in making sense of the moral reasoning of emerging adults, then, is that most do not appeal to a moral philosophy, tradition, or ethic as an external guide by which to think and live in moral terms. Few emerging adults even seem aware that such external, coherent approaches or resources for moral reasoning exist. Instead, for most emerging adults, the world consists of so many individuals, and each individual decides for themselves what is and isn't moral and immoral. Morality is ultimately a matter of personal opinion. It is wrong to render moral judgments of the moral beliefs and behaviors of other people—unless they directly harm you. Everyone should tolerate everyone else, take care of their own business, and hopefully get along.

At the end of this chapter we will discuss in greater depth the larger meaning of these observations. For now, we simply remind readers that there are reasons why emerging adults hold these views, which help make their thinking understandable, even if it is not tenable. One is that emerging adults have observed how purportedly universal, absolutist moral claims have led to horrific destruction and violence. The attacks of September 11, 2001—which took place when this cohort of youth was 11 to 16 years old—is an archetypical case in point. These emerging adults have also heard about the Crusades, Jim Crow America, the Holocaust, Communism's destruction of more than 100 million people, the Rwandan genocide, and so on. At the same time, these emerging adults have not been taught well how to differentiate between strong moral and religious claims that should be tolerated, if not respected, and those that deserve to be refuted, rejected, and opposed. Very few have been given the reasoning tools and skills to discern such important differences. As a result, many emerging adults simply end up trying to completely avoid making any strong moral claims themselves, as well as avoiding criticizing the moral views of others, as we will soon see. But what few of them seem to realize is that such a position makes it impossible to rationally evaluate or criticize *any* moral wrong, including the horrific destruction and violence that helped drive them to this tolerant position in the first place. That is a problem.

Moral Relativism

Does moral individualism automatically lead to moral relativism?[4] Not necessarily—at least in the sense that not all morally individualistic emerging adults subscribe to strong moral relativism. But many do. Moral individualism does seem to have strong intellectual affinities with moral relativism. And those who avoid moral individualism seem to have more to work with intellectually in order to resist relativism, if they in fact want to resist it. But emerging adult thinking about these matters is not often rigorous or coherent. Many hold views that philosophers would say do not rationally belong together. In any case, about three out of ten (30 percent) of the emerging adults we interviewed professed a belief in strong moral relativism. (In our nationally representative survey, 47 percent of American emerging adults agreed that "morals are relative, there are not definite rights and wrongs for everybody.")

Whether this is a high or low number depends on what one is expecting and what one considers problematic (some people, for example, think moral realists are the actual problem). However one judges it, these relativist emerging adults say that there are no real standards of right and wrong, that morality changes radically across history. They told us that different cultures believe and teach very different things morally, and that morality therefore is nothing more than subjective personal opinion or cultural consensus at any given point in time. What people take to be morality, in these emerging adults' view, has no real, objective, natural, or universal basis outside of people's heads. Morality is purely a social construction.[5]

In a discussion about the moral status of slavery, for instance, one emerging adult (who seemed unaware of the fact that there are still large numbers of slaves today around the world) argued, "Who am I to judge? I mean back then, if that's what you believed [that slavery is acceptable] and that's what happened, you know that's your right, if you thought it was right at that time. I wasn't alive then, so I can't really pass judgment on it, though in today's world I would think it'd be utterly ridiculous, like I wouldn't agree with it. But, like I said, it's society, it changes." Another emerging adult made the following claim:

> I think morals are entirely made up, I don't believe in rules or law. I think things like scientific laws are only things that we notice to be true in most instances. So nothing, I don't believe that anything can ever be 100 percent true. I definitely am a power-of-the-chaos-theory, that small little variables can change everything.

So, we clarified, she actually believes in moral relativism? "Oh definitely. I think morals are just a social tool to keep us not killing each other, to keep us in line with our culture, so it can function as a unit, because if everybody had differing views on marriage, or something like that, your culture would fall apart, and you wouldn't be able to raise children in the way that you want them to be raised, or how you want your culture to raise them." True human goods thus disappear. All that is left is *the will*—how anyone *wants* things to be done their way.

When we explained to another emerging adult a simple version of moral relativism ("Some people say that there really are no final rights and wrongs in life, that everything is relative, and morality is simply what people make it for themselves or their culture, and that we can adjust our views of what is morally right and wrong to reflect those changes") and asked her what she thought about it, she said, "I think I agree with that." So, we asked, in the future might it become morally okay, for example, to steal things from others? "Yeah, I mean, you could say that." She then explained her position by defending the possible moral rightness of mass-murdering terrorists:

> I don't know that people, like terrorists, what they do? It's not wrong to them. They're doing the ultimate good. They're just like, they're doing the thing that they think is the best thing they could possibly do and so they're doing good. I had this discussion with a friend recently and she's like, "But they're still murdering tons of people, that just has to be wrong." And I was like, "*But do we have any idea if it is actually wrong to murder tons of people?*" Like what does that even mean? Earthquakes murder tons of people and I'm sure some people believe that God caused the earthquakes and that means there was some purpose for them, they just will never know it. So you could say that people who are terrorists [are okay] who somehow get brainwashed or born into cultures where they're taught that it's all right and necessary and really important for them to kill a bunch of people. In the grand scheme of things that's just because like X amount of population targeted needs to disappear. I don't believe that. But I can see that that could be an argument.

The assumption here is that it is only people *believing* things to be moral and immoral that makes them moral and immoral, at least "for them." What some think of as moral facts collapse into mere subjective moral beliefs, sheer opinions—making morally objective truth claims and judgments based upon them impossible. Thus, if people *believe* something to be right, then for them it *is* right, simply by virtue of their belief. Absent any morally objective standard of moral evaluation, anything could be morally right, then, as long as someone believes it. Even perhaps mass-murdering terrorists. Who is anyone else to judge them? That, again, is the strong version of the professed outlook of nearly one-third of emerging adults today.

Two-thirds of emerging adults, however, were not strong moral relativists; they stopped short of that radical position. This remaining two-thirds of emerging adults wished to resist the radical implications of strong moral relativism. We might think of many of them as reluctant moral agnostics or skeptics. They were not, to be sure, firm moral realists or absolutists. Few of them, in fact, took clear moral stands that they could defend. The majority of emerging adults could not accept total moral relativism, but many of them also could not clearly explain or defend the moral claims that they wished to make or say why moral relativism is actually wrong. Some—more than one-quarter (27 percent) of the emerging adults we interviewed simply waffled on these questions, as in the following case:

> I think I might agree or I do agree [with relativism]. I don't like that I agree with it. I think moral relativism kind of sucks. I think there are things that are inherently right and wrong. At the same time, situations, people change, society changes, culture changes to define, you know, what's moral. There's things that change, but there will always be absolutes.

But what are absolutes and what makes them that was impossible for him to say.

Take, for another example, this case of vacillation: "I don't think anything in life is absolute," one emerging adult told us.

> You can't say, you can feel that something is absolute. You can be like, man, I feel that's ridiculously wrong, you know, you have the right to choose, that's your choice. But, I don't know, absolute's such a strong word. Um, I don't know, I really don't.

What about murder? we ask. His reply: "I mean, in today's society, sure, like to murder someone is just ridiculous. I don't know, in some societies, back in time, maybe it's a good thing." He told us that he is against the death penalty, for example, but also thinks some political assassinations may be okay. Does he feel strongly against the death penalty? we asked. He sighs and says, "I don't know." For this young man, morality is not purely relative. But he finds it hard to identify the basis of moral knowledge or judgment, other than to say that some people might "feel" that some things are "ridiculous."

Another example of an inability to stick with a firm moral claim is this emerging adult speaking on the question of friends drinking and driving. "I don't think it's fine," he said. "I mean, I probably would have tried to help a friend who was driving drunk. But like, they obviously thought it was right and I don't. I wouldn't have done the same thing." So, we asked, are they right (in driving drunk) or are you right (in opposing it)? "That's, that's definitely a subject I would, like, it's like a religion subject." Meaning, in short, that different people have different views and it's impossible to really say which is right. Oh really? we asked, somewhat incredulous. "It seems like it," he replied. More than one out of four emerging adults we interviewed thus fell into this category of those who want to resist the chasm of strong moral relativism but find themselves reluctant to take any strong moral stands.

A similar group of emerging adults who could not affirm strong moral relativism but who often found themselves standing on soft ground when judging moral issues were those who took a "situationalist" approach to morality. All of the same things could be right or wrong, these emerging adults said, depending on the particular context or circumstances. About four in ten emerging adults we interviewed (41 percent) mentioned situations as complicating moral evaluations. In our view, taking into account the facts of particular situations is relevant for making good moral judgments. But to be clear about the kind of situationalism we were addressing, we posed for them a strongly self-centered version of situation ethics, asking whether it is "okay to break moral rules if it works to your advantage and you can get away with it." Many replied with the following kinds of answers:

> I guess it kind of depends on the situation. Like taking an extra vacation day, for me it's not going to hurt anyone. In my job, it's not really going to hurt anyone. Is it morally right? Probably not, no. What's a moral rule, though? A personal thing? Well then I would say that sometimes breaking a moral rule might be all right, depending on the situation.

> I would think, you know, it's still wrong. You don't, it's hard to turn something down when it's turning out to your advantage, but not really sure. Like, I'm sure everyone does it occasionally. You see someone drop five dollars, it's really hard to tell them. I wouldn't agree that it's right to take it, and I think it'd really have to depend on the situation, if

I wanted to do something like that. If it was, like, a seventy-year-old lady, I'd be like, "You dropped that" and I'd hand it to her on the spot. But just some random drunk walking down the street, wasted, and he drops five dollars, you don't need to drink no more, you know? Just situations like that.

Break moral rules? I'm sorry, what do you mean by moral rules? Like, just rules made? [However *he* thinks about "moral rules," we clarified.] I would have to say in some cases, yeah, it would be okay. It just, it would really depend what those rules were. It's on a case-by-case basis.

Often, in emerging adults' answers to our questions, moral individualism, situational relativism, and firm moral commitments jumble together in confusing statements. The following discussion—which condemns killing, acknowledges situational complexity, affirms moral individualism, and verges on relativism—provides an example:

I think that there are some worldwide moral right or wrongs, like killing someone. That's wrong, whether the person deserved it or not, or whether or not it was saving someone. It's wrong to kill someone. But sometimes it needs to be done. Troops or whatever. Whatever you're talking about. But it's complicated. Because even though it may be the right thing to do, it's still wrong to do. Does that make sense? I really don't think that there's a whole lot of right or wrong answers when it comes to it, because when you ask someone else, you're going to get a totally different answer. So it really changes from person to person. I personally think that there's some worldwide right or wrongs that everybody, or at least most people should abide by.

We recognize the real difficulties this emerging adult is grappling with in working out the complexities of the kinds of issues engaged here. Yet we remain concerned that the thinking expressed not only reflects what must have been a very poor moral education and formation, but it is also unable to result in good moral decision making and a morally coherent life. And that, we think, is a form of impoverishment.

Yet another way that some emerging adults—about one in three (27 percent) of those we interviewed—resolve their reservations about strong moral relativism is to say that, while most moral beliefs are relative, a small number of moral truths are *not* relative. This approach seemed to us to reflect better sense than most others. The majority of moral claims are not universally true, these emerging adults said, but vary by culture and across history, whereas a limited number of moral claims are always and everywhere valid. This emerging adult, for instance, distinguished between universal moral truths and more relative beliefs that require more interpretation:

> There's interpretation, everyone has different takes of right and wrong. People will give a level of right and wrong and other people might give it a different level. Like, I smoke weed and there are people who think that's really wrong, and others who think that's okay, or a little bit wrong. And then there are people that are like, "Oh whatever, I do it too." [laughs] So, it's all, I don't know, in how you look at it. Yeah, there are different things that are more open to interpretation, I think. There are moral absolutes and then there are things that people take into consideration themselves and judge for themselves. I mean, you don't kill someone, you don't rape someone, you know what I mean? There are things that are set in stone that you do not do. And then there are things that are more open to interpretation, I guess.

Such a view may be more defensible than many of those expressed above, we think, as a matter of simple moral reasoning. Even so, the lean toward individualism and relativism here is worth noticing. There are perhaps extreme cases, like murder and rape, the thinking goes, in which right and wrong are definite, but beyond those few issues, morality is open to "individual interpretation." For another example, when we asked one emerging adult, a Catholic, whether some things could be wrong for some people but not others, he answered:

> That's hard, because it's really a yes and a no, because with my religion I feel that it's very, it's, it has not changed. And I think that with society today, it probably should change because people are not the same that they were back, you know, who even knows when? Things do change, things progress. For example, stem cell research, it's completely against Catholicism. But I absolutely agree with it 100 percent. I'm in the medical field, and I just I think it's amazing what they can do with stem cell research. So I would say yes, things should be changed, they are relative to certain situations. Some things are and some things are not. Some things are not relative, but some things are.

How, we asked, do you know where to draw the line between changing and unchanging moral truths? "I think, wow, it's, I guess it's based person to person," he replied. "But things that dramatically, like I guess it goes back to the consequences, positive versus negative." This may be a more complex view of morality than many emerging adults hold. But even here, this young man has not considered the problem that it is impossible to evaluate "positive versus negative consequences" apart from some real moral standard that tells what is actually good and bad. He does not realize this, but this consequentialist ethic cannot ultimately help him adjudicate between real universal moral truths and relative moral claims. In fact, few emerging adults who appeal to good or bad consequences to help settle moral issues ever seriously consider how anyone would know or judge what for different people is good and bad.

The following emerging adult provides another example of resolving the tension between moral relativism and moral universals by conceding most of morality to relativism yet protecting a limited set of moral claims as absolute:

> Moral relativism is something that I struggle with a lot. I've spent a lot of time thinking about it. My sister is completely an ultimate relativist, in that [she thinks] nobody is really right or wrong. But I have such a hard time with that, thinking that, you know, is killing someone right? Can that be right in someone's culture? I would say no, there are some things that are universally right or wrong, but then it gets into such a difficult way of defining most of these, you know? That's something I really struggle with, but I would say, I don't know, I'd say for the most part, I'd be a relativist about most things about people's practices or whatever with their lives. Who am I to say that it's wrong? But I think you can cross a line at some point, with difficult things like killing people and stealing, I would say are universally wrong regardless of someone's culture.

The relativity of cultural differences and the aversion to judging any views of other people ("who am I to say?") strongly influence the reasoning here. But in the end, while she admits being a relativist about most things, this emerging adult refuses to let go of all moral truth. In the end, murder and stealing, at least, are believed to be always morally wrong.[6] That, we think, is a step in the right direction, but not one that most emerging adults know how to defend or make consistent with their other thoughts and feelings about morality.

While a significant minority of emerging adults today, about one in three, professes to believe in strong moral relativism, we have also seen that well more than half of emerging adults seem to want to resist relativism. But they also appear to possess few moral-reasoning skills with which to do that. We have called these cases reluctant moral agnostics and skeptics. Some of this reluctant skepticism, however, results, again, from not making certain basic but important conceptual distinctions involving, for example, the ideas of morality being "absolute."[7] The idea of an "absolute morality" is fraught with ambiguity and so is difficult to handle. This, we think, trips up many emerging adults and sends them sprawling toward relativism. "Absolute" in a moral context could, on the one hand, mean *universally binding*, pertaining to all people at all times. But absolute can also entail a *general principle*, which applies to all kinds of relevant situations, and not only to particular cases and circumstances. Different objectively true moral claims and beliefs can entail different combinations of these different meanings of "absolute."[8] When most emerging adults think of morality as possibly being not entirely relative—an idea that most apparently would like to affirm—they often think of morality as therefore having to be "absolute." But all emerging adults rightly know that not *every* moral claim could possibly be "absolute" in both senses of the word distinguished above. And so, because few emerging adults have had an informed adult explain to them such conceptual distinctions, they find it difficult to affirm that morality is not entirely relative. Had they been taught some differences of meaning involved in such concepts, they would be in a better position to find some more reasonable middle ground that is morally realist yet takes into account life's moral complexities. However, without those distinctions, the nonrelativist position—which, again, seems to them to entail an impossible absolutism—appears impossible to hold. Thus moral relativism proves difficult to resist, for explicable though not necessary reasons. To rephrase this very simply, when emerging adults are asked whether they believe in absolutes, they often seem to interpret the question as asking whether they believe in statements like "Thou shalt not kill" and "Thou shalt not steal," or as asking whether they believe in very general moral precepts that apply universally. And they often reply that they do not believe in such simple precepts, thinking that life is far too complicated for such precepts to be anything more than rules of thumb. They therefore seem to be relativists. But they do not need to be relativists on this account. Many may be guilty merely of failing to realize that moral precepts can be universally binding yet still be very specifically tailored to particular situations, because universally binding moral precepts are "absolute" even though they can be endlessly qualified.

Once again, we also believe it would be wrong to interpret these more or less morally relativistic voices as mere self-indulgent rationalizations for emerging adults to live as (im)morally as they please. It would also be highly simplistic to conclude that emerging adults are turning an otherwise morally sound America into some kind of new Sodom and Gomorrah. In fact, there are powerful institutional reasons why emerging adults think like this. And the moral reasoning of emerging adults has deep roots in American history and society. Emerging adults, for example, have been taught from their earliest days to be tolerant of others who are different, to live civilly in a pluralistic society, and to affirm the cultures of often marginal groups. Different Americans have different views about these ideas, but it is true that this kind of educational agenda has been a response to some reprehensible historical facts, like the genocide of Native Americans, Indian wars, slavery, racial segregation, and religious discrimination in America, as well as countless other episodes of ideologically driven massacre, genocide, and war around the world. In short, these messages are well intentioned and, at least in certain ways, we think, important, valuable, and effective (emerging adults, for instance, generally harbor much less racial and ethnic prejudice and feelings of social distance than older Americans, which we consider a moral gain). Unfortunately, at least some of this tolerance-promoting, multiculturalist educational project also seems to have been based upon some shoddy moral reasoning, which it reinforces in turn. Thus emerging adults in our interviews are to some extent simply parroting to us what they have been taught by the adults who have educated them. That does not make sloppy and indefensible moral reasoning acceptable, but it does help to make it understandable.

Moral Sources

One does not have to be a radical moral individualist or relativist in order to exhibit a less than robust grasp of moral issues, weak moral reasoning, or shaky commitment to the idea of moral truth. Examining how emerging adults think about moral sources—that is, the grounds or basis for moral truths—reveals some of the uncertainty involved in their moral outlooks. Whether an emerging adult is a moral relativist or a moral realist of some variety, all emerging adults realize that something called "morality" exists in human cultures and is believed by many to have an authority independent of individual whims and desires. Again, some emerging adults view morality as objectively real, while others view morality as purely a social construction. But none deny the empirical existence of moral beliefs and claims in society. The question, then, is: What do emerging adults believe is the source of morality? Where does morality come from? What is morality's basis?

To these questions, emerging adults offered diverse answers. We wish to highlight two points about what follows. First, most of the accounts of morality's sources offered by emerging adults below are not reasonably defensible. They might make sense to some at first glance. But when analyzed, much of what follows simply does not work; it cannot hold up to basic critical scrutiny. Second, despite claiming to be strong moral individualists, as noted above, most emerging adults' accounts of the *sources* of morality turn out to be not all that individualistic. Almost all of the accounts examined below, in fact, turn out to be highly oriented to the interests, needs, or desires of *social* relations. We are not simply representing different voices here. Rather, this is another instance of emerging adult thinking being not particularly internally consistent. To some extent, too, this seems to reflect the view that, while the basis of morality may come from different sources outside of individuals, it is only each individual who can determine which moral beliefs and claims from whatever sources are true "for them."

For starters, however, fully one in three (34 percent) of the emerging adults we interviewed said that *they simply did not know what makes anything morally right or wrong.* They had no idea about the basis of morality. Tellingly, some of these stumped interviewees could not even understand our questions on this point. No matter how many different ways we posed them or tried to explain or clarify them, our very questions about morality's sources did not or could not make sense to them. They replied to our inquiries by saying things like "I just don't understand, like what do you mean?" and "I'm not really sure what you're saying." Another, when we asked him what he thinks it is that *makes* something right or wrong, simply replied, "These are just not things I think about!"

Others, as illustrated by the following exchange, seemed to understand the intent of our questions about morality's basis, but did not have any answers:

I: What is it that you think makes something right or wrong?
R: I'm not sure, I guess probably what it is and stuff like, I don't know.
I: Do you think it has to do with consequences or laws or what?
R: I don't know, I really don't know.

Still others seemed to hold some views about morality but were unable to describe or explain them, as in this exchange, which picks up with a discussion about moral relativism:

R: I mean, I disagree. I think there are right and wrong things.
I: Do they hold cross-culturally?
R: Well, no, not cross-cultural. Like what may be right here may not be right in another country.
I: So it's relative?
R: I don't know. That is a confusing question.
I: I know.
R: There are thousands of cultures, it is hard. But I am not living in that culture, like here the way we are taught and stuff, I mean there are rights and wrongs, and there are definites in every culture. They may be different in every culture, but you do have definites like . . . I don't know how to describe it.

In short, this person believes in specific moral truths. But he realizes that he does so only because he was raised in a particular culture that teaches certain moral truths. So people like this have difficulty explaining the real source of genuine morality that would apply to all human beings (and therefore why they, or any-one else, has a rational reason to disagree with moral relativism).

In contrast to that 34 percent, most emerging adults were able to offer some account of morality's source or basis. Some emerging adults, for example, pro-fessed to believe in moral right and wrong. Yet their morality does not itself have an objective reference or basis but was defined instead primarily by *what other people would think about someone*. If others would think the worse of a person for doing something, then that would be morally wrong for them to do. Positive and negative social perceptions, in other words, are morality's ultimate ground. So, for example, when we asked one emerging adult what he thought it is that makes something right or wrong, he replied, "Just, well, morals, I guess." We pressed: when he said "morals," what exactly did he mean? "Like morals as in how you want yourself to be looked at," he said, explaining:

> Like if I were to beat someone up and other people would be like, "Oh man! That dude's a savage. He jacked him and he's [bad] for that" or whatever. I don't want to be looked at like that. I want to be looked at as the dude who was able to think for everybody, to be able to think what's right or wrong and stuff, to be the good guy, to be a good man, a decent man in this life. I don't want to be like everybody else. So that's really, morally how people look at you and how you want yourself to be known, to be looked at. That's what I really think of.

It is good, we think, for this young man to want to do the right thing and be thought of well by his associates. But how other people may think of someone itself cannot be the source of real morality, for a lot of reasons—such as that some other people can have a wide variety of reactions to all sorts of moral and immoral behaviors, including condemning people for doing good things (like standing up for the rights of unpopular minorities) and approving of people doing wrong things (like stealing or sexually taking advantage of someone else). Nevertheless, when asked how she decides between right and wrong, one emerging adult explained, similarly, that, "A lot of times I'll be like, 'Well, what would Luke [her cohabiting boyfriend] think if I did this?' Because he's the per-son I live with and I share my life with. If he's not gonna be happy with it, because it's something, a wrong, possibly a wrong decision, then that's the consequence I'll have to deal with everyday." Yet another simply said, "Morally I think about how people would look at me, and that's not that big but it's in the back of my mind." Again, while considering what other people might think about some ac-tion one might take may be a good way to help judge the right moral path, other people's views simply cannot be what makes anything morally right or wrong. Yet about four out of ten (40 percent) of the emerging adults we interviewed referred to how other people would think of them as (at least partly) defining what for them would be morally right and wrong. To the extent that emerging adults feel morally lost in their own minds, looking to the reaction of others (who they presumably trust) may provide what they consider to be mostly reliable guides to determine right from wrong.

Some emerging adults we interviewed described the basis or grounds of morality as whether or not anything *functionally improved people's situations*. If a thought, attitude, or action created a better functional situation, then it was moral, they essentially said. If it made a situation worse, then it was morally bad. This was part of the thinking of six in ten (60 percent) of the emerging adults we interviewed. One, for example, explained (with a dash of individualistic relativism) that, "Wrong are the things that change things for way worse than they were before—and I kinda think again it's totally relative to the person, it depends on where you wanna go and what you wanna do." Another described the morally good in this way: "It just seems like good things are those that benefit and change for the better and help others or yourself, things that are gonna get you to a good place, some place that you should be proud of or that you're gonna wake up tomorrow and be able to tell someone about and not feel ashamed of it." For another emerging adult, who struggled to articulate his thoughts about morality, defining what is moral as situational or a functional improvement tended to marginalize the very language of "morality" and make discussing it difficult:

> R: I just don't know, like, it's not like I'm ever, like, because right and wrong, I mean, there could just be, like, I guess I don't think about my decisions in terms of morality. I probably think of them in other, like, framed other ways, I don't know.
>
> I: What other ways?
>
> R: Like what will be more fun or what will make my friends have a better time or what will make everyone in the situation—this is something I'm always [focused on]—what will make everyone in the situation just like happy together, what will be the less, least tense situation, what will ah, um, [*pause*] I don't know. Yeah.

Likewise, this young man, who also took a consequentialist view of morality, had difficulty thinking about right and wrong in strongly moral terms:

> I don't know if there really is a good and bad. I mean, yeah, there is. Certain things are bad, I mean inhumane, some things. But other than that, basically the world is built on corruption so bad, really it's a fine line. But right and wrong, I mean wrong? You'll go to jail for it. You'll

get killed over it. Something that's gonna affect you in a negative way. It's wrong. Don't do it. But that's about it, you know?

Because situational consequences can often turn out differently than expected, at least some of these emerging adults are not able to govern their lives with moral systems, maps, philosophies, or worldviews that can reliably tell them in advance what is right and wrong. Instead, right and wrong are only figured out after the fact, when one sees the actual consequences of living. Thus one emerging adult told us, "I don't know, I mean the only way I know [whether something is right or wrong] is if you do it and you find out that it's wrong, I don't know, if it has consequences, yeah." Another said, "Outcomes, long term outcomes. I think long term is the most important thing." Yet another agreed with these post hoc determinations of the moral status of anything:

> Whatever is good or pure, it will have good repercussions, even if it's something that is hard or looks bad in the beginning. It can change, it can be like an ugly shriveled fruit, then it grows a tree kinda deal. Whereas something that is wrong usually is the opposite, it looks amazing on the outside, but it's wrong on the inside, so I think you can tell by just the repercussions of what you decided to do.

The crucial distinction that these emerging adults are missing is the difference between the *basis* or *reason* for some moral truth and the *effects* of living according to that moral truth. Right moral living should normally have certain positive, patterned effects, at least over the long run. But that does *not* make those effects per se *the reason why* those things are morally right in the first place. If they are indeed morally right, they should remain so even if they sometimes fail to have those effects. Furthermore, sometimes right moral action does *not* improve people's situations. At times, in fact, it creates major problems. Sometimes right moral action involves real costs and sacrifices—which is exactly why it can be so hard to live morally. Sometimes people doing the right thing, particularly in the context of other people doing morally wrong things—such as, for example, standing up during the civil rights movement for the civil rights of oppressed and segregated blacks living in the South—creates major social conflicts in which people die. So defining morality as that which functionally improves people's situations really does not work.

Another related but more specific basis for morality for some emerging adults is whether it *hurts other people*. For about half (53 percent) of those we interviewed, a moral violation per se is essentially defined as anything that hurts other people physically, emotionally, financially, or otherwise. "Wrong are the things that hurt people," one explained. "There are some cases where of course it's gonna be right, it's gonna be wrong," another said, "as far as like hurting people or getting hurt or doing something that's gonna cause someone some negative effect." Still another told us, "I know what's right and wrong: if someone wants to do something destructive or something like that to someone else, I *know* it's not a good idea." And another said, "I think in a lot of ways if you aren't hurting anybody else, it's certainly more acceptable [to do the wrong thing] than if you were hurting people." Many repeated these ideas, stating that, "I would say that it [hurting someone] is immoral, it's another person's life that you're messing with, that's not yours, that's not yours," and "It's wrong to hurt people, especially if the person being hurt didn't choose it." Yet another put it this way:

> The reason why something is morally wrong in my mind is that it interferes with other people's lives in incorrect ways, harms other people. I think that's the biggest thing. That's why, for example, drinking can be morally right or wrong depending on the quantity or whatever, but underage drinking and driving, it's almost always morally irresponsible because you are endangering other people's lives, you know? I mean that's where the line is really drawn, I think, it's the way it's affecting other people.

These emerging adults did not agree, however, on whether hurting oneself would also be morally bad or whether that was one's prerogative that had no moral implications. Some suggested the first position: "Oh, how it is going to affect people, you know, if it is going to hurt someone or make them feel bad. And if it isn't going to affect anyone, then it's just how it will affect you, like will it be a good or a bad thing for you, you know, morally." Similarly, another told us this:

> I think right or wrong has to do with respect to others as well as yourself. Yeah, I think it comes down to respect, if you have a friend that you're talking bad about behind her back, that's disrespectful to that person. If you have a boyfriend who is cheating on you but you continue a relationship with him, that's disrespectful to yourself, so it would be wrong for you to stay with that person not treating you right. I think that's how you know what's right and wrong.

But other emerging adults who defined morality in terms of hurting people saw nothing necessarily morally relevant about hurting oneself. "Once it's affecting other people," one explained, "their thoughts and feelings have to be put into consideration, you know? But if it's only affecting yourself, the only thing you have to judge by is the way that you personally feel about it." Another shared this view:

When you're doing something wrong and it's only affecting you person-ally, then that's your own decision. I guess that's where I stand on drugs, is that drugs can really ruin lives and they can really mess things up. But if it's just you doing it to yourself, and it's not affecting anyone else, then that's your choice if you wanna mess yourself up like that. But if you're doing something that's affecting, that's messing up other people's lives, it's making their lives worse, I just think that's wrong. I just wouldn't wanna do something negative to impact someone else.

Another distinction made by some emerging adults who espoused the immorality-as-hurting-others approach was the difference between hurting in-dividuals and hurting social groups. This is yet another way, we think, that strong individualism shaped their moral reasoning. For some emerging adults, not only is each individual entitled to define their own personal moral code, but it is also only the hurting of *individual persons* that could make anything morally wrong. For them it was only wrong to hurt *individuals*, and not particularly wrong to cheat or steal from an organization, such as a business. One, for instance, reported having friends who shoplift and say they don't care; he said, "I just kind of laugh and say, 'Hah, well I don't care either,' 'cause Walmart or Target or so-and-so's a big corporation, they have money. If you were stealing from me or my neighbor who doesn't have much money, then you're kind of hurting them more. Whereas, you just steal a DVD from a store, they got 10 of the DVDs, they're not gonna be really hurting." So why does *that* matter? we asked. "They have lawyers and funds that will cover them for these kind of situations," he replied. "So like, yeah, my friend tells me 'I stole a DVD,' I laugh and go, 'I don't care. That's cool.'" Then he continued to explain why, with some equivocation:

You know, it's [actually] not that cool, but it's funny, 'cause you're talking about something I don't care about. But people as individuals, I would never want to steal or hurt someone as an individual, I feel like they're more vulnerable as one person. Whereas like a corporation, like a gas station or something is not one person, even though in reality, in es-sence it is. It's probably like a family-owned business or whatever, even-tually it'll trickle down to one person or a few CEOs or shareholders or whatever. But I think of it in terms of, if it's hurting one individual it's wrong. But if it's not hurting an individual, it's not really wrong.

Likewise, when we asked another emerging adult, in a larger discussion about morality, whether it would be wrong to get on a train or subway without paying the fare, she replied, "It wouldn't be wrong if you didn't get caught." So, we asked, you think that it's the getting caught that makes something wrong? "Yes and no," she answered. "It depends on the situation." Any idea what it might depend on? we pressed. "I guess, given a situation, I mean, something as simple as a train, they charge too much anyway, so it's nothing to hop a train [without paying]." At the same time, she said, lying to an individual would always be wrong, even if you did not get caught. Why? "Because you know it's wrong. I mean, you might have a guilty conscious or not, but the other person believes it's the truth. So you have deceived another person." But why is that different from riding the train without paying? Well, she relied, "you're not deceiving no one by jumping the train." In short, the railroad or municipal transportation system is not an individual, and so one cannot really do moral wrong against them.

Again, without going into much depth, we must observe that whether or not something harms people simply cannot serve as a defensible explanation for morality's source. One reason is that acting morally sometimes involves hurting other people in some ways—think of certain situations that require telling a hard truth, for instance, or of enforcing certain kinds of justice concerning the fair distribution of goods in situations when some people will get less so that others can have more. Another, more basic reason is that *even being able to know or define in the first place what hurts or helps other people* often itself requires reference to certain moral standards and understandings of what is good and bad. Is disciplining a child who lies hurting them? Is denying food or alcohol to an obese glutton or alcoholic loved one hurting them? Is a sports coach putting players through bodily pain during training and practices hurting them? Is telling Southern segregationists that they may no longer enjoy whites-only waiting rooms, bathrooms, and public pools hurting them? Emerging adults may sometimes think so. But we would say they are wrong, even if it feels like it hurts them. In many such cases, it is only knowledge of the moral good that determines what is truly hurtful and helpful to other people. So morality itself cannot be dependent on perceptions of help and hurt as the basis of its very definition.

Moving on, many emerging adults—about 12 percent of those we interviewed—espoused a view that is somewhat related to the don't-hurt-other-people view that can best be described as a "*social-contract theory*" *of morality*. In essence, according to this view, moral truth does not really enjoy any objective existence—nothing that could critique a belief or practice, such as slavery, that is embraced by the majority in a society. Rather, morality is simply the name of a collective social invention agreed to by people in a group or society to advance the hedonic and functional goods of those submitting to the social compact. Their mutually policing moral norms may come to be seen erroneously as objective, natural, or universal. But in reality they are merely agreements by contract—pure social constructions.

Thus, for example, to the question of whether real moral truths exist or whether morality is simply a relative social invention, one emerging adult answered, "Well, I don't know. I think it's mostly about pragmatically needing people to get along with each other." So, we probed, are there ultimately no real moral standards? "Well, you have to draw the line somewhere or you just end up with total anarchy," he replied. "So the government creates broad parameters and then individuals do what they want within them, the government explains at the farthest outside here's what you can't do, in the form of laws, but then within that, individuals can do and think what they want to, as long as they're not too extreme. People should not be too extreme." But what this young man obviously cannot explain, given his own frame of reference, is *why* anarchy is bad, why extremes should be avoided, why individuals should be free to think and do as they want, and why, in the end, social contracts really should be binding on everyone. Pondering those kinds of more complicated questions is way beyond most emerging adults, given the few reasoning tools they have been provided. Nevertheless, some version of the social-contract view of morality is referenced by more than a few of them. Consider, for another example, this exchange:

I: How do you normally decide or know what's good or bad or right and wrong in life? Do you even think there are things that are right or wrong?

R: I don't know if I think in terms so much of right or wrong [but instead more] as things that you wouldn't like them if they happened to you. Well no, that's not true. You can look at something and say that is just . . . Well, it's interesting you say that. I don't think in terms of "this is wrong" so much as that's just not right. I guess there is a lot of the "do unto others as you would have them do unto you" kind of thing. It's just one of those things. You'd like for people to be nice to you, to be forthright with you, because the world is a very unpleasant place if you don't. It seems only fair, I guess.

I: So you're willing to behave in certain ways that put demands on you in the expectation that other people should and hopefully will too, and then we'll all have a nicer life together?

R: Pretty much.

I: It's kind of a social-contract theory?

R: I mean, they won't necessarily [be nice], but you can give it a try.

Note how in this exchange an originally religiously grounded moral command (the Golden Rule) is deployed within a larger contract-theory framework to make sense of moral life. People need not "do unto others" out of obedience to or love for God but rather because if everyone does that the world turns out to be a more "pleasant" place. Morality is thus reduced to a utilitarian strategy to avoid things that "you wouldn't like if they happened to you." That helps explain why this person does not even "think in terms so much of right or wrong." What appears to be morality is actually contingent social contract.

Yet, again, morality of the kind that most people have in mind cannot be defined by social contracts, for many reasons. One is that the theory never adequately states how many people in a group must agree in order to define a moral fact and whether certain kinds of contracting parties matter more than others. If a social contract requires only a majority of people or only a minority of the most powerful, then there is no reason why feeding Christians to the lions for entertainment could not be defined as morally good, or why enforcing apartheid in South Africa could not be entirely moral. Social contracts in this way do nothing to defend the morally grounded rights or dignity of minorities, those who tend to lose in the "voting." The social-contract theory of morality, in fact, has no way at all to explain anything like human dignity and rights. All it can explain are aggregations of populations' desires, tacit agreements to proceed in certain ways, and socially normative behavior that is often mistaken as carrying true moral force. On the other hand, if everyone in a society must agree to establish a social contract, then no morality will ever be defined, since never in human history has *everyone* in a society agreed to anything, particularly on normative issues that sometimes require sacrifices. These are only a few of social-contract theory's many problems in explaining morality. But enough said on that.

Yet another common response of emerging adults to the question about knowing what actually makes anything morally right or wrong was to ground morality in *laws, rules, and regulations.* This way of thinking surprised us, since adolescence and emerging adulthood are not commonly associated with a "law and order" mentality. Prior generations of youth—think of "the Sixties"—are in fact normally associated with rebellion and the questioning of authority. Yet nearly one out of four of the contemporary emerging adults we interviewed (23 percent) referenced obedience to the laws of the land as one, if not the, key way to define morality. The essential idea expressed was that if something is in the law or regulations, then it is moral, and if it is not law, then it is outside the realm of morality. One, for instance, tried to explain his approach to morality this way: "I am an American, in American society, therefore laws apply. I may not agree with them, I may even break [them] on occasion, but when I'm caught, I do pay my bills and whatnot, I pay my dues." Another talked about the morality of not hurting other people in light of the fact that "hurting people goes against the government's laws. We have certain amendments and freedoms and rights and liberties and protections in our society that you can't violate." Yet another emerging adult similarly stressed human commands as the defining feature of morality:

I: What do you think it is that *makes* something right or wrong?
R: Like if it's something your boss tells you to do, they want it done that way, that makes it what you should do.

I: So rules and regulations?

R: Yeah, I guess rules, regulations, laws.

More than a few emerging adults were in fact adamant about the importance of not breaking laws or ignoring rules, appealing to a "slippery slope" argument, like this:

> I think all of the laws, you know, laws aren't really meant to be broken, laws are put in place for a reason. Some laws can be bent, but you know, I'm big on respecting the law. And rules are also put in place, they're not really meant to be broken. They're put there for a reason. Sometimes there's even stupid rules, but I think that even if you did start breaking stupid rules, it's not a good precedent to set, because then you can start breaking other rules and stuff, and then redefining what is a stupid rule.

Another argued similarly that, "if you're breaking rules, I mean, I guess rules are there to apply structure, to keep everything organized, keep the positive consequences or whatever, and if you're breaking those then that's not really fair to everybody else. Plus you're doing it to get ahead, so that's kind of selfish." Almost one out of four emerging adults today thus seem to adhere to a view of morality that is defined essentially by legal and regulatory decrees, by reference to what philosophers call "positive law," the empirical laws of legislators and regulators at any point in time. Many also express a concern with obedience to law that might make their more rebellious baby-boomer forebears, most of whom are not yet capable of turning over in their graves, at least rock harder with agitation in their La-Z-Boys.

If what is moral is defined by or grounded in empirical laws and rules, then it makes sense that many emerging adults view morality as relative—even if this view is inconsistent with moral individualism. What such a view lacks, of course, is the capacity to successfully advance a moral critique of any existing laws, rules, or regulations. If the boss says to do it a certain way, then that is apparently the right thing to do. If it is the law, then it must be moral. Such an outlook, it is worth remembering, underwrote the explanations offered after World War II by thousands of Germans and their collaborators in other countries who cooperated with the Nazis in the mass extermination of millions of human beings. Yet few emerging adults today, who define morality in terms of existing laws, rules, and regulations decreed by authority figures, seem aware of such possible dangers.[9] For many, simply pointing to the law answers the morality questions.

A different kind of answer that some emerging adults offered to our questions about the sources of morality is that *karma maintains justice and right.* A surprising (to us) number of emerging adults we interviewed—nearly one in six (17 percent)—spontaneously referred to "karma" as a way to explain how morality works, why it's best to act morally, and why the universe is ultimately a morally just place. In invoking karma, they meant that good attitudes and behavior will be rewarded in this life and bad people will get what they deserve too. "What goes around comes around," they explained. "Karma's a bitch," another said, making the point that you can't escape its merciless consequences. In a discussion about morality, for example, one emerging adult told us, "Mostly just Karma. I really do believe in Karma. What you give and what you do really does come back to you, whether you realize it or not. It's just, I don't know." Likewise, in a discussion about the morality of returning or keeping lost or stolen goods, one young man explained what is morally wrong about people who just don't care and keep other people's things for themselves, in this way: "Well, then, I guess that's [*pause*] on them. What goes around comes around. I would think it would be [wrong], I wouldn't do it." Another developed this line of thought further:

> You can bend moral views a little bit here and there, but if you bend them too much, it just becomes distorted. There sometimes is a fine line that you can cross over every once in a while, and some people might look at that alright, but I personally don't. I don't think you should [say] it's relative. Because everything has its own positive and negative affect. I kind of do believe in karma, I guess. What you get, what goes around, comes around. What comes around, goes around, I should say. And if you're going to do something negative to someone else, it's going to come back at you in another, maybe even in a harsher way.

Talking about karma like this does not mean these emerging adults have any real interest in or knowledge about Hinduism, Sikhism, or Buddhism or believe in reincarnation. Many did not even seem aware of those possible connections. Rather, karma appears to have become for some a pop-culture way of explaining the fair operations of good and bad in the world. Karma functions as a reminder for emerging adults that they can't get away with bad stuff. It catches up to you. It pays off in the future to do the right thing now. Bad people will get theirs. Everyone basically gets what they deserve. Karma thus helps keep some moral justice in the world. So it serves as the basis of morality in this outlook. To be sure, karma does not exactly explain the sources of morality. Rather, it sidesteps those questions as perhaps unanswerable and instead suggests that, whatever morals are actually based upon, those who obey them benefit and those who do not pay the price.

These are many, but by no means the only accounts that emerging adults give for the source or basis of morality. Most emerging adults do subscribe to one or another of the above views. But other emerging adults appeal instead to other kinds of moral sources—religious ones, for example, such as God or the Bible. In fact, about 40 percent of the emerging adults we interviewed—a not insignificant minority—claimed that their own moral views were somehow based in God's commands, the Bible, or other religious knowledge or sensibilities. And another 24 percent said that they did not follow a religious moral system directly, but that religion probably operated as a general ethical influence in the background of their lives. Those are significant numbers.

But we would be wrong to believe, based on these numbers, that all or most of these emerging adults understand, embrace, and live out religiously coherent moral traditions and practices. Remember that many of the categories described above are not mutually exclusive. It is thus entirely possible, and in fact often empirically the case, that sizeable chunks of these "religiously moral and ethical" emerging adults are also strong moral individualists. Some of them struggle with, and even subscribe to, some version of moral relativism.[10] And more than a few operate with syncretistic outlooks that mix more traditionally religious moral elements with some of the other views noted above, including more pragmatic, functionalist, social-contract, laws-based, consequentialist, and karmic views of morality.[11] This is not to say that religion, God, or the Bible does not matter to any emerging adults today. For many, they do. It is merely a caution against assuming that simply because emerging adults make reference to them as moral sources, they are necessarily living lives with a high degree of religiously grounded moral knowledge, coherence, or consistency. Very many are not.[12]

Moral Compromises

The majority of emerging adults report that they believe that people ought to do what they think is the morally right thing in any situation and obey the law, and that they usually try to do that themselves—to the extent that they understand morality. That is what we expect. But significant minorities did, in fact, leave the door open for acting otherwise. In our nationally representative survey, 16 percent of American emerging adults agreed with the statement that "it is okay to break moral rules if it works to your advantage and you can get away with it." That number increased considerably among those we personally interviewed: one in three (34 percent) of those we interviewed said that they might do certain things they considered morally wrong if they knew they could get away with it.[13] In our interviews we explored how they thought about this. Here are the kinds of things they said. One young man, in justifying lying and cheating, claimed that the dog-eat-dog world in which he perceives he lives sometimes requires dishonesty:

> I don't think lying is wrong necessarily. It's life. People lie. That's my view on the whole thing. Everyone's done it. It's not going to go away.

People are brought up not to cheat. I think from a moral standpoint, yeah, it's wrong. But, I don't know, people cheat. That's how a lot of people have gotten ahead in life, especially in this country. It's like a cutthroat world out there. Do or die. Get it done, or move over. You know what I mean? There's no room for weak people, almost in a sense.

So how, we asked, does he personally respond to that world?

I don't agree with it, but I live in it. I will do what I can to get ahead in this world while I'm here. Society doesn't always make sense, you don't always agree with it. It's just what it is, though. And it's hard to have one person make a change to something that's much bigger than themselves.

Another shared this general outlook. When asked how he knows right from wrong, he replied, "What formula? I guess it's society, what's interpreted as right or wrong in society. You just know, like cheating, you know it's wrong. Everybody does it, whether it's with your girlfriend, or a test, or your taxes, or, you know, everything. There's so many corrupt practices going on these days, you know."

Some emerging adults claim not only that adults in society regularly lie and cheat, but report that some of those adults also explicitly teach and encourage them to do the same. Consider, for example, the following interview exchange with an emerging adult who said he would sometimes break moral rules:

I: Okay, so what is an example of a moral rule that wouldn't be wrong to break?

R: Cheating. If you cheat on a test. My high school football coach used to tell me that "if you ain't cheating, you're not trying."

I: He said what?

R: "Not cheating, not trying."

I: So he was encouraging you to cheat?

R: Yeah. Because he knows we probably didn't study, and it was his class he was teaching, so.

I: Okay. So you think that's okay if you can get away with it?

R: Yep. I mean it's bad, but if you can get away with that, use it to your advantage.

Many emerging adults, however, simply said that it is hard to make the right decisions in the middle of difficult moral situations. In response to our question about whether it is ever okay to break moral rules, one emerging adult laughed and said, "Um, let's see, I don't know if I think it's okay. I think I've done it. And I think people do what's easiest for them at that time and think it's okay, I guess." Another explained his drunk driving this way:

R: Recently I got pulled over for a DUI, so that situation was definitely wrong, and at the time I just wasn't thinking in the right mind.

I: How did you decide to do that?

R: I didn't decide, I just . . . I mean, I figured I'd done it plenty of times before and not gotten caught, so I figured I'd be able to make it away this one time.

Yet another confessed, "When I was younger I always kind of like psyched myself out of believing some of the things I did were wrong, just because it seemed fine at the time."

Others spoke about breaking moral standards more in terms of the very human experience of slipping up and making mistakes, as with this young man talking about religion and sex:

Religious beliefs affect my views about sex, because like the Bible says premarital sex is wrong. I'm not gonna say that I haven't done it before, I have, though I don't do it often at all, to tell you the honest truth. That was a problem with me and my girlfriend at a point in time, she's like "Yo, I haven't had sex with you in a month," and da-da-da, and I'm like "Yo, easy, you feel me [i.e., understand]? It's not that serious, you feel me?" Premarital sex, she knows it's wrong, because her mom is yelling at her about going to church. And, yes, yes, I agree with what religion teaches, you know what I'm saying? But of course we all gonna make mistakes and fall, of course.

Yet others took an approach that more consciously calculated costs and benefits of different courses of action:

Well, it depends what the situation is. If doing the right thing won't [help you], you know, it's easy to do the right thing as long as doing the wrong thing is not going to help you. You know what I mean? If the outcome will be the same for doing the right thing or the wrong thing, obviously you're going to do the right thing. I'm still keeping this in a competitive context. If doing the right thing is not benefiting you as much as doing the wrong thing, then that's a tough decision you have to make.

So, we clarified, ultimately moral decisions are about what would benefit him the most? "Right," he said.

Some emerging adults told us that their economic poverty forced them into violating their own moral standards. Usually these people seemed to regret their behaviors, but also felt they had no real choice. One, for instance, spoke about the tradeoff between selling marijuana and not eating:

Yeah, sure. For instance, selling drugs. Not necessarily morally unsure, you know what I'm saying? I'm saying basically that's what it is. Can't find a job, still got to eat, still got bills to pay. So I start selling weed. Okay, it's gonna get you in trouble, right. But at the same time, if you don't, you don't eat. So there's really no right or wrong line there, because you either don't eat or risk your freedom. I mean it's a choice that has to be made. [So how did you decide what to do then?] I had to eat. I had to eat. You know what I'm saying? It's a chance you got to take. It's a gamble.

Another spoke of having to steal food:

Well, there was a time where I was actually homeless, where I had my truck and stuff, but I actually had no money. I literally stole breakfast, lunch, and dinner. Now compared to if I have money and I steal something, versus where I'm actually hungry, I have no money and I need to feed myself, I view those very differently. I literally need food and have no way to provide it for myself, and no one's going to provide it for me. So I'm going to have to steal this or I'm going to go hungry.

Such hard financial conditions, according to another emerging adult, sometimes require making the "sacrifice" of breaking moral rules: "The mentality I have is, it wouldn't be hard to do what's right at all if I was in a position to do what's right, if I was [economically] stable. But since I'm not and it's still a work in progress, you know, sacrifices have to be made. I mean you have to do what it takes to get where you want to be."

To be sure, these voices do not represent the majority of emerging adults. Most emerging adults, again, profess that they believe in and normally try to do the morally right thing, as best as they can understand it. Most emerging adults do not routinely give themselves the legitimate option of selectively violating moral standards. But some do. A significant minority, in fact, does.

Happiness and Instinct

Another way to approach questions of moral behavior is to ask emerging adults how they actually would decide how to make moral choices in situations of uncertainty. In our survey, we asked emerging adults this question: "If you were unsure of what was right or wrong in a particular situation, how would you decide what to do? Would you most likely (1) do what would make you feel happy, (2) do what would help you get ahead, (3) follow the advice of a parent or teacher or other adult you respect, or (4) do what you think God or the Scripture tells you is right?"[14] Thirty-four percent of the survey respondents said they would "follow the advice of a parent or teacher," and 18 percent said they would "do what God or the scriptures" says is right. Nine percent—almost one in ten—reported that they would resolve their moral questions by doing "what would help them get ahead." The kind of thinking associated with this last answer is represented in a number of the quotes given in the previous few pages—namely, that it's a competitive world; everyone cheats, lies, and steals; that is necessary to succeed; you have to take advantage of limited opportunities; and so on.

The most frequently chosen answer to this survey question, however, was *"doing what would make you feel happy."* Nearly four in ten (39 percent) emerging adults we surveyed chose this answer. Slightly more of those we personally interviewed (41 percent) said the same thing when we asked the same question in interviews. Why? What did that answer mean? For some it comes back to the problem of really knowing right from wrong in the first place, which is then often resolved by falling back on moral individualism. One explained it this way:

> I would do what I thought made me happy or how I felt. Because I have no other way of knowing what to do but how I internally feel. That's where my decisions come from. From *me*. My decisions come from inside of me.

Others took a quasi-utilitarian approach to moral decision making, seeking to maximize pleasure: "I guess it depends on the situation, but probably what would make me happy. Because you only have one life, might as well be happy. Every second you spend mad or upset or angry you could spend being happy and have a whole lot more fun with your life." Others gave answers suggesting a similarly egocentric orientation: "I would probably do what would make me happy, what made me happy. Because it's me in the long run." And yet others, as in this answer, talked more about the power of personal gut feelings and emotions to inform their moral choices:

> Normally you're not like, "Oh, I'm gonna go commit a murder today." But then there's certain things where I'm like, "Oh, screw it, I'm going with what I think is my gut feeling." And that might not necessarily be the right thing. But if it's me fighting against my gut feelings or my emotions, that's where it gets really difficult. If it's emotional, I have a difficult time fighting that off. I usually give in.

It is important to note, however, that most emerging adults do not think about moral decision making as resulting primarily from cognitive deliberation

or actively considered judgment. Instead, most (72 percent of those we interviewed, cutting across a range of different types of answers on other questions)
describe their moral knowledge and behaviors as *being based upon "instinct."*[15]
Most report that they *automatically* know through embodied reaction what is
right and wrong in any situation. As one said, "From inside, neurons, nerves,
what my body tells me." Another reported: "You can kind of just tell instinctively. You can feel if it's good or bad." "It's pretty much common sense," one told
us. "You know what to do and you go with your common sense. Go with your
intuition." Still another told us, "I can usually just tell right away, don't have to
think about it very hard, you just know. It's hard to describe."[16]

Different emerging adults described this "instinctual" moral knowledge and
response in different ways. Some spoke in simple physiological terms. When
asked about where her sense of right and wrong come from, for example, one
reported, "I don't know. Probably like our adrenaline. Like, I get, my stomach
starts hurting. My heart starts beating. And all physiological things start happening. So that's where I get it from, mostly." Others spoke in more vague subjec-
tivist terms that they think might be related to religion: "I guess that's just an
internal feeling—whether it's, some people would say it's God or just a spiritual
thing or your conscience, those are all really the same thing when you think
about it, all kind of the same general thing in just different ways of saying it." Yet
others spoke about morality as if it were hardwired in human genetics: "We all
have a good, like a core, a core belief. We all have like a set of right and wrongs
that's like in the strands of our DNA. That's how we know that killing each other
is wrong, or hurting others or cheating or lying are wrong, not because it's in the
Ten Commandments, but because it hurts people, or because it hurts you, and
because it has negative repercussions." Many emerging adults agreed that morality is somehow "innate" to human nature, claiming:

> I think everybody has a sense of right and wrong, unless you are clini-
> cally insane or chemically imbalanced. It's common sense for most
> people what's really [moral]. There is a lot of gray in between, but on
> the far end of each spectrum you know what's absolutely wrong and
> right. I think it is just kind of innate for any person with a healthy mind.

Therefore, when someone acts morally, does the right thing, they will naturally
feel a kind of internal serenity:

> In my heart, I could feel it. You could feel what's right or wrong in your
> heart as well as your mind. And most of the time, I always feel it in my
> heart and it makes it easier for me to morally decide what's right and
> wrong. Because if I feel about doing something, I'm going to feel it in

my heart and if it feels good, then I'm going to do it. But if it doesn't feel good, I'm going to know, because then I'm going to be nervous and tensed and it's not going to feel good, not going to feel right. So it's like I got that feeling, as well as the mental.

Likewise, when someone does the morally wrong thing, they will instinctively feel badly about it in body and mind:

> I guess it's just kind of an emptiness, an unhappiness, and a dissatisfaction with life, and then thinking, "Wow, this isn't what I wanted with my life, I'm not happy." For sure, like I feel, like I pretty much know, when it's wrong and if I decide to do it, I'll feel bad about it, and it's kind of like an ache, like, "ergh." But in the end [when you do the right thing] it's a lot better than feeling bad about it, and you know it's one less time that you gave in to the enemy, that you gave in to, you know, your human nature, so, it's a victory even if it's small.

Some emerging adults spoke about this instinctive moral knowledge as their "conscience," which they often said had a firm grip on their lives. "You just listen to your conscience," one said. "Your conscience will tell you where the boundary is—well, a normal person's conscience will tell them where the boundary is. People aren't exactly stupid. They can figure it out." Another reported: "I think for me, personally, if I do something wrong and I know it's wrong and I don't rectify it my conscience, I have a conscience that will get at me and it'll stay at me for a while until I rectify it." Another explained, "I guess my conscience. Like, if I feel like I'm gonna do something that I'm constantly gonna keep thinking about and possibly have regrets about it, then I won't do it. I don't wanna live my life with any regrets, so I try not to do anything that I think I'll have regrets about in the future." For some, having a conscience internally meant external social controls and punishments should not have to matter in making moral choices:

> It doesn't matter if you get caught or not. You should have the conscience to say that it's not okay, regardless of whether somebody else saw you do it or not. At the end of the day you did it, so I mean just because you can run a red light doesn't mean you should just because there's no cops around. I don't agree with that at all. I don't like that kind of outlook.

But for some, even belief in the power of conscience cannot overcome the relativity involved in moral individualism, since what anyone's conscience makes them feel bad about is probably relative to what they think is right and wrong in the first place, as this emerging adult explains:

> I think your conscience will get you. Your conscience will tell you that you shouldn't have done it. But I guess different, it goes back to different people have different standards. If they can, so they think it's right. [So some people might do something other people think is wrong and not have any conscience, any guilt, because it's not wrong to them?] Uh-huh. Yeah.

The point is well taken. Consciences usually only work as well as they have been morally formed. People generally do not feel bad about doing things they genuinely believe are not wrong. So the existence of people's consciences per se does not guarantee the living of genuinely moral lives.

Some emerging adults are also aware that their instinctive moral reactions have little or no rational justification behind them, or at least that they themselves have not figured out the legitimate reasons for their moral instincts. To them, morality seems merely to be society's operant conditioning of behaviors. One, for example, explained:

> It's like I'm conditioned to immediately say, "Well, that's wrong," but when I actually think about it I'm like, "Well, why is it wrong?" It's honestly something I've never really been able to figure out, because really we are conditioned to think a lot of things like society tells you to think like this, and you do. And there are certain things that most people don't really deviate from too much, just because everybody thinks the same way. And I don't really know where it came from. I don't really know why we see this as right or wrong. It just is. My brain just automatically screams, "No, stealing is wrong, even if it doesn't hurt anybody, that's wrong, you can't do that." It's just, I don't know, when I actually think about it, I don't really know why. I honestly don't really have much of an answer for that.

Some other emerging adults, as with this case, explain human morality as nothing more than the social expression of natural human survival instincts:

> If you and I were on a deserted island somewhere, the morals would be different, because there is no guidelines in the way if we were born there. On this desert island, we actually would be different, because we would do what we have to do to survive. You know, when it comes down to it, the only real "morals" are [merely survival] instincts. I don't

think we have [what most people take to be] morals in our instincts. I think it's more that we have instincts that tell us to do what's best for the survival of ourselves and our species. Like our instincts would not tell us to just kill other humans for the hell of it, you know, because it doesn't make sense biologically, you're killing off the species.

Such a morally reductionist view does not necessarily mean that emerging adults who hold this outlook feel entitled to transcend or violate society's moral codes, however, simply because they believe they have "unmasked" them as being only about functional survival. Thus, the same emerging adult continued with this explanation:

> I mean all that stuff is like, the way I see it is like we have these rules and these guidelines because this is how you were grown up in. I feel like we're not growing up on a deserted island, we are here, we do live in this community, we have grown up a certain way. That's the way that we were raised and the way we're going to believe. So basically I don't think it's the intrinsic part of our nature, but it doesn't mean it's not important.

Society's moral orders, in other words, may fool people into thinking that morality really does have an objective ontological status with real directive force, when in fact that is simply a misrecognition of what are merely survival instincts. However, given the controlling power of society, even realizing that does not matter. There is no way to eradicate the power of instincts that give rise to moral sensibilities and no way to escape the society that inculcates moral norms. So everyone in the end has to live with the morality taught by their particular society.

This section's observations about morality being known "instinctively" are curious. In very many ways, emerging adults today express many of the difficulties that beset modern and postmodern moral philosophy—skepticism, relativism, subjectivism, and the interminability of debates due to the inability of any one school or approach to decisively win the arguments. That is not surprising. However, that the vast majority also believes that moral knowledge can be instinctively known is surprising, in at least one sense, which is that—despite all the individualism and social constructionism that is evident in so much emerging adult moral reasoning—on this point most emerging adults seem to be giving voice to something like the very premodern notion of a *natural law*.[17] Very few know about this theory, and not many more would likely subscribe to it if they did. Yet the way many emerging adults speak about moral knowledge as being instinctive, automatic, prerational, embodied, common sense, and perhaps even genetically rooted suggests a possible connection to the premodern idea that the universe inherently contains moral truths that all but the most morally deformed people cannot fail to know. Such a natural law may exist, according to different theories, simply because that is the way reality is, as some ancient Greek philosophers believed, or because a creator God purposefully designed it that way to reflect his goodness and character, as various theistic traditions have taught. Of course, "moral instincts" can be explained in other ways, including as the result of evolutionary natural selection. Still, we find it interesting that so many emerging adults insist upon an experience of moral knowledge that seems to hew so closely to a traditional natural-law theory, even when they know nothing about it theoretically and are otherwise so very modern and postmodern. Could it be that many emerging adults today are, along with all of their other assumptions and views, also nascent, unschooled, crypto believers in a natural law? If so, the incongruity of it would not be impossible, given the lack of coherence in much else they had to say.

Moral Dilemmas

Yet another way to gain some perspective on the moral reasoning of emerging adults is to engage them on the question of moral dilemmas. A moral dilemma is a complex situation that involves a conflict between moral imperatives, such that choosing one would violate the other. Psychologists, philosophers, ethicists, and other scholars interested in moral life and reasoning often use moral dilemmas to help sort out how people process difficult moral issues. In our interviews, we also raised questions about moral dilemmas. We asked emerging adults to tell us about any experiences they have had facing moral dilemmas recently and how they went about resolving them. In the context of a larger discussion about moral rights and wrongs, goods and bads, we asked this question: "Can you tell me about a specific situation you've been in recently where you were unsure of what was right and wrong?"[18] Their answers were revealing.

First, one-third of the emerging adults who we interviewed (33 percent) simply could not think of any moral dilemmas or difficult situations that they had personally confronted in recent years. They replied, simply, "I really don't know, 'cause I've never had to make a decision about what's right and what's wrong," and "Nothing really is coming to mind. I haven't had too many really huge moral dilemmas that I've had to navigate through in my lifetime, I don't think. Nothing is coming to mind right now." Others said, "Not really when it comes down to like moral fiber," and "Not really, unsure. Being logical as I am, I have most of it down to a logical right or wrong things. I don't know." After a long pause to think, another answered our question this way:

> I'm trying to think about some time when I decided not to steal something. I mean, not that I decide to steal things very much. [laughs] But I'm

trying, that's the kind of default thing my mind goes to. Hmm. [*pause*] Not really. I think the reason why I can't is because, up until a couple weeks ago, I'd only been basically faced with, my immediate task has been to read this stuff, learn this stuff [in high school]. I haven't really been out in the world. I don't know, I can't think of anything that has happened recently where I've really been torn up about it. I'm totally blank on that one.

What this absence of moral dilemmas may mean more broadly we discuss below.

Second, nearly one in three (29 percent) of the emerging adults we interviewed offered what they thought were examples of moral dilemmas that they had faced. But these in fact turned out to be not moral dilemmas having to do with right and wrong, but rather some other kind of practical decision they had had to make. These situations or problems they described to us actually had little or nothing to do with moral conflicts. Some of them concerned simple household decisions, such as whether to buy a second cat litter box:

> Well, I guess just today, this cat I'd gotten recently, it started to develop an area of wanting to use as a litter place that's not the litter box. I've been cleaning it up and trying to use that spray stuff to get away the smell of where she's gone, but she seems to keep going there. So I kind of already had the idea in my head that I did go to my mom to confirm if she thinks this is probably the best idea. I'm thinking of getting a second litter box to give her. So the best way to phrase that is, I guess, I made the decision but confirmed it with my mom.

Note: the "moral dilemma" here was not, say, whether to take the cat to a shelter or euthanize it, but simply what to do about it urinating in the wrong place. Other kinds of examples offered merely concerned whether the emerging adult should make a particular consumer decision:

> Well, I guess, renting the apartment thing, whether or not I would be able to afford it. So I just sat down and write down pros and cons, and work out the budget and see if it was doable. [So was there anything about moving that concerned the *morally* right thing to do, or was it just about finances?] It was just figuring out the finances.

Others' stories concerning money had to do with risk taking that might involve fines:

> Like "Should I park here?" you know, for 20 minutes when I only have enough change for 15, you know, should I risk getting that parking

ticket? [*laughs*] Choices like that. [So how did you decide what to do?] [*laughing*] It's usually what costs less money, say, as a college student that guides my choices, you know. I try to be more healthy when it comes to choices about like that, I guess.

Still other examples offered had to do with self-acceptance and the nerve to dress up among peers:

I mean mostly with me, it's being myself and being comfortable with who I am. Like today, this is a true story, you know, dressing, putting on dress shoes and khakis and being comfortable going to class in a tie. You know what I'm saying? I feel like in my heart a man should dress for the job he wants. That's what they say, right? A man should dress for the job that he wants. I want to be in the public eye, I feel like I should dress the part. So that's the way I feel, so an issue or a challenge for me is not worrying about what others think of that. Because not everybody my age feels like it's important to wear a tie.

Yet other examples of pseudo moral dilemmas *could* have been real moral dilemmas if the issue was engaged differently, but it was clear that the emerging adults really only had in mind things like technical cost-benefit analyses. Consider, for instance, this case about drilling for oil:

Oh yeah, I've got a good one for you: offshore drilling. I mean it's not an individual situation but a lot of conversations I have, you know, friends whose parents are senators and congressmen and that sort of stuff, so we talk about that kind of thing and I think there are just situations when you don't know what's right or wrong. The cost-benefit analysis that has to be done and that sort of thing, so.

Finally, some faux moral dilemmas simply have to do with trying to break bad habits, like driving badly:

Pulling out in front of somebody when I was driving and I probably shouldn't have, but I did anyway. If I make myself nervous I'm gonna get in a car accident. I've done that once and I never want to do it again. Just kinda like fast or jerky, or if people make me mad I just get stressed and go around them really fast. And I shouldn't drive like that. I know it and I do it anyways. One of these days I'll get pulled over for speeding, I'm sure. My insurance is already really high so I shouldn't speed, but I do it anyways.

These cases make it clear that many emerging adults do not have a good handle on what makes something a *moral* issue or what the specifically *moral* dimensions of such situations are. The idea of distinctively moral goods and bads, rights and wrongs, is not engaged. What comes to the fore instead are straightforwardly practical, utilitarian, financial, and psychological dilemmas.

So, including (1) those emerging adults who could not think of any moral dilemma that they had faced, (2) those who offered examples that were in fact not moral dilemmas, and (3) those (not discussed here) who simply declined to answer the question (about 3 percent), two-thirds of the emerging adults we interviewed (about 66 percent) proved simply unable to engage our questions about moral dilemmas in their lives.

The remaining one-third of emerging adults we interviewed did manage to tell us about genuine moral dilemmas they had faced recently in their lives, specific situations in which they were unsure of what was morally right and wrong to do. Of that one-third, about 35 percent described moral dilemmas they had faced concerning personal relationships (many of which had to do with whether or not to break up with a romantic partner), about 25 percent described dilemmas that involved alcohol or drugs (such as whether to drink and drive), and 20 percent described facing moral dilemmas in workplace situations (such as dealing with inappropriate or harassing behavior by colleagues). Another 10 percent described moral dilemmas concerning abortion, adoption, or other child-related decisions. And the remaining 10 percent described moral dilemmas involving choices about future schooling or work, which seemed to involve genuine moral issues. Some of their examples of moral dilemmas were somewhat trivial. Others were truly profound, difficult, and troubling. For the purposes of this chapter, it is not necessary to spell out specific examples of these moral dilemmas; the reader can imagine them. Our primary point here is that only a minority of emerging adults—about one-third—can, in the context of a three-hour interview including a long section discussing morality, speak meaningfully about any struggles, conflicts, or dilemmas they have faced in their moral experiences and decision making. The rest either think they do not face any moral conflicts or uncertainties, think that they do when in fact they really do not, or do not understand what "moral" means.

Some Reflections

Our presentation of emerging adult voices on the topic of morality is, we admit, not perfectly balanced, in the sense that not every perspective and argument was given its exactly proportional weight or space in this chapter's exposition. We have highlighted a number of what we think are significant dominant and minority voices of particular interest. And we have backgrounded some of the more conventional viewpoints. We could have quoted more emerging adults saying that there is a moral right and wrong, that people should be good, that God gives commandments, that the Bible tells them how to live, and so on. They certainly exist and are part of the larger story. But we do not think that quoting them at length would have added much insight or value to our analysis. In mainstream American culture, those views are fairly standard, representing the default—what's expected. Many Americans may not actually believe them, but they still represent the inherited, conventional, predictable, baseline positions. So reciting them here would contribute little. Instead we have focused on what we think are more interesting and important themes expressed by different types of emerging adults. And we have provided estimates of the proportion of emerging adults that express those themes, in order to help place their numbers in a larger context.

What we have found, in short, is that moral individualism is widespread among emerging adults and that a sizeable minority professes to believe in moral relativism. We also found that emerging adults resort to a variety of explanations about what makes anything good or bad, wrong or right—many of which reflect weak thinking and provide a fragile basis upon which to build robust moral positions of thought and living. We learned that a substantial minority of emerging adults admitted that, for various reasons, they do violate or would consider violating their own moral standards and those of society if it worked to their advantage and they thought they could get away with it. We found that the majority of emerging adults say that they do not or would not refer to moral traditions or authorities or religious or philosophical ethics to make difficult moral decisions, but rather would decide by what would personally make them happy or would help them to get ahead in life. Finally, we discovered that the vast majority of emerging adults could not engage in a discussion about real moral dilemmas, but either could not think of any dilemma they had recently faced or misunderstood what a moral dilemma is.

So what does all of this tell us? First, we think the widespread moral individualism and solid minority presence of moral relativism among emerging adults today tell us that the adult world that has socialized these youth for 18 to 23 years has done an awful job when it comes to moral education and formation. Moral individualism and relativism are simply intellectually impossible and socially unsustainable positions. Any college sophomore philosophy major should be able to handily deconstruct them both. Yet the majority of American youth have entered emerging adulthood committed to moral individualism. And a substantial minority of them have done the same with moral relativism. On these two elementary points, these emerging adults are simply lost. They are morally at sea in boats that leak water badly. That is not an acceptable situation.

But if these emerging adults are lost, it is because the larger culture and society into which they are being inducted is also lost. The forces of social reproduction here are powerful. That so many emerging adults today are adrift in their moral thinking (though not necessarily in how they live, we think) tells us that the adult world into which they are emerging is also adrift. The families, schools, religious communities, sports teams, and other voluntary organizations of civil society are failing to provide many young people with the kind of moral education and training needed for them even to realize, for example, that moral individualism and relativism make no sense, that they cannot be reasonably defended or sustained, that some alternative views must be necessary if we are to be at all reasonable when it comes to moral concerns. Colleges and universities appear to be playing a part in this failure as well.[19] There are many explanations for this situation that deserve to be better understood. But for the moment our point is simply this: the adult world of American culture and society is failing very many of its youth when it comes to moral matters. We are letting them down, sending many, and probably most, of them out into the world without the basic intellectual tools and basic personal formation needed to think and express even the most elementary of reasonably defensible moral thoughts and claims. And that itself, we think, is morally wrong.

Consider one example of this kind of intellectual failing. Central to many of the confusions in emerging adult moral reasoning is the inability to distinguish between objectively *real* moral truths or facts and people's human *perceptions* or *understandings* of those moral truths or facts. The error of not distinguishing these two things is this: the *realities* themselves are confused with, and therefore dependent upon, people's *cognitive grasp* of them. What *actually* exists is conflated into what is *believed* to exist. But those are different things that must be kept separate. For example, the moral truth that human slavery is a categorical moral evil stands true whether or not people understand and believe it. Many people before the nineteenth century did not believe this, but that itself did not make slavery morally right. When people do not believe moral truths, we rightly say that they are wrong. Slavery *is* a moral evil. The truth status of that fact does not depend on people's subjective recognition or assimilation of it, any more than the existence of germs or the Grand Canyon depends on people knowing about it. Whatever people know or believe, it is true that germs and the Grand Canyon exist and slavery is evil. As Flannery O'Connor once wrote, "The truth does not change according to our ability to stomach it."[20] What most needs to happen, then, is for people to conform their minds and lives to the reality of those truths. In short, moral realism is the only position that makes sense.

Yet most emerging adults do not understand that. Some cannot even begin to grasp the distinction made here. They think that people believing something to be morally true *is what makes it* morally true. They assume that if some cultures believe different things about morality, then there is not a moral truth at all. These mentalities naturally lead to moral skepticism, subjectivism, relativism, and, ultimately, nihilism. Are we surprised then that these are precisely the directions in which we see many emerging adults today actually heading? Among the many problems here is that few of them have thought very far through the intellectual impossibilities and practical consequences of their approaches. Why? Not because emerging adults are dumb. It is rather because many representatives of the adult world who are responsible for socializing youth have in the previous two decades not asked them to do that or shown them how. And why not? Because, we suspect, a lot of them do not know how to do that themselves. In which case, we should be thankful that—since behavior often lags behind the implications of thought—many people act more morally than they are able to justify.

Much of this is institutionally located. Good and bad ideas do not float about in the air. They are the products of particular institutional practices. To modify an observation by Karl Marx, the ruling ideas are the ideas of the ruling institutions.[21] Take public schools, for one example. Schools are one of the most powerful socializing institutions of youth in American society today, along with families and the mass media. Public schools are the dominant institution among all school types. Before we interviewed our respondents as emerging adults, we had previously interviewed them twice, when they were still teenagers, some of them when they were as young as 13 years old. So we know a great deal about their lives before they entered emerging adulthood. One big theme that stuck out in our previous interviews was the fact that the schools, especially public schools, that our younger respondents attended studiously avoided talking about potentially controversial moral issues. Over and over again, these teenagers we interviewed reported that their teachers always sidestepped and evaded questions and problems that might generate disagreement or conflict in the classroom. "No, my teachers avoid controversies like that like the plague," they would typically say. "Anytime anything that might make trouble or hurt someone's feelings come up, they say we aren't going there," others confirmed. "Nope, we can't talk about religion or them hot-button moral issues in school, 'cause they don't want to open up that can of worms" was a typical report. In short, it appears that most schools, especially public schools, are not teaching students how to constructively engage moral issues about which people disagree. Quite the contrary, schools are teaching students that the best way to deal with difficult moral problems and questions is to ignore them. The moral pedagogy of most middle and high schools clearly seems to be: *avoid, ignore, and pretend the issues will go away.* Needless to say, that is naive and impossible. It actually resembles highly dysfunctional families that have sets of issues that nobody is allowed to bring up or discuss and that are instead carefully tiptoed around.

All of this is sociologically intelligible. Middle schools and high schools usually have some degree of cultural diversity among their students. These days, especially, teachers and school administrators mostly feel pressure to get their students to perform well on standardized tests. They also more generally want to minimize any sort of trouble or conflict in school, to have their work go smoothly. Given the mass nature of education and limited resources, simply maintaining order becomes the number one goal. Many teachers and principals have enough difficulty simply contending with basic forms of misbehavior and academic underperformance. So the idea of purposefully and directly engaging students for good educational reasons, in moral issues over which people disagree seems like asking for trouble. Red flags fly up all over the place. Teachers, many of whom perhaps are not sure themselves how to think well about moral problems, envision out-of-control arguments in the classroom and students' feelings getting hurt. Principals foresee angry parents and lawsuits. At which point the discussion is shut down. And so the opportunity to provide a basic education in moral reasoning is treated like the Black Death. Cutbacks in American higher education in programs in the humanities in favor of increased investments in science, technology, engineering, and mathematics may contribute to this tendency as well.

To be clear, we do not think that American public schools should be in the business of promoting one particular *substantive* moral position on specific moral issues. Private schools may do that, but not public schools. But *all* schools certainly should be promoting the particular position that *it is good to learn how to think clearly and coherently about important issues, including moral issues.* That is what education is all about. Schools do not need to teach *what* in particular students should believe on every moral matter. But they certainly could, and, we think, should, teach *how* to reason well when it comes to moral problems.[22] Every school could teach how to identify rival presuppositions, how to civilly question and critique differing positions without creating explosive conflict, and how to eliminate certain arguments for their lack of intellectual merit. Why cannot schools be places that model how to have a good, constructive argument? Why can't teachers show that we need not be afraid of all disagreement, that it is possible for people who differ about matters they care about to talk things out and perhaps move forward together? This may be asking a lot. But if centers of education cannot do this, then what hope do we have for sustaining our larger pluralistic society? Knowing how to think well in the most basic ways, including about morality, is as important for our nation and society, we believe, as learning algebra and having a football team. We have to be able to rise to the occasion—or else live with the consequences of the kind of moral outlooks seen in this chapter.

But it is not just schools. Another factor is that, with the advent of globalization, the Internet, digital video, and cable and satellite television, this cohort of young people has exponentially more information, narratives, and political, ideological, and moral claims at its fingertips than any generation before. This mass of information, stories, and claims is also less filtered and evaluated by institutional gatekeepers—book editors and news executives, people who might guarantee some level of accuracy, significance, and value—than it ever was in the past. Therefore, the most important and reliable information, stories, and claims instantaneously flash onto the same screens along with the most bogus, irrelevant, and misleading ones. In short, most emerging adults today are inundated with more competing information, narratives, and truth claims than any person could possibly assimilate, assess, and synthesize. And along with this flood of information comes a plethora of morally relevant beliefs, claims, and arguments. Making good sense of it all can be very difficult, if not impossible—especially when adult institutions, like families, schools, and congregations, are not providing youth with the kind of critical reasoning skills needed to do that well. So an overwhelmed incoherence often prevails and emerging adults retreat to the kind of seemingly safe moral positions that we have observed in this chapter.

Moving on next to the accounts offered by emerging adults about the source or basis of morality, again we find little reason for encouragement. One-third said they simply didn't know what made anything right or wrong, good or bad. Others offered ideas—that moral action is determined by what other people will think of the actor, for example, or by whether it improves circumstances functionally—that make little sense. Others espouse views, such as positive laws and rules defining morality, that at least seem to possess some level of consistency but in the end reduce morality to sheer power and will, without apparently realizing it. Similarly, the social-contract theory of morality that some emerging adults propounded descends from a long line of serious thinkers (although these thinkers have usually sought to explain the basis of civil society and political life, not morality), but it also proves unable to sustain a thick notion of what morality is or to explain why people finally should act morally when that involves personal cost. Furthermore, while not hurting other individuals is certainly an important part of most moral traditions, it is not really possible to ground morality per se in a "no hurt" rule. For one thing, as noted above, in many cases the definition of "hurt" itself depends on some substantive morality. What is or should be hurtful or not often depends significantly on what one thinks is ultimately truly good or bad in life. Finally, whether or not karma is real and operates as advertised, in the end referencing karma does not answer the question of morality's source; it only says that, wherever morality comes from, some kind of moral justice will prevail in the end. These critiques and the others mentioned above obviously only just begin to touch on a few of the problems involved in emerging adults' accounts of the sources or origins of moral truths. That will have to do for present purposes. The point, at bottom, is this: a large proportion of emerging adults today are lost, confused, or misled in their thinking about what makes anything morally good or bad—and yet they are generally not aware that this is so.

Furthermore, that sizeable numbers of emerging adults feel free to engage in moral compromises and violations under the right circumstances does not shock us. We are moral realists in more ways than one. We think that fact is neither new to the world nor the end of the world. However, we also do not believe that the moral orders and experiences of societies remain constant throughout history. Things can definitely get morally better and worse. And the difference between better and worse can matter profoundly for the potential flourishing of human life in those societies. Therefore, we think it is worth examining that one in three emerging adults admit being prepared to violate the moral right or good if it helped them and they could get away with it. We do not think it likely that such attitudes are unrelated to other aspects of their problematic moral reasoning noted above, including moral individualism, relativism, confusion about moral sources, and so on. We also have similar reactions to our finding that seeking their own happiness and getting ahead in life constitute the primary means for the majority of emerging adults for deciding moral issues in contexts of uncertainty. Our view of human beings did not lead us to think it would be dramatically otherwise. But that itself does not mean that happiness and getting ahead represent good primary moral decision-making criteria that serve either emerging adults or our culture and society well.

Finally, we think the widespread inability to address the question of moral dilemmas indicates an anemic view of what even counts in emerging adult life as moral or as concerning morality. We know from the rest of the interviews that most emerging adults in fact face all kinds of real moral challenges, conflicts, temptations, difficulties, dilemmas, and sometimes tragedies in their lives. Some of the remaining chapters in this book make that clear. It is not the case that emerging adults today do not have to grapple with serious moral dilemmas. We know that. But it also seems that very many emerging adults hold views of moral right and wrong, good and bad, that make many of the truly moral features of different life experiences invisible. Stated differently, most emerging adults today seem to live in morally very thin or spotty worlds. Most of what goes on around them seems to appear to them as amoral or extramoral—as mostly concerning basic issues of functional costs and benefits, psychological impacts, and utilitarian calculations. Morality, for many emerging adults, mostly concerns extreme things, like murder, rape, and bank robbery. For many, driving drunk, doing drugs, cheating on a partner, cheating in school, stealing, and having abortions also qualify as moral issues. But most of the rest of life seems not to have many moral implications or challenges involved. Much of life seems to them to be a neutral zone, in which moral goods and bads are absent or irrelevant.[23]

It is this learned blindness to the moral dimensions of much of human life that enables many emerging adults to say with straight faces, as one interviewee did, "I don't really deal with right and wrong that often." Rather than seeing so much of human personal, interpersonal, and social life as infused with significant moral meanings and implications, as it most definitely is, many emerging adults segregate "moral" matters off to the side, as part of a narrowly defined set of issues or problems, like driving drunk, stealing, and murdering. And that produces a moral myopia that in turn undermines the ability for robust moral reasoning.

In such a world, doing drugs, for example, becomes a matter of individual moral "interpretation," which in the end boils down to one's personal opinion. Completely removed from moral consideration, in that case, are the many real moral ramifications of doing drugs in the present war-on-drugs world. Emerging adult drug users do not consider as a moral issue, for example, the massive bloodshed that the drug trade causes in other parts of the world, such as Mexico, among those involved in illegally supplying drugs to meet the immense U.S. demand for them. They do not think morally about how their drugs are implicated in the promotion of gangs and gangster warfare that kills thousands in the United States and beyond. They do not weigh the moral implications of the hundreds of thousands of American men and women—often emerging adults themselves—who sit in prison for narcotics convictions, peers who have risked incarceration to make a small share of some of the money that they spend on their drugs. Drug-using emerging adults do not consider the tax dollars spent combating the illicit drug industry that might otherwise be used for much better purposes. All of that is invisible. Rather, whether to use drugs is either defined as not a moral issue at all or is narrowed down to things like whether drugs will be bad for one's health and future relationships and job prospects. This is what we mean by the learned blindness to morality.

Complicating this picture, very many emerging adults (like most other Americans, as we know from other interviews of other research projects) are somewhat schizophrenic when it comes to morality. On the one hand, most emerging adults know that nearly everyone breaks rules, that the world is full of questionable people, and that even they themselves are far from perfect. They know that they sometimes do the wrong thing. In this "inclusively immoral" world, it is not really a problem to think, do, say, and advocate the morally wrong things, however, because "everyone is like that." Nobody is any worse than anyone else.

On the other hand, many if not most emerging adults tend to define what is wrong or immoral as *extreme* cases—"murderers, rapists, and bank robbers" being an almost archetypical representation of what or who is immoral. This has the agreeable effect of defining most emerging adults as not immoral, as never doing anything of questionable morality. This "exclusively immoral" world effectively "others" those who do moral wrong as being very far away, very much unlike the ordinary people that most emerging adults view themselves to be. When those who are not moral are only terrible people, then one is automatically exempt from being not moral, since not many view themselves as terrible. One therefore clearly belongs to the category of moral. Emerging adults (again, like the rest of adult Americans) tend to keep both of these understandings of morality in play at the same time. As a consequence, they are normally able at any given time to acknowledge all of the moral problems and failures in their lives, yet without having to feel too bad about them or to think of themselves as nonmoral people. That too affects their moral reasoning.

Having defined moral problems away to the far extreme, as having to do with "murderers, rapists, and bank robbers," emerging adults can then afford to be rather blasé about the necessary moral underpinnings of any functioning society—including even a liberal society. That the social order that emerging adults enjoy works as well as it does can simply be taken for granted. That schools, banks, corporations, and the rest function as well as they seem to is simply assumed to be normal. Functional order and social prosperity are taken to be the natural default, not valuable accomplishments that take real collective human effort. The idea that a democracy or a republic or any humane society requires that its citizens continually invest in the common good, or even actively contribute to institutional functionality, by sustaining and practicing moral virtues, such as acts of care and goodness, that go beyond simple procedural justice, is either inconceivable or else sounds laughably old-fashioned. Consider, for instance, the reflections of this emerging adult in our discussion about the value or purpose of morality: "I would like to have an answer like, 'For society to function.' But I don't necessarily think that's true." In her mind, society functioning is a given, a natural fact, to be assumed without asking much morally of its citizens. This is for her in part because nobody in her experience actually seems particularly immoral or destructive: "I don't feel like I personally know any mean or evil people. I have never met anybody that I've watched do something just out of spite and evilness." We are glad this is true for her. But she has obviously not studied much history or read much in the newspaper. So, we probed, the threat of social disorder doesn't really seem real to her? "It doesn't really. Sometimes the world is a scary place, but I think there are enough sane people to hold it together," she answered. The question of morality is thus transformed from a thick one about goodness, right will, and wise choices, to a thin one about sanity and reason. In short, morality as it has been perennially defined in human history and experience can simply be set aside, and all will surely be well with the world.

One thing in all of this that we think emerging adults need to realize is that moral relativism and complete tolerance for every other point of view actually do not respect or honor those points of views; quite the opposite. People often think that they are showing consideration for different beliefs when they say "whatever." But what they are really, if unintentionally, saying is, "I don't care enough about what you think or believe to pay it any attention. Your view doesn't make any difference, it doesn't deserve to be taking seriously." To really respect and honor someone's point of view requires taking it seriously enough to actually learn about and consider it, question it, and perhaps challenge it if it seems problematic. Sometimes opposing what seems to be a bad idea is the greatest respect one can show it. By contrast, as Wendell Berry points out:

> If I merely tolerate my neighbors on the assumption that all of us are equal, that means I can take no interest in the question of which ones of us are right and which ones are wrong; it means that I am denying the community the use of my intelligence and judgment; it means I am not prepared to defer to those whose abilities are superior to mine, or to help those whose condition is worse; it means I can be as self-centered as I please.[24]

That understanding turns the tables on the standard assumptions of many Americans today. We think that undermining this widespread pseudo respect for different ideas and beliefs in the form of passive tolerance of them is a key part of strengthening the moral imaginations of emerging adults today.

To repeat what we said in the introduction, whether or not the situation we have described in this chapter is any better or worse than it was among young adults in previous generations is not our interest. Our concern is the state of things among emerging adults today and what it means for the future. Even if it could be shown that young adults of past generations were less morally thoughtful and coherent than those today—which we highly doubt—the fact is that the world we live in itself has become much more complicated, pluralistic, and arguably morally challenging than it was before. And that ups the ante when it comes to dealing well with moral issues. To take the simple position that "things have always been bad" is entirely unhelpful. Comparisons to the past may be interesting, but they do little to help us address the difficulties of today and tomorrow. What matters now is how well equipped we are to address the challenges of the present and the future. On that matter, when it comes to moral reasoning among emerging adults, we do not find the evidence reassuring.

To be clear, again, we are not suggesting that all or most emerging adults are moral reprobates. Some of what some of them say makes real sense. Some of what others say in fact seems to be trying to give expression to real moral difficulties and challenges in the world. A few emerging adults are quite clear-headed and impressively articulate. And many others in fact live decent, and sometimes morally very impressive, lives. Our central point does not have to do with moral degeneracy. Our main point concerns moral education and training. American emerging adults are a people deprived, a generation that has been failed, when it comes to moral formation. They have had withheld from them something that every person deserves to have a chance to learn: how to think, speak, and act well on matters of good and bad, right and wrong. Therefore, in Charles Taylor's words, with which we opened this chapter, "We have to fight uphill to rediscover the obvious, to counteract the layers of suppression of modern moral consciousness."[25] It is not that emerging adults are a morally corrupt lot (although some of them are). The problem is more that many of them are simply lost. They do not adequately know the moral landscape of the real world that they inhabit. And they do not adequately understand where they themselves stand in that real moral world. They need some better moral maps and better-equipped guides to show them the way around. The question is, do those maps and guides exist, and can they be put into use?

‖ 2 ‖

Captive to Consumerism

The only thing that consoles us for our miseries is distraction, yet that is the greatest of our wretchednesses. Because that is what mainly prevents us from thinking about ourselves and leads us imperceptibly to damnation. Without it we should be bored, and boredom would force us to search for a firmer way out, but distraction entertains us and leads us imperceptibly to death.

—Blaise Pascal

What do American emerging adults think and feel about the mass consumer society in which they have grown up? Are they comfortable with mass consumerism? Do they like it? Or do they have concerns about the environmental impact of mass consumerism or the misplaced values and priorities that some critics see in consumer materialism? What role does the buying and consumption of material things play in the lives, values, and goals of emerging adults today? This chapter explores the place of mass consumerism and materialistic visions of the good life among emerging adults. After a brief view of some survey statistics, we explore in some depth today's emerging adults' views of mass consumerism. In that discussion we focus on how critical or uncritical they are of our culture of material consumption. We then shift to examine emerging adults' outlooks on what makes for a good human life, and how material consumption fits into that vision.

First, in our nationally representative telephone survey, we asked emerging adults some questions about materialism and consumerism. The findings help to provide a larger context for the analysis of our follow-up interviews with them. Among emerging adults ages 18–23, 65 percent said that shopping and buying things give them a lot of pleasure. Fifty-four percent said that they would be happier if they could afford to buy more things. And 47 percent felt that the things they own say a lot about how well they are doing in life. These are survey questions about which some respondents likely feel a social-desirability bias not to

70

give answers that would make others view them as materialistic or shallow. Nevertheless, between one-half to two-thirds of emerging adults said that their well-being can be measured by what they own, that buying more things would make them happier, and that they get a lot of pleasure simply from shopping and buying things. A majority of emerging adults today thus appear quite positively disposed to materialism and consumerism, at least as far as surveys can measure that.

What about our in-person interviews? What did we learn there? Our discussions with emerging adults focused on possible practical and moral questions concerning mass consumerism. What do they think about the general topic of shopping, buying, and consuming material things like clothes, cars, music, etc.? How do they think or feel about the consumption of material products that nearly all Americans engage in? Are there any limits to what people should possess? What are they, and why? What are reasonable goals when it comes to buying, owning, and consuming things in their own lives? What we found is that few emerging adults expressed concerns about the potential limits or dilemmas involved in a lifestyle devoted to boundless material consumption. Most are either positive or neutral about mass consumer materialism. Only a few have reservations or doubts.

We went into this consumerism section of the interviews expecting at least some emerging adults to display a heightened awareness about environmental problems associated with mass consumer economies. We thought we would hear a variety of perspectives, including some "green" and "limits-to-growth" viewpoints—especially since a sizeable proportion of those we interviewed are in college. We expected at least some of them to speak critically about the emptiness or dangers of all-out materialism, even if that talk was only rhetorical banter for the sake of considering all possible sides. We also went into our interviews expecting to hear emerging adults talk about the political and military complications of such dependence on foreign natural resources like oil. And we expected some to emphasize the importance of personal, inward, subjective, or spiritual growth or richness over the material consumptions of products. But we heard almost none of that. We actually started off in these discussions very cautiously, determined not to be leading in these directions with our questions, since we assumed that many emerging adults would be primed to criticize mass consumerism. But when we heard no such critiques, we began to press harder. Soon we were nearly pushing the emerging adults we interviewed to consider any plausible problematic side to mass consumerism, if they could. They could not.

Even when we started deliberately leading emerging adults to address such questions, very few wanted to go there. Most emerging adults simply had very little to say that was critical, nor were they worried or even much aware of the possible questions or concerns about mass consumerism. For the vast majority, mass consumerism was good, end of story. Some others thought that mass consumerism may have some problems, they admitted, but none that they can understand or that need to affect their own lifestyles and goals.

Mass Consumerism—What, Me Worry?

For nearly all emerging adults, mass consumerism is either an unqualified good in life, or it may have some problems, though none that they can understand or do anything about, and so therefore none with which they should be concerned.

Perfectly happy. Contemporary emerging adults are either true believers or complacent conformists when it comes to mass consumerism. Most like shopping and buying things. Most enjoy consuming products and services. It is the way of life with which they are familiar and content. What problems with mass consumerism could there be? This was the general outlook of emerging adults on mass consumerism. But different individuals expressed it in slightly different ways, emphasizing somewhat different themes, even if a good amount of overlap among them is clear. One group was unabashedly enthusiastic about mass consumerism. They strongly emphasized its importance in driving the American economy and improving people's way of life. One, for example, said about mass consumerism, "It's important, keeps the economy going. Going into too much debt is always a very negative thing. But you gotta do what you can, stimulate everything." Another argued:

> Some people like that stuff, you know? The way I think about it is, I see the people all going to the mall wasting their money. But then again, it's not like they can afford mansions, not like everyone can be Bill Gates. So, lots of people get that simple pleasure in life, a lot of people's pleasure in life derives from that consumerism. So, if you have to spend 70 hours a week in retail to afford that, I'm not really going to criticize. Consumerism is good for the economy.

Should there be any limits at all to what people consume? "No," said one, "in our capitalist society, none. [Just] if you can afford it." In response to those who might say that materialism is bad for the environment, that mass consumerism may reflect misplaced life priorities, or that it undermines relationships or spiritual life, another emerging adult replied:

> They're probably right. But at the same time I guess this is one place where I'm just like, "This is the world we live in, either get on board or

be unhappy." I don't really know what to tell you. I guess I just really don't agree with people who are like, "Let's go granola." That's really unnecessary. You don't have to live that way anymore. You have the opportunity to live better. That's why your parents did what they could for you, and their parents did for them, is to give you this. We are improved. Be improved.

Here we find a vision for self-improvement, for growth and transcendence beyond the old. But the improvement in this case does not concern self or morals or social justice, but rather material lifestyles and personal consumption. Yet another emerging adult we interviewed reflected a similarly uncritical mentality:

I am the ultimate American when it comes to that, I mean, I got 500 bucks in my pocket one day, and two days later, I'm looking to make my next 500. I spend my money, man I am great for the economy. If I won the lottery I would stimulate the economy on my own. Because I spend my money that I don't save, unless I set [a savings goal] of what I make, I spend.

Likewise, this young man sees a synergy between the enjoyments of personal consumption and the health of the national economy: "I buy a lot of movies and CDs. I joke that is what I do, instead of my friends who buy cigarettes and beer. I don't know, whatever makes people happy—it's like, our society is based on buying stuff, so I guess it helps." Does he think there should be any limits to what people maybe should possess? "Again, to each his own. I don't like buying a lot of stuff, but if it makes you happy, that's what your hobby is, and you can afford it, whatever."

Another set of emerging adults did not talk about helping the economy but rather more individualistically about how shopping and consumerism make them feel good, help them be respected, and build self-confidence. Consider the following representative quote, for example:

It feels good to be able to get things that you want and you work for the money. If you want something, you go get it. It makes your life more comfortable and I guess it just makes you feel good about yourself as well. You want to get some, you work for it and you can get it. I think it's a good thing to buy what you want if you work for it, because when you work for something, then you gain that accomplishment, it's not like you were just given money, I want to get this, you know, I'll buy that. It's like you actually work for that thing so you feel that you deserve it, you earned it. You earned that thing that you wanted. You weren't just given it.

Here working, earning, buying, and enjoying are key to achieving self-respect. In this second case, consuming material goods is a basic source of personal happiness and self-esteem. "Buying stuff really makes me happy. I know how bad that sounds, but seriously." Why does that sound bad, we asked? "Because you shouldn't be that materialistic, you shouldn't define your happiness on the things that you have or want." Why not? What is wrong with that, we pressed?

> Okay, when I'm having a bad day, a bad week, whatever, there is nothing that makes me feel better about myself more than going and buying myself a whole new wardrobe. I feel like a better person, I feel prettier, I feel more intelligent sometimes, I feel cleaner, it's just a great feeling. I feel self-sufficient 'cause I bought it on my own.

Note that the last response does not actually answer the question asked, about why being happy with shopping sounds bad, but rather ignores it and presents more information justifying the need to shop. Exchanges with other interviewees were similar: "I love shopping, I love music. I think it's fine. You know, maybe not necessary to buy a $10,000 purse or whatever, but I like shopping, I can't really go against it." Does she think there are limits to what people should possess? "I don't know, I mean, if you want it, buy it. There's certain things that are just, I think, unnecessary. But, you know, if you think it's necessary in your life and you can afford it, more power to you." Might mass consumption be destructive to society in any way, we ask? "I love to shop. My sister doesn't, I do. I love to shop, I love going to the mall, I like buying things. I don't consider myself materialistic, I don't depend on my material things to make myself who I am, but I do love to shop." Again, the answer to whether mass consumption might be destructive is simply "I love to shop." The premise of the question itself is apparently invisible.

A third theme among emerging adults on the topic of mass consumerism is the avoidance of making any evaluative judgments of anyone's consumption habits. It is entirely an individual matter and should be driven by whatever makes people happy. Thinking collectively about these concerns as a society is either inconceivable or illegitimate. It's up to individual people. Consider, as examples, the following quotes. "I think everyone has what they like," one young woman declared.

> If you have a thousand shoes, that is all you. If you want a thousand shoes, cool, that is all what you want. I personally wouldn't want a thousand shoes, I love shoes, but I wouldn't want that many because I don't value spending my money on that. But I don't want to judge someone else and say you can't or shouldn't have that.

In response to the idea that a person might own 12 mansions and 20 cars, another emerging adult said, "I think it's kind of silly, but hey, to each their own." Yet another said to a similar question, "I don't really have any positive or negative feelings towards the issue. People should get things if it works for them, if that's what they want." So is any amount that people buy too much? "No. I don't feel like that. I think people should do what makes them happy." She then continued:

> I guess I don't really think about consumerism as far as its effects on society. I think I don't like to have too much stuff like clutter. I do get rid of stuff a lot. I like to shop. I'll be honest with you. I am a woman. I like to go shopping. [But] I don't really think about long-term effects on society and mass production and mass consumption.

Finally, another only qualified the "happy individual" criteria with her personal problem with rich people who do not also give to those who have material needs:

> I'm definitely a consumer. I like to buy things. I like to have things. Yeah, I think it's great, capitalism and giving consumers choices are all good. I mean, you can have too many cars, too many boats, two planes, which is kind of over the top. People can definitely get excessive in a lot of ways. There is definitely a limit. But, it's whatever makes you happy. If somebody needs all those things, then they need all those things. But if they're not giving back to people who are more needy then, yeah, I've got a problem with that.

Yet even in this example, it's still ultimately "whatever makes you happy."

As seen to some degree in earlier quotes, a large group of the emerging adults—about one out of four we interviewed—also emphasize "whatever makes you happy," but clearly added the qualification of "within your means." Anybody can buy whatever they want, in other words, as long as they can afford it. The only possible limit to mass consumption is the danger of consumers going into too much debt. The standard line here is, essentially, as one emerging adult stated, "I'm not really concerned about mass consumption. If you have the money, you can buy what you want in society." Another told us, "I don't have any particular thoughts on that, not really. But I think sometimes it's ridiculous how much stuff costs, like $80 on a pair of shoes, it's just dumb." What, we asked, about any possible limits on consumption? "I don't think so. If you have the money to buy it, regardless how I think about the product, you should still have the right to buy it."

Even emerging adults who complain about consumption fads in the end come back to the issue of purchasing power, as in the following quote: "A lot of people focus on material things, me included. We look at labels, as far as what one person, this celebrity, wears I want to wear. A lot of people pay attention to material objects and name brands and stuff." So are there any limits, we asked, to what people should possess? "I don't think that there are any limits. As long as you can afford it. People talk, you know, 'You shouldn't buy this, you shouldn't buy that,' but if you've been successful and well enough off, I think that you should indulge yourself." It is not only upper-middle-class emerging adults who think that money justifies consumption. Emerging adults who are just struggling to get by financially also share the same view: "I wish I had more money, no, I have a really hard time. Me and my husband have been trying to be really good, but it's gotten to the point now where I feel bad like if I go even to Wal-Mart to buy me a shirt; but if I go out and buy my kids stuff, I don't feel as bad like that." Does she think there are any limits to what people should possess? "I think if you have the money, you can own whatever you want."

It's not only that money can purchase anything you desire. Some emerging adults, including the woman quoted above, seem to assume that humans can consume endlessly, since, they believe, if a product is man-made, then it can be remade infinitely:

> I'd say if you got the money, get it. Just don't go invest all your time and money in materialistic stuff, because there is always going to be something newer and better. If you can afford it, go ahead and get it. I don't really too much worry about massive consumption because, if you can buy it, then I am pretty sure that it was made by man, so it can be made again. Unless it's like gas, 'cause like I know, the oil is running out or whatever and so, that's like halfway made by man—they turn it from petroleum into gas. But see now they're making cars that don't even have to run off of gas. So just park it in your garage and plug it in.

Natural resources are apparently endless, and when they are not, technological developments will overcome our limitations. Therefore, the only factor that matters is "if you got the money." Similarly, this emerging adult explained, "If you have the means to have what you need and some of what you want, I don't think there's a limit, that's fine. Like nobody's limiting Donald Trump from buying this state [New York], but he has the means to have the things that he needs and the luxury of having things that he wants." Are there any potential problems, then, when it comes to the topic of mass consumerism?

> I do think there's too much jealousy when people are like, "Well, she got a Range Rover for her 16th birthday and all I got was my brother's old Camry," you know something like that. I think that's the problem, when

people start being jealous of people who are more fortunate. There's always gonna be jealousy. I'm not trying to say that it's gonna be like everybody is, "I'm happy with my beat-up old car with no windshield." But I think everyone just needs to accept what they have or strive for better or they just need to stop [complaining].

Again, any problems that might exist—other than a possible inability to afford things—has to do with individual attitudes. People should either live within their means or try to increase their means—and avoid jealousy and envy.

Another variant on the common "mass consumerism is completely fine" theme emphasizes the inevitability of materialism and mass consumption. These emerging adults are less likely to think that mass consumerism is necessarily a good thing. They do not evaluate it with the same positive zeal as some of their peers quoted above. But they do think that it is necessary to the functioning of our economy and thus an inevitable part of life that we ought to accept and enjoy if we can. One, for example, observed, "I think that's in my everyday life, so I don't know about the topic but it's in everybody's everyday life. I don't know." Another said, "Um, it's capitalism, kind of a way of life. It's [*laughing*] kind of what America has evolved into. America sort of centers on it, it's necessary to survive." Yet another said, "I don't know if this is just naive, but I think somebody is making it, so it's kind of good, they have a job because of it. Somebody's making that car, wherever it's being made, they have a job, they're earning money hopefully. I don't know, I guess that one is a little too big for me." Still another explained how consumer spending was necessary for the economy:

After learning a little bit about economics, see, it's a good thing. In high school economics I learned about gross domestic product. Basically, the more people spend, the better the economy. The economy is like a bathtub with three faucets. The biggest faucet is consumer spending. [Another] one's government spending, and the other one is, I think, business spending. Then there are three drains. One goes back to consumer spending, the other goes to the government, and the other is personal savings. So in a recession the problem is people holding onto their money because they're scared, when what they really need to do is spend money to put more into the bathtub to help the economy.

Finally, this emerging adult acknowledged that a lot of consumerism wastes money but is justified anyway because it creates jobs and makes people happy: "I think people who spend a lot of money spend it in the wrong stores that don't really help out the economy. But it does give jobs to people based on money, so that's good. I see people buying frivolous things [and wonder] why would you waste your money on that? But, if that's going to make them happy, I suppose [it's fine]." Are there any limits, we asked, to what people might possess? "That's personal feelings, if they can live with wasting all their money when people are starving. But no, there shouldn't be restrictions." But, we pressed, might all of this material consumption be bad for the planet? "It's probably not good, [but] you're not going to change how people are." In short, mass consumerism is part of an immutable way of life and individuals operating as consumers within the system have no responsibilities to consider other than their own desires and happiness.

Another small group of those we interviewed expressed no problem with mass consumerism per se, but said they wished that wealthy people would be more generous in their voluntary financial giving to the needy. The following example of this view was expressed by an emerging adult woman:

> I go back and forth on that. On the one hand, you know, capitalism, you get what you can, which I am all about, you work hard and you get the benefits. But I think you have some responsibility when being well-off to help those who aren't. If you look at Bill and Melinda Gates, no one cares that they own a huge place, because they have done so much good and people think they deserve their place. Which I think is fine. They take so much responsibility for people, and I think that's amazing, like if they wanted to, they could own everything, but they choose to do good, which I think is the ideal for people.

Likewise, this one mentioned—in the course of describing her own excessive shopping and expanding wardrobe—the importance of the wealthy "giving back":

> Oh my lord, I have an addiction to shopping lately that's developed ever since I started working in retail, and it's gotten bad. I think that we are definitely a consumer nation. It can become a problem, I don't know, I think that when you really look at it on the grander scale it's probably really detrimental. But it's doing wonders for my closet [*laughs*]! But I do think too much wealth is outrageous, and I really do think that it's important to give back [to the needy].

How, we asked, would someone know that they have too much money or too many belongings? "I don't know," she replied, laughing.

Inconsequential concerns. So far, the slightly different approaches named above, which are all essentially quite content with mass consumerism, account for 61 percent of our interviewed emerging adults. Another 30 percent, equally male and female, fall into the category of expressing some concerns about mass consumerism but thinking that they can do nothing about it. In the end, mass consumerism remains in place and their lives remain unchanged. With these people, then, we begin to hear some critiques of mass consumerism, but nothing that makes any difference in the end. They suspect that there is probably something wrong with excessive material consumption. But they do not fully understand what that might be; they tend to think that whatever might be wrong is *someone else's* behavior or attitude; and they are not actually affected much if at all in their own consumption behaviors.

One version of this general outlook focuses on something being wrong with people owning too many material possessions. Typical of this position is the statement "I think sometimes people are ridiculous with what they buy, but if that's what they want to do and they have the money and they worked for it, that's their choice." This evaluation moves us a bit beyond the "perhaps unnecessary" or "a little silly" mentioned by the previous group toward a more overtly negative evaluation. Yet what exactly is wrong with too many possessions is not usually explained. And often the perceived benefits of mass consumerism to the economy are injected into conversations here as well. But something about owning too much does seem to bother some emerging adults, though rarely enough that it makes any difference in their own lives. In any case, like the previous group, these emerging adults think that each individual is only responsible for and accountable to themselves for what they buy and own—nobody can say anything to or about anyone else. For instance, one said, "I do believe there is such a thing as excess material possessions. But am I the one to judge how much someone should have? No. I think some people just overdo it, if people are buying stuff to make themselves happy then I think that there's something a little off." Part of what is going on here is emerging adult ambivalence of thinking *other* people sometimes consume too much, while also wanting to be able to buy a lot of things themselves, as with this case:

> If someone has too much money or too many houses? Yes, I think there should be a limit, because some people have five houses and millions of dollars while other people are living on the streets. I don't think that's fair. However, I think if I was a person with five houses and all that money I wouldn't quite see it the same way, so and I think people who work hard deserve to be paid well. But, I don't know, that's a hard one to balance. I'd actually like to have five houses, I'd like to have that, I don't know, I think that's a little too much. I'd like to have a nice large house, be financially comfortable, have maybe two cars, jets, a boat. I mean I'd like to have all that stuff one day, and that's why I feel, I don't think there should be a limit, but at times I still, where I am now, I think there should be limits, but I don't know.

And this:

> I think we are an overly materialistic society. At the same time, I like
> new things. It's tough because I do enjoy having new things. I think it's
> also very important to sustain a strong economy just from a political
> standpoint. At the same time, from a religious standpoint, I've got to be
> wary of material [things] or being overly materialistic. I mean, I feel like
> such a hypocrite talking about this, but I do see definite problems with
> how consumer centered our society has become, that's mostly the con-
> sumer part of it but the disposable part of that consumerism, you know,
> people keep a cell phone for six months and then trash it for no good
> reason, it's just out of control. There're definitely negative impacts from
> that on countries and on the environment, whatever, on ourselves even.
> But I think, again, I mean, I enjoy the act of shopping, I enjoy being able
> to purchase things that I want. So, I don't know. But I think there's a
> point where it gets out of hand.

This mildly conflicted viewpoint of both believing that Americans are too materialistic and feeling the personal desire to enjoy materialism are expressed well
by this emerging adult:

> I'm probably somewhere in the middle on consuming. I do think
> that there's just too much stuff. We buy too much and make too
> much, but it makes the world turn better and then people get paid
> and have jobs because we buy too much stuff. I don't know. Yeah, we
> should buy less stuff. But it's not going to happen. So I'll keep buying
> my $4 coffees from Starbucks and, you know, I'd be in a $60 jeans
> from Abercrombie that I don't really need but really want and just go
> home with.

In short, this group of emerging adults responds: sure, there may be problems,
however vague my understanding of them is, but nothing is going to change,
so go out and enjoy spending money. Central to their inability to envision
any change in our mass consumerist way of life are three key assumptions
of liberal individualism. The first is that everyone, including the rich, has
fairly earned their money through hard work. The second is that no person
or society has the right to impose any external restrictions on any other individual. And the third is that people are naturally driven by self-interested
acquisitive motives, which ultimately cannot be denied or deterred. All three
of those assumptions are evident in this emerging adult's uncertain assessment of mass consumerism:

I think there should be limits to what people possess, but there are people out there who work harder than others. It's almost like, how is that fair if we say there's a limit on what you can own? There are some things that we hear people buy are kinda ridiculous, like a $20 million yacht. It's like something that you use once a year, maybe, and you say, "Oh, okay, that seems a little odd." But, yeah, it seems unfair to put limits and say, "Hey, you can't buy that." But at the same time, too, there is a reason that some of them have that money, because they have worked harder. They have earned their way to get all of that riches and stuff. It's like how can we, who don't have it, say, "You can't get that." You know, if he really wants that, then, you know, that's what he's gonna get.

Another told us, "I don't know, we're a consumer society [*laughs*]. I guess ideally I would like a very socialist society where everybody sort of shares everything but I guess I couldn't place a threshold. Certain things just seem ridiculous to me, when people own so much or have so much money who don't think that they can just live kind of regularly." But greater moderation or equality are ideals that will never be realized.

Among these emerging adults, some others tend to worry about the relationship of mass consumerism to human happiness. A few emerging adults suggest that material possessions are simply unable to provide people with happiness, as in this case: "I think people are so miserable in their lives that they're trying to buy happiness, and the advertising and marketing people get rich off of the unhappiness and insecurity of people. They sell an image people want so they buy and buy and buy in a desperate attempt to fill a gaping hole of miserable cynicism." Still, this problem with happiness is conceived as one that concerns other individuals, not the one speaking. Another emerging adult talked about people working jobs that make them unhappy in order to be able to afford the consumer purchases they want:

We're definitely a materialistic society and the average American usually is a consumer. We're all consumers, technically. That's what gets to me sometimes. I work eight hours inside a building. I don't think human beings were meant to do that, sit inside for eight hours and just move your hands. That seems so terrible. It doesn't have anything to do with hunter-gatherer survival, basic survival. So it feels like sometimes we're just wasting our lives away, just so we can buy that new car, new house, kind of thing. We work to live in this country. If you don't work you're going to have a terrible life, living on the street kind of thing.

So does he think consumerism ought to have any limits? "There aren't any limits, not really. I mean in a capitalistic society you just want to get ahead, so the more you have, hey, more power to you, kind of thing. Go for it." This same person also said, "I would like to have a house, a car, the American dream kind of thing, just a set-up job, decent pay kind of thing." Finally, one emerging adult voiced concerns about the misplaced priority of seeking happiness through shopping itself:

> I think about it, because some people buy things unnecessarily. Like, I've met people that are buying underwear or shoes because they didn't feel like looking for or washing their own clothes. That's ridiculous to me. I personally get what I want. Like, I've had my Air Nikes, my uptowns for almost two years now. But I don't really wear them that much and they're in good condition. So there's no need for me to buy one every summer, just so they can shine when the sun hits it. That's how I feel about it. Some people will just buy because they like buying or because they're having a sale or whatever, so they shop.

A related issue that some emerging adults voiced, echoing a theme above, concerns mass consumerism's ability to tempt some people into living beyond their means. This is a stronger response than the "as long as you can afford it" idea we heard above. One, for instance, emphasized paying bills before going out to buy a new car:

> I guess if you can own it and comfortably support yourself, fine. I think you shouldn't be buying things if you need to spend your money on more important things. Like you shouldn't be buying a car if you already have like bills you need to pay or something. You don't need like 12 mansions, that's excessive, certainly excessive. But I don't feel they should be limited, because although it's selfish and greedy, I don't believe it's our right to be able to like tell them what to do with their money.

"To each his own," said another. "To some people shopping is their thing, but I think you have to be very careful with that, like, I mean frivolous and just throwing money away, just be careful, you know. On the one hand, I feel like if it's your money, you made it, you should be able to do what you want to with it. But I also think someone has to hold someone accountable, you know, you need to be cautious with what you buy." At the same time, this person wants to be able to buy whatever he decides he wants to buy:

> For myself, I want to be basically financially able to do what I want. If something came up, my family members needed something, being

able to help them. Married. Kids. You know. Luxury isn't necessary. What's most important to me is, if I wanted to, is to be able to go out and buy a nice boat, that would be nice. Just being able to. I'm not really into boats, so I wouldn't buy a boat. But if I wanted to, that would be more important.

Another set of emerging adults worry some about the problem of inequality when it comes to consuming material goods. But again, their individualistic assumptions ultimately make inequality impossible to address. And they personally do not worry enough about it to make any changes in their own lives or to work on changing social structures. Usually, concerns about inequality of consumption are framed in extreme terms, as with this comparison of people with 100 pairs of shoes and those with none:

> I see myself as someone who loves to shop. But I also recognize that I need to be careful with that. I own more things than I need, and really need to be able to part with a lot of things. There's a lot of people who need shoes and I have over 100 pairs that I don't need. So yeah, I am worried about how consuming we are as a society, but not worried enough to change my ways yet.

Likewise, this emerging adult used the idea of 15 pairs of sunglasses to illustrate her point: "I definitely feel like people spend way too much time and effort in buying things for themselves and don't really take a step back and think, like, you don't really need 15 pairs of sunglasses. You could give that money to something else. I really think that people have definitely lost their priorities." In theory, the following emerging adult thinks helping homeless people is more important than buying new shoes. But in the end those kinds of calculations prove difficult to make, given individualistic assumptions about never limiting individuals and people's absolute right to the money they earned through hard work:

> Oh, I'm sure there is a limit. But, I don't really know how to put a limit on anybody. I even have close friends who sure spend a lot of money. I guess probably where it becomes a problem is where if you don't pay your bills. Or if you were standing in front of a homeless person who can't eat and you'd rather buy those shoes. I mean, people work hard for things and you should be a good financial steward, but I don't know where to put that line on other people. I know that I have lines that I draw.

This emerging adult thought it was crazy—although also legitimate—to splurge on nice clothes when others have a hard time buying food:

People that go out and spend a thousand dollars on clothes are absolutely crazy, and I don't plan on doing that anytime soon. If it makes them happy, they're crazy, but they can go ahead and do that if they can afford it, since I've known people that do that and then end up in trouble later. Just the whole idea of being able to go and spend a couple thousand dollars on clothes in one shopping experience when other people are having problems buying groceries, just that whole concept is crazy for me.

So what, we asked, should they do with money instead? "Whatever they want to. I mean, I think it's crazy for them to do that, but if they enjoy it and they want to, they can." Again, consumerism is critiqued here, but the problem with it resides not in the larger system or culture but in other individuals who are excessive in their consumption.

A few other emerging adults mentioned—and usually only mentioned, without elaborating—some concerns about the negative environmental impacts of mass consumerism. But again, they do not think they can do anything about it. One, for example, mentioned the environment in a discussion that wove in multiple themes noted above:

I have a particularly negative attitude towards commercialism overall, just because I'm not a big shopper and I just think it's very wasteful. It's great for the economy, but it's very wasteful. I don't think it's right for someone to have like 30 airplanes and five Hummers, or whatever. But I think it's their right to do that. I would disagree with it, but I'm not too worried about it. I'm just worried about the repercussions of the environment and things like that. But for people's personal lives, I think it can transform people into more consuming beings, but, as much as I dislike that, I don't have a problem with it.

Another spoke of environmental concerns, but mostly to point out that they are inconvenient and nobody is doing much about them:

The more you buy, the world is getting worse and environmentally we're not really doing anything big to change it, because it's kind of inconvenient I guess to do anything about it. Eventually we're going to have to, but I think right now everybody is just like, "That will happen 100 years from now, so why even worry about it kind of thing?"— keeping their heads in the sand kind of thing.

This emerging adult suggested that he is not concerned with the environment, although it could become "a little more important":

Talking about the environment and stuff like that or what? I mean, not really, honestly, I don't really have too many concerns with things. When it comes to environment, I think that could be a little more important when it comes to that, I guess. Not consuming too much, recycling, reusing, and all that stuff.

Likewise, this emerging adult thinks, wonders, and worries about environmental issues, but in the end is not concerned because "it will all get sorted out":

Sometimes I think about mass consumption. Sometimes I wonder. It seems like so many companies are making things that really aren't worth having, like why does the company make that? It's just one more thing to be bought and thrown away, because it's not going to work once you get home. Sometimes I worry about that. Like all the money that must go into that. And then where does all this stuff get disposed to? I'm sure all of that will get sorted out. It does not keep me up at night. But I think about it.

In addition, one emerging adult voiced a concern about the possibility of the exploitation of labor in a globalized economy.

I don't know, consuming is good for the economy. I don't like to do it but it's fine if people want to do that. I'm more concerned with the production end, the way things are produced. Unfortunately, in order to have a moving economy you got to produce things with cheaper labor and sometimes internationally exploit. I'm concerned about the exploitation factor. But I think material consumption is, on a whole, good. It helps. Again, the whole consumerism thing is kind of ridiculous, but it's part of what makes this country, that people go out and buy ten pairs of shoes in a three-year span, and if they have the money to do that then they can do it, unfortunately. I do not have the set limit on what people should buy, but if you have ten houses, that's too much.

What we have found so far is, first, that 61 percent of emerging adults we interviewed have no problems or concerns with American materialism and mass consumerism. These emerging adults are essentially quite happy with our social system of shopping, buying, consuming, and disposing. Second, another 30 percent of emerging adults mention certain concerns about mass consumerism, but none they think they can do anything about and none that especially affects how they personally think or live. Whatever possible problems may be out there, they do not "keep them up at night." In either case, it is hard to criticize others for overconsumption when you yourself enjoy shopping and want to be able to buy anything you might want in the future.

Structuring and governing the outlooks of nearly all of the 91 percent of interviewed emerging adults represented above is the dominant cultural paradigm of liberal individualism. In this outlook, individuals are autonomous units who act and choose independently of each other. Meritocracy ensures that people earn what they deserve, so those with abundance are entitled to dispose of their wealth exactly as they please, however excessive or crazy it may be. People can hold personal opinions about what is good and right for others to consume, but they have no right to voice these opinions—who are *they* to say?— much less to have them place limits on anyone else. Almost inconceivable are notions like a common good, human interdependence, systemic reform, or voluntarily embraced cultural alternatives of visions of the good life and society. All that society is, apparently, is a collection of autonomous individuals who are out to enjoy life. The idea of people changing their own lifestyles or of mobilizing for collective social or economic change is nearly unimaginable. Individuals can make their own choices and should not spend beyond their means. But individuals cannot really influence other people or make a difference in the larger world. That is beyond them. Some may be aware of problems of waste, inequality, environmental degradation, the exploitation of overseas labor, or misplaced life values and priorities. But there is nothing to be done about those. They are beyond individual control, so they will either work themselves out or will simply impose their negative effects in due time.

Criticism and consumer choice. The vast majority of American emerging adults, then, have few or no problems with materialistic mass consumption, at least of the kind that make any difference. But there was a smaller minority of emerging adults who did, in fact, voice some real concerns that, at least for a few, appear to make a small difference in their lives. These concerns did not focus on inequality, the exploitation of overseas labor, or misplaced life values and priorities. They nearly all addressed instead problems around the environmental impact of mass consumerism and waste. This is the minority of emerging adults that is at all tuned into the negative impacts of excessive consumption on the environment or other aspects of life. And at least a few of them actually try to live personal lifestyles that somewhat reflect those concerns. What that mostly consisted of, however, is their exercising individual consumer choice: shopping in thrift stores, not going to the mall, or generally buying fewer things than they might otherwise purchase—nothing too drastic. This more critical group represents 9 percent of all the emerging adults we interviewed, and is split evenly among men and women. The proportion of those, however, who mentioned that these problems actually affect their personal behaviors is much smaller than that—perhaps only a few percent of all those we interviewed. In any case, their comments on these matters are worth examining, to get a flavor of what somewhat more critical emerging adults sound like.

One emerging adult told us,

> I'm sort of an environmentally conscious person, sort of opposed to overconsumption, mostly because of the waste that it generates. People are very quick to just replace things and use nonrenewable resources instead of fixing their stuff, they'll just throw it away and get a new one. Or on a different scale, clothes, they go out and buy lots of clothes, which I sort of do too.

Did he think there are limits to what people should possess? "I think so. Like, I'm not a fan of couples with no children having 12-room houses. So I guess there is like a limit and I feel like sometimes you can redirect the money to something more important." And how does someone know what the limit is? "What you truly need. Not necessarily like you should live with the bare minimum of need, but if you're comfortable, then you don't necessarily need like a sixth car kind of thing." Whether this particular emerging adult actually limits his own consumption, he did not say. Another emerging adult spoke similarly:

> I think our society is far too materialistic, that there's a lot of problems with it. It's not something that's sustainable. Environmentally, we live in a way that's kind of selfish, taken against the world backdrop, and people put a lot of their personal happiness and satisfaction in life on material acquisitions, things that they've got. And I don't think that ultimately makes people any happier.

For a few, as in the following case, traveling overseas opened their eyes to new perspectives:

> I can compare German to American society, and say that rampant materialism is a problem in the United States. People become more and more concerned with the distractions in life, the iPhones, MTV, pop music, sports, all this. When I was in Germany, I felt it was a very healthy society. Every person walking down the street, regardless of their profession, would be able to talk to you about German classical music or literature. I don't think that's the case in the United States. I don't know if that's a problem or not, but, being abroad myself, I see it as a problem.

What, then, should Americans do about that?

I really believe that people should understand personally what they need, instead of feeling they need something because somebody else says so. Advertising is a really disgusting thing in our society, we're constantly bombarded by things, magazines and product placement. You see this beautiful person wearing a Polo shirt and so you feel you need to go buy it. Obviously, as an economist you hope the American spending machine continues, because it creates a higher standard of living. But you go to a place like Germany, which is a wealthy country, and people there are mostly concerned about what they need on a day-to-day basis, clothing, food, friendship. Sometimes I think material goods become a substitute for basic needs, and that's kind of what's contributing to the sickness in American society.

Again, however, this emerging adult did not talk about anything specifically different in his own life. The implication seems to be that greater awareness will make the difference. Another emerging adult also emphasized the importance of awareness and education:

I see nothing wrong with having material things, 'cause it's what we do, we like to have things. The key lies in realizing that they're just material things and they mean nothing to you, they're just things. So to value interpersonal relationships, to value yourself and life instead of putting your life in your car, job, or big-screen TV, I think that's ridiculous. It'd be better if we lived in a more recycling culture and actually using things, rather than just throwing them out when we're done. I think that's contributing to what's destroying the environment and not appreciating it.

Do you think, we asked, there should be limits to what people own? "I don't think there should be limits. I think people should just be educated about their actions and about what happens when you throw out that TV or watch TV all day, you know, just understand what they're getting themselves into."

Another emerging adult emphasized the importance of not shopping too much and not letting possessions "go to your head." He explained: "Sometimes I buy into consumerism, mostly I don't. Recently, my friends went to the big mall around here and invited me, and either I'm seriously too tired or I just can't get excited to go buy clothes and get tons of stuff. I never have been, because when I get tons of stuff I never get around to using it all, if I buy a lot and never use it, what's the point of buying it in the first place?" And what of his more general view of mass consumption?

I think it's wasteful. And too much stuff can go to your head and make you think you're important when really you're just the same as everybody else. Over time you're probably never gonna wear all the clothes you buy, never gonna play all the video games, so if you keep it to almost a minimalist type of stance, just try to do what you think you can or would want to do or buy, I think that's all you should do.

So what are his views about placing limits on acquiring possessions? "I think there should be limits, living a comfortable life, sure, that's the beauty of being an American as far as liberty in this country involves. But too much stuff is just gonna go to your head in the end. That's where religious charities and stuff come into play, where you can donate part of your money." Thus, even those who express concerns about excessive consumerism are reluctant to do anything that might challenge a comfortable life, as this same person explained:

I'd like to live in the future a comfortable life, get married and have some kids eventually, be comfortable with my job. I think just living a comfortable but not overexcessive life is definitely reasonable. I mean, look what happened with the depression in the '30s, which was because of mass consumption. Yeah, too much can seriously go to your head, not that you should give away all your possessions and live on the streets, but you should definitely still have a comfortable life, but not overexcessive.

Thus, many of the emerging adults who are the most critical of mass consumerism, including the following one, recurrently focus on being practical by buying useful products in moderation: "I think you should buy what you need and stick with it. If you enjoy doing an activity and you need equipment for that, then do it. Don't get really hard core and greedy about it, just get what you need and just be happy." Again, we asked, what makes something "hard core?" Where should one draw the line?

If you have things you bought on a whim but don't use ever, I think that is where I would draw the line. And I have stuff like that too. You should definitely think about it before you buy it, like, "Do you need it? Yes. Okay. Go for it." Or do you only just want it? Are you going to use it more than once or twice? If not, then, okay. That was fun. Toss it in the garbage or let it sit in the closet and collect dust for two years, and then you find it again you're like, hmm, I don't need this.

For nearly all of the most critical emerging adults, we see, the primary if not exclusive solution to the problem is becoming a more discriminating consumer and getting rid of excess possessions. One, for instance, who was one of the very few who mentioned any of this fostering any changes in their personal lives, said:

> We waste a lot. I don't necessarily think you should have only one out-fit. But I think a lot of people are oblivious about how much they really do consume. I watched a documentary about how much we throw away, which was challenging to change our minds and make different decisions, which I try to incorporate it in my life. I catch myself throwing away a can or buying something that I really didn't need. It's hard to get away from in our society, but I do wish it was something that would change. Our world is not going to last very long if we keep throwing all this junk on it. A lot of young people have never known anything else [than materialism] and it seems like it could define you these days, whether you have the Gucci handbag or from Kmart. It's sad how important brand names have become.

She herself tries to recycle cans, buy less, and not be controlled by the power of name brands. Other than that, she only wishes things would change and feels sad about the state of things. Similarly, this young man has translated his concerns into efforts to buy clothes at thrift stores:

> I definitely think mass consumption is a problem. Right now in the ocean there's a pile of trash the size of Texas that has all gathered because the way the currents go, it all goes in one spot the size of Texas. That's not cool. I'm not a fan of trash everywhere, and especially in my city, I see things dumped all over the place, and this is the only place we have, so it'd be nice if we tried and kept it looking nice. But I definitely shop at thrift stores and stuff, 'cause there's definitely overproduction, over-consumption, over-everything. Then people buy lots and lots of things that they don't need, and then they don't understand why gas is so expensive. All this stuff is shipped here in huge tankers that use gas, that's why.

The mildly evaluative language here—such as "not cool" and "not a fan"—is not very pointed. But, unlike most emerging adults, at least this person has modi-fied his behavior in some specific way. Important to some critical emerging adults, too, is reducing the amount of possessions one owns, as this young woman explains:

> I think Americans have this way of buying a lot more stuff than they really need. I've tried not to do that. My parents' house is full of stuff

because my mother is a stock person, but my father and I are not, so we try as hard as we can to not accumulate stuff. I moved from my little apartment, packed everything up, and it all fit in the back of my dad's truck, and I like that.

So what exactly, we asked, is the problem with owning lots of stuff? "I don't know, people with 8,000 pairs of shoes are a little ridiculous, but I don't really know that I can place numbers on 'This is okay, but this is ridiculous.' It's a problem I guess in terms of the environment, but people are now learning not to buy stuff and that's interesting, like you don't see hardly anybody with giant SUVs anymore." What possessions does she need, then, to be happy?

> I don't need a whole lot to be happy now. You want to have a roof over your head, to have a car, to have Internet. You need to have Internet, that's just, there's just no other way. Like your house is not really actually a habitable house if it doesn't have Internet. You could live without water or trash, but not without Internet. Right now my boyfriend and I have a big-screen TV and satellite and we have nice computers, so we have everything that personally I need to make me happy.

Emerging adults have a difficult time seeing anything wrong with high-tech communication and entertainment gadgets. To them, the Internet is a basic necessity.[1] But, again, being aware and making responsible consumer choices— while acknowledging the importance of strong consumer spending for "the economy"—is the heart of environmentally conscious emerging adults' strategy for countering the negative effects of mass consumerism, as this one explained:

> It's not okay to hurt the environment, we shouldn't build things that destroy habitats. We should protect habitats when we build new developments. But consumerism keeps the economy going. It's a helpful thing that we're such mass consumers, we need to buy things to help stimulate the economy, so it's a good thing to buy, actually. We need it for our economy. But, yes, there also seems to be a climate shift going on, it's not necessarily global warming. But the fact is nobody can change the entire economy, so the only thing we can do is know what we're doing when we buy things and be aware of the choices we make, to not make consumer choices that are going to harm the entire human population.

Very few emerging adults could or would see possibilities beyond being "aware" and careful in consumer purchases. Only one who we interviewed directly criticized massive wealth and income inequality in America as it affects people's ability to consume too much:

> Even if Bill Gates had given half his money to charity, he still has too much. I think that some people have way too much money. And what do you need all that for? Nobody needs to be a millionaire or even earning a high hundred thousand. Why do you need to live any higher than middle class? Like why can't everybody have the same amount of money and just be happy with a nice house and a yard and a pool? That's what my family has, right? I don't need any more than that. I'm never gonna have more than that. I'm gonna have a nice house, a car, and a sweet TV and that's it. Like, my family doesn't make a ton of money and I still have enough to afford a nice CD collection. Why do you need millions of dollars or even $400,000? That's too much money, in my opinion. People make like hundreds of millions of dollars, that's gross.

Extremely few emerging adults would go that far, to challenge absolute differences in wealth among Americans, to suggest that there might be a cap on the top income earned. That is a somewhat radical view that violates the assumptions of liberal individualism, as described above. At the same time, it is far from clear that he has any specific plan or proposal in mind to reduce income inequality and excessive consumption, or that this view affects his own life in any challenging way. What might be done to curtail the excesses of wealth, he does not say. Meanwhile, even he hopes to enjoy a comfortable middle-class lifestyle—to have a nice house, a car, a "sweet" TV, and a nice CD collection.

Visions of Ideal Lifestyles

In the next set of questions in our interviews with emerging adults we addressed the issue of what makes for a good life when it comes to lifestyle and goals involving the ownership of material possessions. Specifically, we asked, "What is your idea of a 'good life' when it comes to the ideal kind of lifestyle you might have? What are your goals when it comes to buying, owning, and consuming in your life—or maybe living modestly or simply?" Few emerging adults we interviewed took us up on the "living modestly or simply" possibility. Again, few express interests or purposes or goals that are dramatically unlike that of securing material security and comfort for themselves and their families. The vast majority of emerging adults once more came out strongly in favor of a financially unconstrained, materially comfortable lifestyle spent by them and their families consuming a variety of rewarding goods, services, and experiences.

Material comfort, security, family, and happiness. When asked about what makes a good life in terms of an "ideal kind of lifestyle" and about goals when it comes to "buying, owning, and consuming," most emerging adults expressed some variant of this answer: "A family, a nice car, nice house, my own practice, be happy, stuff like that." Such responses were remarkably similar across sex, race, and social class. What nearly all emerging adults want and expect out of life when it comes to buying, owning, and consuming is to be financially and materially comfortable. Emerging adults elaborated this outlook in a variety of ways:

> Have a nice house that belongs to me. Have a nice, reliable, dependable vehicle. Have something to play with on the weekends, maybe a boat, a four-wheeler, or a bike or whatever. And be able to provide for the family, and, basically, the best way to put it is, I'm comfortable. I'm not struggling, I'm not rolling in money, but I'm comfortable. Something could happen tomorrow, put a little bit back [into savings], I'm OK.

And:

> I guess I'd like to have nice things, I don't know, I wouldn't really need them but I'm not going to say that if there's a sale that I don't spend money that I shouldn't. I definitely want to be comfortable. I want to have a house and a car and that stuff. My parents just bought a boat, which now I think is a nice addition [*laughs*]. So I think I definitely want to be comfortable.

Most, though not all, emerging adults describing their ideal, materially comfortable lives usually deny an interest in becoming super rich. Many appear to think that wanting to be rich might be too greedy and that it comes with troubles of its own, as this one explains: "I don't want to hurt for anything, don't want to struggle. But, I don't want to be so wealthy that I have to worry about robbers and stuff like that. I just want to be okay in life, I guess, I'm the kind of person that just wants a middle-class kind of life." Another said, "I want to have a nice car, I want to have a boat. Those are things I want to have later on in life, toys, but nothing in excess. I mean, it's whatever makes you happy." Yet another spoke along these lines of balancing enjoying the kind of job they want with the imperatives of material comfort:

> I think ideally I would have a job that would allow me to, you know, be able to explore the outdoors, like rock climbing, hiking, camping, that sort of thing. I would have a job that would let me do that as well as travel and do missions work. And, you know, also live a comfortable life

in a house, but it doesn't have to be like 5,000 square feet for two people. You know, just a decent living where I never want for anything but something comfortable, not necessarily depriving myself of anything.

Others, however, such as this one, are more explicit about wanting a clearly upper-middle-class status: "Comfortable lifestyle, obviously married, to be able to educate my kids. I want to earn, between me and my wife, at least a quarter of a million dollars a year. That's a number, I guess, I'd be satisfied with making that." Still others who come from somewhat lower social classes express lower expectations, but still focus their goals primarily on financial and material comfort and security. One, for instance, told us, "I like what my family has now, except for our house would be fixed up and everything paid off and that would be the good life. I don't need anything more than that." Another said,

> I'd like to have a house and, like I said, a decently, a car that the service engine light doesn't come on every five blocks. What I want most in my future is stability, to be stable. I want to have somewhere that I call a home and, you know, probably take up a hobby or two, and, materialistically speaking, I wouldn't mind some kitchen gadgets, washer and dryer, matching dining room set, a nice TV, maybe—well I have a nice TV now but I want like [nicer].

In either case, most tend to emphasize financial security as part of the expected picture: "Having no mortgage, making sure you're secure, if something bad happens, you have some type of savings to help you out, or making sure if you have a kid you can take care of them, provide. I guess just being financially stable is my one big goal." In some cases, as with the following, "security" includes the idea of family stability along with material comfort, with both being kept in a judicious balance:

> To have a nice home, to be relatively comfortable, I don't have to have, like, fancy whatever. I mean, if I can still provide security for my family and myself and my future, then hey, good on it. I'd much rather have a small house and be happily married and kids than have, like, a McMansion and be twice divorced.

Even so, the ideal here clearly involves both family happiness and material comfort and security. Then again, some emerging adults are not shy about expressing their larger material ambitions. One, for example, told us:

> A good life for me would be to have more than enough money than I actually need, and live like a kid the rest of my life. That would be my

little heaven in today's reality. Yeah, it's consuming a lot of stuff, but at the same time, if you can afford it, what is money anyway? Money is meant to be spent, so why not? You only live once, and if you have the chance to live in excess, why not?

What about any concerns this emerging adult may have about potential problems in mass consumerism?

I think it's hypocritical by a lot of people, just because if they had the money, would they really spend it on all the stuff that sounds righteous? Come on, this is the world. Everyone is human. If you had that kind of money you'd be doing the same thing. That's what I think, especially with the spending money. It's there for you. If there was $1 million on this table, I would be flipping out right now.

Another described the kind of life he would like as "being able to spend and do whatever you want."

I mean, that's nothing I would ever achieve unless I win the lottery. But, you know, if I could have $5 million, that would be amazing. That's a good life. I would be happy if I could go on vacation two or three times a year, send my kids to private school, never have to worry about paying bills. I guess if I reached a point of never having to worry about affording a house, cars, and paying my mortgage and paying my bills, then I'll be happy.

What, we asked more specifically, would be his ideal life scenario?

Finish top of my class first year, transfer to NYU or Columbia, land a job at a big law firm after the three years and then work at one of those big law firms for a few years, find my way into the sports entertainment industry being an agent. Meet a girl somewhere along the way and love, you know, who knows what love is these days? Be a sports agent and accumulate so much money that I could become a high school basketball coach and spend time with my kids and my family.

Some emerging adults refer specifically to their own "American dream":

Realistically, a good life would be a house, a big yard, and a dog and you know, what is it? 2.5 kids or whatever. A husband, a kid or two, two vehicles and that's it, it's my American dream and to have a good job and you know, be able to afford insurance and not struggle, and I don't care about being wealthy, I just want to be comfortable.

Being materially comfortable is a key element in most emerging adults' life goals. This can mean different things to different people, but for some it means a solidly upper-middle-class lifestyle, as this one expressed: "Ideally I would just like to have what I would say is comfortable for me, which I guess you would define as an upper-middle-class existence, of course, and being able to afford things for my family and my kids, and not really have money be an issue, is really what I'd like. That's what I hope for." Most also expect that their material comforts will only increase as they grow older:

> Now, just nice clothes, I would say. The car doesn't matter to me because my car is all right, but I'd say clothes. Eventually, I want to live in a big house and have a really good car, that's why I'm going through college to get a job, so I can get these things I haven't had.

Another told us:

> I would like in my life to have a house, houses in multiple countries, be well enough off to be able to do that, to be able to go on trips, have enough money so I can be generous and donate money, and also be well enough off, I guess, say wealthy, that I can travel and do things I want to do, and involve my family. Also have a car that I like. I guess some material objects, yes. Where I've come from is a very materialistic area, I had a lot of competition in high school about whose dad made what, whose parents drove what car, what you'd buy, what clothing brand you wore, everything.

One emerging adult woman finishing college at an Ivy League school observed this about her peers:

> You have people that opt for the money, specifically, investment bankers. They're going to be working 80 to 100 hours a week and they had internships from the previous summers living in New York. You ask, "So how'd you like it?" They say, "I hated it." And then, "So why are you doing it?" They answer, "'Cause I get paid over $100,000 a year," and then, "but you know drains me out." They get two weeks of vacation a year, which they don't take because they don't want to fall behind. So they are accumulating money. What are they getting out of it? They really have no answer for that question. But money, everybody needs money. That's a big factor in how you live your life.

This emerging adult is rather unique among her generation for her critical awareness of the emptiness of living only for money. But in the end she does not offer an alternative, and she herself is moving along a similar kind of career development path as the peers she describes.

A handful of somewhat alternative voices. A few of the emerging adults we interviewed did make an effort to speak about simplicity or moderation of material consumption or of giving money away generously, although they usually also mixed those themes with other thoughts of greater comfort or luxury. One, for example, spoke about both possibly being satisfied with the material basics in life as well as being financially secure and being interested in owning a luxury sports car:

> It would really be nice to have food, shelter, clothing and transportation, that would be really nice. But I guess if I can't have those things, there are some people who are happy without them. But for a good life, no debt, maybe a mortgage, but I would love to pay it off soon and not have that. I would say live modestly within my means. And no sports car, although a Lexus IS would be so sweet [*laughs*].

Another talked about the importance of family and relaxation, as well as her lack of interest in accumulating a lot of material possessions, within the context of her simultaneous concern with financial security and material comfort:

> I really would like to be financially secure when I'm older and not have to worry about making mortgage payments or even my kids or anything along those lines. But I do think it's important to balance getting everything you need financially and enjoying your family and taking time off to relax. Because you only have one life so you have to enjoy to the fullest. As far as shopping, I really don't want a ton of things. I'm very minimalistic. We just cleaned our house and I threw out everything. I don't like a lot of things around. So I don't want multiple houses. I would rather just keep it to the bare minimum, things that I'll use but not a ton of other things.

With this kind of material moderation, one house will suffice. The larger point is to enjoy life to the fullest, which the narrow pursuit of material things can obstruct. Finally, one emerging adult dreamed a bit about not only being financially comfortable but also having enough money to give to charity:

> My ideal life would just be like financially being comfortable and not having to worry about paying bills and things like that, and being able

to buy things when I need them. I don't know. Actually, preferably I'd like to have a lot of money and be able to give it away, that would be my ideal life, would be like being able to donate to charities or even create charities. But I guess in terms of like material things, just having like a good-sized house but not like too big, but comfortable.

Another small number of emerging adults, particularly some from less well-to-do backgrounds, spoke more single-mindedly about the virtues of living simply or modestly, which is all they desire. One young woman said that all she wanted was "a house, somewhere to stay, you know, something to drive and a family. I want just a little, small house, something simple." A young man told us, "I don't need a huge house; I know that I can't afford a big huge house right now. Maybe eventually [I'll get one], but it really doesn't matter to me if I have a mansion or if I have just a ranch somewhere." One spoke of his interest in downsizing his housing even now: "We're going to sell this house when we leave and hopefully move into a two-bedroom apartment that's small, because this is way too much. We have too much room and we don't do anything with it and that's wasteful." The same person also expressed relatively modest retirement dreams: "Our goals when we retire, we want to have a house somewhere, wherever we decide to put our roots in and hang out there for a while, until our son is out of the house and, if we have any more kids, they're out of the house. Probably then just buy a little house in the mountains and then get an RV and travel around, but that's really it." Another emphasized the importance of living within his means:

I think there are more ways to be happy than to buy things. I learned this from my parents, but I live under my means. We don't have a huge house, we buy only the size that we need, I'm not going to go out and buy a Jaguar or use money for that, I don't want to be one of those people who buys a huge house and has a huge mortgage they can't pay off and an expensive car and then they can't pay for their kid to go to college. That's where I am.

Another likewise told us:

You know I wouldn't say I have to have something to be happy. I could ride a bike to work if I needed, I could get by without the truck. There's things that make you happy, just normal, and I enjoy them, like my nice clean apartment, I mean I enjoy things. But I think even without all that I would still be happy. I don't think material possessions make a person happy, if you have a productive job, a productive relationship, then the material things just help that out. But if you replace negative feelings with your job or with material things, then that's not going to make you happy at all.

The number of emerging adults who spoke in terms of moderation and contentment like this was very small, however.

Besides these, only a small handful of other emerging adults expressed any kind of genuinely different vision for what a good life would be for them. One rare example talked about the importance of music, agriculture, community, and relationships in life:

> As long as I have my music equipment, someday I'd like to own a house, whatever kind of house that may be. Really I'd like to be able to work the land, get involved with a small group of people to be part of a community, and just be content. I don't have too many huge hopes. I don't want to be a millionaire. If that were to happen then that'd be an interesting life, but I try and keep my dreams real. I want to be able to do my music. I like to be part of nature and have my friends and somebody I love.

Another talked about her life goal of working in academia and of interests in socially responsible consumption:

> I want to be a professor. So having a job in academia is something that's important to me in terms of having a good life. But that's not a material possession. I don't expect more than a professor's salary. I think that that would be fine for me, having a place to live, having a means of transportation, being able to be able to have enough money to make choices about how I spend my money, in the sense that I really like organic food and I like buying fair-trade clothes and stuff when I go out shopping, but that's just like a lot more expensive, it's almost like a luxury to be able to do that. So being able to do that. Like, I don't really want a lot and I actually don't like big houses. I don't think they're cozy and they waste a lot of energy and that kind of stuff.

Even in this case, however, having a decent salary and financial discretion in purchases is definitely a priority. Another emerging adult talked about the central goal of being happy, content, and having good friends and an enjoyable atmosphere in life:

> Money would be nice, but to me it's not everything. For my personal lifestyle, I just want to be somewhere where I'm happy. Like, if I end up

living in this little shack and have not much to my name, I'm happy because I have good friends, and I'm in like a nice enjoyable atmosphere, then I consider that a good life. If your idea of being happy means having a lot of material possessions, fine, do what you please. But for me, it's just as long as I am content with where I am in life, it's all good.

Likewise, this young man said the good life would involve family, farming, and self-sufficiency:

If I didn't have a truck, a drum set, if I didn't have anything but the clothes on me, it's fine. Like I said, material stuff doesn't really bother me that much. My ideal situation would be probably having a little house, a garden, yeah, just, you know, having a family, I guess. I don't really want a lot of stuff, so maybe just like a little house, little garden, grow some stuff. Like a farm, so I could literally be self-sufficient. I could grow everything I need, I wouldn't have to buy it from anybody. That'd be nice.

Finally, one emerging adult told us, "I think it would be really cool if I could live out of a backpack and be comfortable, so that's what I think I would aspire to. But I don't know if I can achieve that." But, again, these most distinctively alternative views of the good life are rare. Very few emerging adults spoke like this. Instead, again, the typical viewpoint sounded more like this: I would like to have a house, a car, the American dream kind of thing, just a set-up job, decent pay kind of thing. That is absolutely how the vast majority of emerging adults think about a good life, living well, and being happy.

For the most part, then, in thinking about what a good life is, about what their own well-lived lives should look like, when it comes specifically to buying, owning, and consuming, emerging adults did not think very expansively or critically or creatively. Nearly all focus on a certain version of the standard middle- or upper-middle-class dream that is centered not only on family but also on financial security and material comfort and consumption.

An Aside on Ripple Effects in Higher Education

What we observe in this chapter about emerging adults' captivity to consumerism and materialism is connected, we think, to a loss of vision and understanding of the most important value and purpose of higher education. We step aside here to briefly note that loss. Ultimately, society should invest in higher education because of the rich intellectual and personal development it fosters—and for the richer qualities of life reaped as a result by students and their families, workplaces, political communities, places of worship, and other people and social institutions whose lives they touch. Higher education serves a crucial common good in fostering breadth, depth, complexity, and richness in all dimensions of social, cultural, political, and economic life. What is ultimately the most important question about college education is, therefore, not what students can "do with it," in immediate and practical terms, but rather what college education *does to its students* deeply and broadly. It is about expanding people's horizons and depths of understanding, engaging students with the big questions that matter most in life, giving them tools to think and learn and communicate well, and passing on the richness of scientific and humanistic inquiry and understanding.

The most important payoffs of college education do not concern career promotions and higher salaries. They have to do with forming thoughtful, critical, appreciative, careful, capable, and interesting family members, neighbors, citizens, workers, leaders, teachers, artists, researchers, and friends. In short, the truly important product of higher education is better people, not bigger promotions and paychecks. That is in part because better people—broadly defined—help over the long run to produce better lives, better politics, better cultures, (genuinely) better economies, better societies. This is the real value and purpose of higher education at its best. And it is the job of leaders of colleges and universities to be making this case continually to prospective and current students, parents, faculty, trustees, alumni, legislatures, secondary-school educators, and the general public. Unfortunately, this is also an understanding of higher education that precious few emerging adults today grasp or value—in large measure, we think, because leaders in secondary and higher education are losing sight of this vision. The humanities especially are being marginalized, despite their central, long-term importance (at least when conceptualized and taught well) in strengthening the fabric of democracy.[2] As a result, nearly all emerging adults now assume a very different view of higher education.

Most, though not all, emerging adults believe in the importance of finishing high school and getting a college education. Large numbers want to do well in school, go to college, get a degree, and put it to good use. But for most, the reasons they value college seem to have little to do with the broadly humanistic vision of higher education described above. Rather, their motivations have almost entirely to do with the instrumental advantages it produces for them as competitive individuals—as well as the fun they want to have while in college. What really matters to emerging adults is getting the credits, earning the diploma, and becoming certified as a college-educated person so that they can get a better job, earn more money, and become a good salary earner and supporter of a materially comfortable and secure life. Not very many emerging adults talk about the intrinsic enrichment of an education, of the personal broadening and deepening of one's understanding and appreciation of life and the world that expansive learning affords. Few emerging adults talk about the value of a broad education for shaping people into informed and responsible citizens in civic life, for producing members and leaders of society who can work together toward the common good. An articulation of an understanding of the enduring worth of a broad liberal arts education for the development of people and the sustaining of good, humanistic societies is rarely heard among this age group. For most, instead, higher education is good—besides, again, the fun one can have in college—because it promises to help secure for individuals more rewarding jobs, higher income, and, thus, greater expected personal prospects for material and psychological well-being, security, and happiness. For some, that means actually learning specific information and skills. One emerging adult, for example, said, "Right now I'm studying marketing, but I think I am going to change it to finance and accounting, so anything in business really. Because business is a very solid thing, businesses are going to be around for a long time. There will always be jobs, and I like math, so, accounting." For others, higher education is just so many formal but substantively meaningless hoops to have to jump through, whether in classrooms or over the Internet. Thus, another emerging adult, for instance, told us:

> Once I did find a job [I realized] it would be so much easier to do well if I did have a degree, just because of the way access is given people. People just recognize you more if you have a degree. That's why I decided to go back to school. But really, my heart is in the work that I do. If I didn't need to be in school, I wouldn't.

Either way, those who can afford college are mostly happy to do it, because of the instrumental goods it will deliver to them as individuals. As one respondent said, "So many people are out of jobs and losing their houses, it's really kinda bad around here, so that's a reason why I want to go to school, so I can make sure I get at least a decent job."

There is, of course, nothing wrong with some young people never going to college at all—college is not for everyone.[3] And among those who do go into higher education, there is also obviously nothing wrong with young people getting the training, credentials, and skills needed to secure jobs that will contribute to living good lives. But any college or university training and education that does take place we believe needs to happen within a larger context of broad personal and intellectual development designed to help challenge and enrich visions of what a truly good job, life, and society might look like—visions which make jobs themselves even worth doing and life itself genuinely good and worth living. Our observation, however, is that such an expansive understanding of the true value and purpose of higher education is disappearing—it has, in fact, nearly disappeared among college-age American youth today. That is not primarily the fault of the youth. It is partly the fault of too many leaders in higher education losing sight of the best vision. Taking its place instead is a culture and system of higher education driven by individual careerism and pragmatic instrumentalism. And this is accelerated by shrinking public support for higher education, the growth of private big-money influences and corporate interests, the demands of "the Economy," and—behind much of this—the imperatives of materialistic mass consumerism. If this is correct, then these changes represent the massive loss of a profoundly rich educational heritage; an erosion, if not collapse, of the intellectual foundations justifying liberal, humanistic education; and the certain diminishment of the quality of personal, cultural, and social life in America for decades to come.

What, Finally, Is a Good Life?

Lastly, and returning to our main theme, in the concluding section of our in-depth, personal interview discussions—long after we had discussed consumerism and ideal lifestyles, on which we just reported—we approached the matter of materialism and mass consumerism with emerging adults somewhat less directly, by asking the question "What, ultimately, do you want to get out of life? What would living a 'good life' look like to you? What is it that you really want to accomplish or experience in your life before it's all over?" People throughout history have of course wrestled with these big questions and have come up with a variety of answers. Some say the good life is one spent in pursuit of moral virtues. Others say the good life involves exploring the vast wonders of nature and the diversity of human cultures to the fullest. Some talk of developing the full potential of one's personal gifts, talents, and abilities. Yet others believe a good life means learning control over one's individual desires, impulses, and passions. Still others emphasize the importance of loving relationships in family and among friends. And then again, some view the good life as one of love and justice before God. However the views vary, by most accounts offered by the people generally considered the wisest among us, the good life involves some kind of transcendence beyond one's own self. To live a good life, in other words, means progressing on some kind of journey to become something more that what we already are. It means realizing some higher purpose or value, often of a personal and perhaps even spiritual nature. To live a truly good life, in short, entails engaging with some important reality beyond oneself and transforming oneself in a way that enhances morality, understanding, or important relationships.

We did not focus the thinking of the emerging adults who we interviewed in this section specifically on consumerism or materialism. The topic here was rather their broadest views of what makes for a good life, of what they themselves ultimately want to get out of life. We also had by this latter section of the interviews already discussed their views of consumerism and materialism, so they may have also been ready not to reengage those topics, in order to avoid being repetitive. What they had to say in this section as a result tended to be somewhat broader and more diverse than what they said in the previous section about consumerism and materialism—as we would expect. Even so, when asked about a "good life" broadly conceived and what they want to achieve in life, the ideas of material success, financial stability, not having to worry about money, being successful in work, being able to provide for family, and having money to spend on valuable experiences and products were expressed again as significant themes in the majority of their answers. Thus, even when emerging adults are not directly asked about these subjects, for most, financial success, material acquisition, and consumer enjoyment surface as important ideas defining what makes for a good life and goals to achieve.

To get a larger perspective, we must see that nearly all emerging adults, when asked about their views of a good life and what they ultimately want to get out of their own lives, gave answers that mixed together a lot of different kinds of ideas, interests, and values. Rarely did they report only one goal or vision for a good life. Instead, most gave some combination of concerns, like having families, enjoying friends, traveling and experiencing the world, being happy, being financially stable and secure, enjoying the fruits of work, and enjoying material possessions, being a positive influence on others, and achieving in education and career. The most frequently mentioned of these ideas—voiced by about 60 percent of those we interviewed—concerns close relationships: getting married, having children, and enjoying good friends. They said things like "just [having] a full, happy family," "being with the person I love," "rais[ing] healthy children," and "hav[ing] great friends." Many of these explicitly mentioned wanting to avoid getting divorced—not saying that they want to get married but rather "just staying married." As an aside, some emerging adults spoke of marriage and family not in terms of their loving and caring for *other* people—as most did—but rather as others loving and taking care of *them*. One, for instance, said, "I'd like to have had a wife that loves me and kids that admired me." Another observed about his goal of marriage, "I feel like that is something that would really fulfill me." Yet another said, "I want to have the most loving, caring wife." Some emerging adults thus seem subtly to look to marriage and family more for what it can do for them than for the care they can invest into the others who they love—an approach that hardly seems conducive to achieving marital success.

In any case, seldom did anyone we interviewed mention family alone as defining their vision of what they ultimately want to get out of or accomplish in life. Usually, marriage and family were combined with a few other goals, values, and interests. Often, however, these were stated in quite vague terms. Among the about 40 percent of emerging adults we interviewed who mentioned their desire to travel, for example, one told us , "I would love to travel and meet different people." Another, who was among the roughly 40 percent who also talked about wanting to "be happy," said things like "When I'm older I just want to still feel great about everything" and "Happy. I don't want to be depressed." About one-quarter of the emerging adults we interviewed spoke of wanting to help others or of being a positive influence in others' lives—as with this one: "I would like to have some positive influence on something, whether that be people or dogs or babies or I don't know, something, somewhere, some kind of positive influence." Roughly one in five mentioned developing their own careers, reaching educational goals, or learning some skills or knowledge as part of their hoped-for good life. Thus, one said, "I'd like to make a mark [in some industry]. I kind of crave attention, in that I really want to make a mark that's noticeable." Much smaller minorities of emerging adults expressed other elements of their views of a good life. Eleven percent mentioned wanting not to have any regrets at the end of their lives, of making the most of all of their life opportunities. "I don't want to have any regrets, but I know there will be some. I want to get everything I want, to do everything I want to do." Nine percent, as in the following example, spoke of knowing God or making God proud, deepening their life of faith, or being more religious: "I want God to be satisfied with what I did and for him to look back and say, 'Well done. I'm proud of you.'" About 5 percent talked about an interest in creating art, performing music, or making films and so being acknowledged by others for their creative works. Two percent mentioned being physically healthy or having a healthy family. Two percent talked about becoming a better person. One percent said they wanted to make their parents proud. And another 1 percent mentioned simply wanting to come up with some goal or purpose in life at all.

So there was some diversity here. But amid that there were also central, dominant themes. The most typical answer combined a desire to have a successful family, to be personally happy, and—as we will see next—to enjoy the financial ability to be able to consume the material goods and experiences one wants and not have to worry about money. Career success, financial comfort, and sometimes even becoming wealthy were sprinkled throughout 57 percent of the interview answers in this section, usually along with some other themes mentioned above, of course. One emerging adult told us that what she ultimately wants to get out of life is "having a beautiful family, my own house, my own car, and not having to worry about money." Another said, "I want to have a good job, be able

to support myself, have a nice house, be able to do the things I want to do, probably get married and have kids." Yet another told us, "I'd like to be successful, well-
off, provide for my family. Along the way maybe travel a little bit. Still play golf,
go camping, visit places, stay at home, hang out with family more, go to the park,
stuff like that." Some emerging adults spoke explicitly about wanting to get a lot
of money. One, for example, said, "I want to make money. I really want to make
money. And I want to leave a legacy." Another reported:

> Six-figure income, yeah, 'cause I love money. That's my thing. It's attrac-
> tive. You can have anything if you have your money. I just wanna be,
> like, financially set and everything. Nothing else.

Another agreed: "I want to be rich. It'd be good, man. Uh huh." But, again, most
of those overtly seeking money mixed their desire for wealth with other goals.
Thus one said, "Be wealthy, be happy. I want to travel a lot." Another reported:
"Probably getting married, having kids, being able to live where I wanna live, and
being able to afford the things that we wanna do. I'd like to travel the world, just
to see different places, different things, meet different people, seeing new things,
experiencing new things." Still another told us:

> Just having a good job, being stable, not having to worry about things,
> bills and all that, without struggling, being able to pay for the bills. And
> being able to go out once in a while, take a break, just being there with
> the good things that you want on your own time. And just working,
> having a good job, being able to spend time with family. I think that'll
> be a good life. To have a home, to travel. I definitely want to travel to
> different countries, see the world. That's probably about it, just to know
> my wife, too, and then love her.

Some seemed happy to settle for more modest versions of material success than
others. "Somewhere where you're comfortable," said one, "like financially comfortable, where you're just content[4] with where you are. And I definitely want to
travel more, see the world, see what it has to offer." Another also took a similarly
modest view: "What I would like to accomplish is basically being better off than
my parents were." And yet others, as in this case, professed to want money not so
much because it meant a lot to them personally but because they know it is
"what matters" in the world: "What do I want? A relationship with God, good
steady pay, make sure you can pay everything off, because money, apparently, to
the world, is worth the world."

Again, in this section of the interviews, where we did not explicitly ask about
money or material comfort, not all emerging adults described the ideal life that

they hoped to live in those terms. Some talked only about family, friends, being happy, education, religious interests, and "making a difference." Then again, 57 percent of the emerging adults we interviewed *did* spontaneously bring up the subjects of money and material consumption during their discussions of what they ultimately want to get out of life. And this was despite the fact that we had already talked about materialism and consumerism in an earlier section of the interview—in up to 88 other questions on other topics in the interview guide *prior* to this concluding point in the interview—making the discussion here feel somewhat repetitive.

Stated differently, when it comes to the nature of a good life believed to be worth living, to what in the end they want to get out of their lives, most emerging adults are rather limited in their horizons to a typical set of answers. In addition to having a nice family and being personally happy, another main goal of the majority of emerging adults is to have the financial means to possess and consume material goods, enjoyable services, and fulfilling experiences. Presumably, the last of these is also expected to contribute both to personal happiness and having a nice family. Only small minorities mentioned goals such as becoming a better person, being healthy, creating and performing art and music, serving community or country, or growing spiritually. These observed facts are totally consistent with the generally pro-consumerism survey statistics cited at the beginning of this chapter. They also comport with what emerging adults said in the discussions about materialism and consumerism examined above. And all of this, we think, tells us something sobering about the moral and spiritual visions of our culture when it comes to the goods of life and about the parochialism of the horizons into which we as a society are socializing our youth.[5]

Conclusion

We do not suggest that any of these issues or potential problems, much less their answers, are simple and easy. Nor do we do expect 18- to 23-year-olds to be brimming with realistic programs and solutions to address complicated economic and environmental problems. What we did expect to hear more of from emerging adults, however, is a broader array of visions of the good life, a better-informed awareness of the possible problems of mass consumerism, a greater concern for consumerism's impact on the earth's natural environment, and some existential wrestling with the personal implications of these challenges for their own lives now and into the future. Of these things we heard very little. The majority of emerging adults are content with mass consumerism and materialistic and self-fulfillment-oriented lifestyles—as long as they can also enjoy these things with their spouses, children, and friends. They do not see any problem with this. A substantial minority senses that consumerism entails some problems, but they are not very clear on what they are and are not particularly bothered by them. Fewer than one in ten emerging adults we interviewed voiced any kind of focused discontent or more intense criticism of mass consumerism. And only a minority of those spoke of actually changing their own thinking and behaviors accordingly. Most of what they actually did as a result of those discontents and criticisms was to try to maintain a greater awareness about overconsumption, to discard some of their excess possessions, and to be careful not to buy too many products that they did not really need.

Some cultural commentators today look to young Americans as our hope for a brighter future. Today's youth, some think, represent a new generation of alternative thinkers who will act as creative agents of change to push the nation in directions that are greener and more just.[6] We wish that this was so. What we have found, however, suggests quite the opposite—at least when it comes to mass consumerism and environmental stewardship. Nearly all emerging adults in America today have fully bought into mainstream economics and culture. Indeed, they may be even a little behind the curve on where social change seems to be heading with regard to a greener future. Very many emerging adults we interviewed could not even understand the issue or problems that we interviewers were asking them about. The idea of having any questions or doubts about the cycle of shopping, buying, consuming, accumulating, discarding, and more shopping appeared to be almost unthinkable to most of them. Most seem quite consumed with consumerism. Emerging adults have in fact been very well raised by parents, teachers, and the media to perpetuate the kind of standard materialistic values and lifestyles into which they have been socialized. They want and expect material security and financial comfort. They view recently invented, high-tech communication and entertainment gadgets—like iPhones, laptops, high speed internet, and big-screen televisions—as basic essentials in life. They view individuals as autonomous decision makers out to maximize their privately held values and preferences. They believe that any money that they or anyone else earns is entirely their own to do with exactly as they please. Notions such as the common welfare or of living a good life not defined by material consumption rarely cross their minds. Shopping, buying, and consuming as a way of life is thus presupposed by most emerging adults, and owning some of the nicer things in life is a natural part of the purpose of life. Most simply want and expect to live comfortably, working hard to earn money and using their earnings to happily consume products and services to their satisfaction.

If there is a problem here, as we think there is, the fault is not primarily that of emerging adults. They are simply mirroring back to the older adult world, to mainstream society and culture, what has been modeled for them and what they have been taught. Emerging adults have simply been good learners and now are eager to enjoy the benefits of their material abundance and consumer choice. So if there is a problem here, it is a problem of mainstream American culture and institutions. If we have questions about what we have learned in this chapter, they are questions to be put to all Americans. What really is a good life? What does it consist of? What more than anything else makes life worth living? What is of real value? Why do we feel so compelled (or what about our systems compels us) to consume and dispose of so much stuff? What are the moral and spiritual presuppositions of that kind of lifestyle? And what is that way of life doing to the earth's capacity to carry flourishing and healthy human life well into the future? These are no little questions. And what we have learned about and from emerging adults only presses them upon all of us more urgently.

|| 3 ||

Intoxication's "Fake Feeling of Happiness"

Drugs are merely the most obvious form of addiction in our society.
—Christopher Lasch

Intoxication is an important part of emerging adult culture and of the lives of many individual emerging adults. Why? Exactly why is intoxication so prevalent and important among 18- to 23-year-olds? Why do so many American emerging adults feel the need to become high, stoned, buzzed, and drunk? What is wrong with simply living life *not* recurrently intoxicated? And what might the answers to these questions tell us about our larger American society and culture?

Fears and complaints about adolescents and young adults doing drugs, drinking alcohol, and smoking cigarettes are nothing new. Dismay and alarm about these issues have been around for a long time. In fact, the issue of booze and drugs among youth has become perhaps an almost endemic ritual in our culture. Every day, month, and year, many young people feel compelled to get high, stoned, buzzed, and drunk. And every day, month, and year, some old people feel compelled to worry, raise concern, and develop new programs designed to reduce substance abuse. In a few cases, certain aspects of these problems have improved.[1] But in general the underlying situation remains much the same, year after year. Intoxication remains a big part of American emerging adult life and culture, despite many educational and governmental programs trying to change that. So what besides the obvious is going on here?

First, let us consider the actual extent of the substance-use issues in question. According to our NSYR survey data, nearly one in five (19 percent) of our surveyed 18- to 23-year-olds report drinking alcohol either a few times a week, once a day, or more often.[2] But drinking alcohol per se is not necessarily a problem. What *is* a problem is heavy drinking. Of the 78 percent of all emerging adults surveyed who do drink alcohol, 60 percent report having engaged in binge drinking at least once in the previous two weeks.[3] That is 47 percent of *all* emerging adults. And nearly 10 percent of those who drink at all reported binge drinking *five or more times* in the previous two weeks. Clearly, a sizeable minority of all emerging adults binge drink, and one in ten of those who drink binge drink very frequently. Furthermore, more than 12 percent of emerging adults surveyed by NSYR reported smoking marijuana either once a week, a few times a week, daily, or more often; 18 percent use marijuana monthly or more often. Regarding other drugs, 6 percent of 18- to 25-year-olds abuse psychotherapeutic drugs and nearly 2 percent each uses cocaine and hallucinogenic drugs. Altogether, about one in every five (20 percent) 18- to 25-year-olds use one or more illicit drugs (including others not mentioned here).[4] Finally, 33 percent of emerging adults smoke tobacco cigarettes, 55 percent of whom (18 percent of all emerging adults) smoke daily.

Furthermore, the percentage of adolescents who drink a lot of alcohol and smoke marijuana and tobacco *increases* as they grow through the teenage years into emerging adulthood. According to NSYR data, the number of emerging adult binge drinkers is about 8 percent higher than what the same youth reported three years earlier, when they were 15 to 20 years old. And it is more than 17 percent higher than five years earlier, when the same sample of youth was 13 to 17 years old. Even so, the pattern of heavy drinking starts for many during the teenage years, as 60 percent of all youth ages 15 to 20 who drink reported having gotten drunk at least once during the two weeks previous to the survey. The number of emerging adults smoking marijuana also increased more than 3 percent over the number reported three years earlier, and it increased almost 9 percent over the number of those who as 13- to 17-year-olds reported using marijuana "regularly." The abuse of any illicit drug also increases 10 percent in the jump from ages 12–17 to 18–25.[5]

Viewing the numbers from a different angle, by single age group, the proportion of youth who *never* drink alcohol drops from 86 percent at age 13 to only 16 percent by age 22—a 70 percent decline in never drinking. The proportion of teenagers who have never gotten drunk[6] declines from 67 percent at age 13 to a mere 14 percent by age 19—a 53 percent decline in never having gotten drunk. While 96 percent of 13-year-olds have never smoked marijuana, that number drops 27 percentage points for the same sample by age 23, to 69 percent. And the number of 13-year-olds who do not smoke cigarettes is 98 percent, which drops 31 points to 67 percent by age 23. Some of these numbers are depicted graphically in Figure 1. The point is that significant minorities of emerging adults regularly or recurrently seek to intoxicate themselves through substance abuse, and the proportion of youth who do so increases as they grow through the teenage and into the emerging adult years.

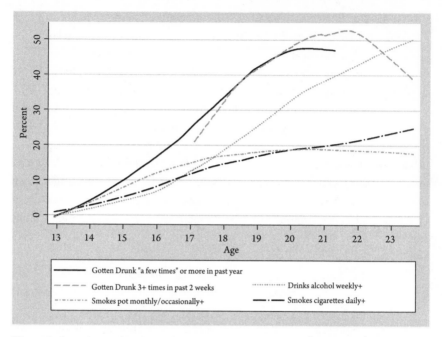

Figure 1 SUBSTANCE ABUSE BY AGE, 13- to 23-YEAR-OLDS (PERCENTS). Source:
National Survey of Youth and Religion, 2003, 2005, 2008.

What practical consequences do these substance abuses have? Consider
some facts about the matter of college alcohol drinking. More than 80 percent of
all college students drink at least some alcohol, including 60 percent of students
who are 18 to 20 years old. More than 40 percent of college students report
having engaged in binge drinking at least once during the two weeks prior to
their being surveyed—a number that reaches above 70 percent at some surveyed colleges with strong drinking cultures. This has consequences especially
for the drinkers, but also potentially for others around them. Among 18- to
24-year-olds, binge drinking and driving while intoxicated increased between
1998 and 2001. The number of students who reported driving motor vehicles
while intoxicated, for example, grew from 2.3 million in 1998 to 2.8 million in
2001—a 22 percent increase. The number of alcohol-related deaths also
increased among this age group between these years. In 2001, among students
ages 18 to 24, there were about 1,700 alcohol-related unintentional injury
deaths—an increase of 6 percent among college students since 1998, controlling for changes in the total college population. In addition, about 599,000 college students between the ages of 18 and 24 each year sustain unintentional
personal injuries while under the influence of alcohol. Furthermore, more than
696,000 students between the ages of 18 and 24 are estimated every year to be

physically assaulted by another student who had been drinking.[7] More than 400,000 college students ages 18 to 24 also report having had unprotected sex as a result of drinking alcohol. More than 100,000 college students every year report having been too intoxicated to know whether they had even consented to having had sex. Finally, more than 97,000 students between the ages of 18 and 24 are victims of alcohol-related sexual assault or date rape.[8] Clearly, alcohol abuse among college students is no small problem, and no laughing matter to be shrugged off with banal comments like "kids will be kids."[9] Alcohol consumption is a leading cause of death among youth, particularly teenagers, and contributes substantially to adolescent motor-vehicle crashes, other traumatic injuries, suicide, date rape, and family and school problems.[10] A recent study by the Independent Scientific Committee on Drugs published a report describing alcohol as the most harmful drug to users and to others around them of all 20 drugs examined.[11]

Beyond these statistical rates of drinking and smoking and their consequences, it is also worth considering that intoxication through substance abuse also figures prominently in mainstream emerging adult *culture*. To be sure, a majority of emerging adults are not binge drinkers and drug users, but they nevertheless have to negotiate a cultural world among their peers in which partying, drinking, buying drugs, getting buzzed, getting wasted, getting high, getting stoned, and the like are centers of attention, often encountered among friends and acquaintances. These become issues and choices they are forced to engage, and the substances for which are always available for consumption, whether in the foreground or the background. For three decades, for example, 83 to 85 percent of U.S. high school seniors report that in their lives marijuana is "easy to obtain."[12] While only some emerging adults seek recurrent intoxication for themselves, in other words, nearly all emerging adults occupy a shared culture in which intoxication impinges in one way or another on nearly everyone's life and thought. So, again, we ask: what is going on here? Why the need for intoxication? What does it mean? The following pages examine what emerging adults told us in our in-depth interviews about drinking and drugs in their lives— accounts that we think are instructive.

Approaches to Intoxication

The emerging adults we interviewed turned out to have an array of different attitudes toward and uses of different intoxicating substances. We present the major types here. Remember that, in speaking about quantitative proportions, our personal interviews with emerging adults are not nationally representative. What is nationally representative is our survey data and statistics reported above.

Nevertheless, our sample of interviews does represent a roughly accurate picture of American emerging adults, so estimated proportions are worth at least mentioning. More importantly, the interviews provide insight into the way different types of emerging adults think, feel, and act on the subject. The first two types we discuss are cases we do not find troubling. The subsequent types become more problematic.

Nonusers. A little more than one in five of the emerging adults we interviewed (22 percent) we label "nonusers." They were slightly more likely to be female than male, and a little younger. Almost 30 percent of them tried drinking alcohol once when they were younger. Only four nonusers (out of 46) we interviewed smoke cigarettes occasionally, and one more used to smoke regularly but has quit.[13] This group represents a mix of mainly two sorts of emerging adults. One is highly religious, coming particularly from conservative Protestant (evangelical, fundamentalist, and Pentecostal) and Latter Day Saints (Mormon) backgrounds. The second sort of nonuser includes emerging adults who have seen the lives of family members damaged or ruined by some addiction. Many in the highly religious category, however, either do not explicitly mention religion as a reason to avoid alcohol and drugs, or they reference their religious beliefs only vaguely, in passing. They are more likely to focus their explanations for abstaining on health concerns, other damages that addictions cause, or a desire to maintain control over their lives. Most of these approach alcohol and drugs with extreme caution. Some do consider that it might be fun to drink socially when they are of age, but most emphasize alcohol and drugs' power to destroy, saying that consuming them would not be worth the risk. Stepping back and examining their larger situations, it seems to us that the influence of their social ties and significant relationships, which are, of course, often formed through religious associations, are the primary reason they avoid alcohol and drugs.

The second type of nonuser, those who refrain because of bad family experiences with addictions, offered answers that were straightforward. "I've seen how my dad's side of the family has been, because they were really big on drinking and drugs," one said. "I know that it messed up my dad and his twin brother a lot, my uncle." Another explained: "My twenty-first birthday is coming up, but I won't drink; I promised myself I would never touch alcohol, because my grandpa was an alcoholic and my uncle was an alcoholic, so I know it runs in my blood and I just don't want to risk it. That's what I'm scared of, becoming addicted or smoking or drugs, I just don't want to chance it." Yet another explained:

> My grandpa was an alcoholic and a smoker, and he just died from, his body was, like, riddled with cancer. The smell and the expense of smoking, it's just not even worth it. What it does to you, down the road, it's not worth it. And drugs and stuff, that's a way to escape. And I mean,

for me, if I need to escape, I can just go and pray or find, emotionally or mentally, [support] like, that's the way it is.[14]

Some nonusers also joked about other "addictions" in their lives, such as Diet Coke, running, visiting museums, or playing video games, saying that they "just do not have the time for one more addiction"—suggesting, again, the larger presence of intoxicants in emerging adult culture and the apparent need to actively justify, even if only by joking, one's choice to abstain from them.[15] Many nonusers, especially those who have not suffered family histories of addiction, express the morally individualistic position that it is okay for anyone to do anything as long as they are not directly hurting anyone else. Even most of the religious nonusers said that their views only pertained to them, that others were free to do as they please.

Occasional substance users. Occasional users, who represented one in four (25 percent) of those we interviewed, enjoy the occasional glass of alcohol and sometimes the infrequent joint.[16] Many do not oppose smoking marijuana, but they are definitely against harder drugs, which they think damage one's health. Occasional users try to balance fun and responsibility. Many are aware of the possibility of, as one put it, "screwing up your entire life because you had too much fun."[17] They want to fit in with partying crowds (discussed below) just enough, but most also tend to maintain important social ties with others who have patterns of substance use similar to theirs. Like nonusers, occasional users strive to maintain self-control, but they are more outspoken in defense of alcohol and drugs, feeling a need to justify their limited use. They speak about the need to keep control of their actions when under the influence, but also, often more tacitly, the need to stay in control of where their life is headed. Their desire to maintain self-control generally prevents them from binge drinking or overusing pot. Ten (of 53 interviewed in this group) recalled experiences of getting drunk or high, which they typically regretted and had no intention of repeating. Some occasional users (8 of the 53) limit alcohol to only very rare occasions, while a few (3) say they enjoy a cold beer after a hard day of manual labor. The 4 out of these 53 who use pot do so less than once a month. Compared to the "partiers," described next, for occasional users, intoxicating substance use isn't nearly as exciting. Their social world does not revolve around red plastic cups and half-smoked joints. They are like nonusers in pragmatically seeing their behavior today shaping the life opportunities they will have later. Also, like nonusers, occasional users rarely directly judge the substance-use behavior of others. They tend, rather, to maintain personal standards for their own behavior and not hold others to similar standards. Occasional users are an even balance of male and female, and tend to be a little younger. They tend to say things like this:

I'll say, let's go get a drink. I don't drink very often. I probably go once a month, at that. And it's just with the guys in the [police] academy. I've become really close with departments and so we'll go hang out and have a drink, just to catch up on things, me and my old friends. But I'm not one of those people who go to party every week and get smashed and loud. I mean, that's a bad example.

And, "I've always seen alcohol as a social, holiday kinda thing, always saved it for birthdays, New Year's, special occasions like that. It's just never been an every-weekend thing for me." Or: "I haven't gone out lately, and mostly when I go out I like fruity beverages. I don't even like hard liquor, so to me, I don't feel like I have to drink. It's just if I'm in the mood for it." One last example:

> You come home, you're dog tired, and you know what? A cold beer sounds just absolutely the best thing in the world. I probably hit one or two of those, maybe three times a month. One month you could go by never pulling a beer out of the refrigerator. And some other days you could be, "Man that was hard work, I could sure use a cold one," you know, ease off the nerves and tensions of the day.[18]

Nonusers and occasional users, who together account for about 46 percent of the emerging adults we interviewed, represent relatively reasonable and healthy approaches to alcohol and drugs, we think.[19] The other types of emerging adults, however, are, in our view, more problematic.

Partiers. Those we call "partiers" were 22 percent of the emerging adults we interviewed, more than one out of five. They were equally men and women and spread across all age groups. They are also much more likely to smoke tobacco regularly. Partiers drink alcohol frequently, and when they do, they typically binge drink. About half of them also smoke pot, and very few of those who do not are against marijuana in principle. Seventeen percent of them have also used harder drugs, and slightly less than one half drink between one and three times a week. Eleven percent of them report using more than one drug, consuming a variety of intoxicants.

Partiers like alcohol and drugs, they say, primarily because they help them to be more social. "You get to release your inhibitions and a lot of people just go out [drinking] and they feel like they're able to socialize better," one explained; "It's a social thing." This is a major theme in partiers' discourse. That alcohol relaxes them socially and reduces their inhibitions is the main reason partiers offer to explain their heavy drinking. As one said, "I don't know why I started, but it's kinda like a social lubricant, 'cause I am a pretty quiet person, and alcohol does kinda help me loosen up and become more open to people. I don't like to talk a lot either, so if I have been drinking I'm really social, which is good for me." Another partier said that it would be socially alienating for someone not to drink in college. "My friends do it" is another recurrent theme. Another common response was that life without alcohol is simply boring. Partiers also explained their heavy substance use as a way to help them relax, because it is part of "the college experience," because it helps them to be less judgmental, because of dating stress and romantic breakups, and because of financial stress, difficult family relationships, and unfulfilling jobs.

Partiers were different from the two groups discussed above in being much more likely to have begun drinking alcohol or taking drugs earlier in life—22 percent of them reported beginning in middle school and 59 percent of them in high school.[20] One we interviewed got initiated as a young middle school student, with "help" from older siblings and friends:

> When I was 12 years old, I had an older sister whose friends thought it was really funny to see the little sister drunk. So they would feed me shots and stuff, and me being 12 years old, I'd be like, "You guys want to hang out with me? Okay!" They were 16, 17, so I was like, "Okay, yeah, let me do it!" I remember everybody went, "Let's go swimming," so I stumbled downstairs, put on my bathing suit, go and jump in the pool and realize that everyone else is naked. And I'm like 12, like, "What? What is that? I've never seen that before!" [*laughs*] There were like a couple times of that [drinking shots], and then I was like, "What am I doing? I'm like 12 years old, I should not be drinking!" So I actually quit for a good two years before I actually started sometimes [again] with my friends drinking.

Few of our interviewees actually describe the partying lifestyle itself in any depth. That seems to be partly because many of their parties seem, by many of their own accounts, pretty boring (despite much talk about their being "fun"), and partly because emerging adult partiers do not always remember what happens at their parties. Many parties seem mostly to involve people sitting around getting drunk, making weird faces for pictures to be posted on Facebook, and "meeting people" but never really getting to know them. By most accounts, the intoxicants (alcohol and sometimes drugs) are the main point of parties, the real goal the use of which often seems to be to relieve boredom.[21] But despite the lack of detailed reporting about party life, we can piece together some images of it from various comments offered by the emerging adults we interviewed.

One clear theme is that parties are not about good friends happily celebrating life and their relationships together. Parties are simply about getting drunk and maybe high. One emerging adult explained how much he drinks this way: "If it's just at a buddy's house, we're just hanging out, having a beer, just relaxing. But at a party, it could be a 12-pack, just sit there and get obliterated for the night or something." Such partying can also clearly consume a lot of time, taking over entire weekends and some weekday nights. "It's pretty much a weekend thing," one reported, "sometimes Thursday night, maybe if not Thursday night, then Wednesday night." Another said, "I drink alcohol at parties. I don't drink every day [laughing], just a couple times a week and two or three times a weekend, during the week maybe once or twice. But, [I'm] not [an] alcoholic." In college, there seems very little to prevent hard partying, even in dorms, as one told us:

> It's definitely prevalent at college. We usually drink on Fridays, as a hall, stay in [the dorm]. There are [RA supervisors] but [laughing] I mean, you'll find a way around, that sort of thing. It's pretty easy to. Some friends did get caught but, you know, we had a decent ability to not get in trouble. I mean, we weren't completely rowdy, we [just] got drunk.

Emerging adult partiers who are not in college often explain their partying life-styles as driven by stress, blues, and boredom. One, for instance, explained her recent increase in drinking this way:

> Just being stressed and depressed, and sometimes I feel like I need a drink. I just been going to work, taking care of my son, and it kinda was stressing me out, and I was messing with a boy[friend], and I'm like, okay, I'm getting kinda bored, I need a drink. So I was like, I just had to go out.

Another told us, "I started dating a guy that sold pot, and so being around it all the time, I smoked a lot more. It was strictly out of boredom. It was seriously just out of boredom." Yet another reiterated this theme:

> I didn't have a job at that point, and I hadn't really started going to school, because that was in the middle of the semester right when I came back. So I was just hanging out with friends and their friends, who also didn't have jobs. We just kind of all hung out all the time. We didn't really have anything to do, so we would just go mess around and drink, like, all day. It was just something to do.

Some emerging adults talk about parties as a way to meet new people. "Up at school," one reported, "drinking's a way to get out and meet people—go to parties, that kinda stuff." So, we asked, she finds that helpful? "Uh, it's not really helpful," she replied; "it's just one of the facets of just meeting people, go out, go to a party." Apparently, meeting people outside of intoxicated parties is difficult in college. In any case, rarely do emerging adults seem to form meaningful, lasting relationships at parties. Casual sexual hook-ups are more what party "relationships" are about. "I don't know," one explained, laughing, "you know, in college, drinking, hooking up happens." Asked whether a hook-up could ever turn into a serious relationship, one college fraternity brother said, "Not really, because if you're hooking up with someone at a party or something, you're really not paying attention to any of the qualities or personality or anything." In short, when "meeting people" at parties, who they actually are or what they are actually like is irrelevant.

Intoxicated partying fosters not only casual and often risky sexual encounters but also a variety of other forms of "stupid" activities and behaviors. Many partiers are naive about risks they take, recurrently risking danger and embarrassment. Indeed, risk and inanity are essential parts of the partying scene for many, where building reputations for being "badass," being able to "hold your liquor," entertaining fellow partiers (and friends the next day with stories) with idiotic behavior, and courting danger as a badge of honor are prized. Some others, however, such as the following emerging adult—exceptions that prove the rule—try to be more careful: "I drink around people who I trust. I don't drink around strangers or anything like that, just around people I trust, so if I do stupid things [when drunk] they just laugh at me and get over it because they do stupid things too." Some partiers go so far as to plan and implement "risk management" strategies before their partying begins. Responding to our question about how much he drinks, one explained it this way: "It depends on what the celebration is like. If it's a party, and we know we're staying here for the night, I'm getting drunk [*laughing*]. I'm not going nowhere, no worries." But, he said, "If we're at a bar, it's like, 'All right, who's driving?' and whatnot." An unwritten code of independence and responsibility governs most partiers' behavior, he explains: "Nobody wants to get too drunk to where you're a burden on your friends. Well, I mean, some people don't care and they do. But I would never wanna just get so drunk to where people had to take care of me, in a situation where we're like in public." But that code matters less when the party is not in public, as he explains: "But I don't mind, like if we're at a house, I'm telling 'em, 'Look, I'm gonna get drunk and you might have to take care of me for the night.' I ain't got no problem with doing that."

Sometimes, however, events at parties do not unfold as anticipated. One emerging adult college student we interviewed, for example, recently got into a fight at a party and was badly beaten up: "Two months ago, I got in a fight. Six kids jumped me and broke eight bones in my face. I had to go back home [for health insurance coverage] and get my nose reset every day." How did that happen? we asked. "I was walking home with a friend and we saw a party across

the street and said, 'Oh let's go in,'" he started. He was already under the influence of alcohol when he arrived at this party. "We went in and couldn't find the
beer, so we left." That's when the trouble began:

> There was a kid climbing a tree on the way out and she's like, "Goose
> someone.[22]" and I'm like, "No, you goose someone," and she's like, "No,
> you goose someone." So I goose someone. He got upset, and him and
> his six friends just "did work" on me. My nose was all swollen shut. I was
> messed up, had to go to the hospital, blowing blood out my nose. They
> broke two orbitals, a [cranium] plate, a nasal bone, these were broke
> [*pointing*], plus messed up my sinuses and broke some teeth. It sucked,
> I'm upset. Now I'm sad, I'm turned off by people. No shitting. Don't get
> in fights with five or six people. You're not gonna win, apparently.

Whether involving fights or not, college is a key institution in the life of many
partiers.[23] "Here in college," one said, "it's ridiculous how much your life revolves
around alcohol, you know?" Another recounted, "I went in high school to a
boarding school, where it was available but I never did it, we figured out how to
have fun without it. And when I got to college, nobody knew how to have fun
without it. So that's when it started." For many partiers, college is not so much a
time to develop personal and intellectual breadth and depth and to learn how to
critically engage the world. It is more typically viewed as a kind of holding pen,
a place of limbo students occupy until they receive the diplomas that will usher
them into "the real world." Because in their minds they have not reached the real
world yet, partying hard is perfectly acceptable and encouraged. College is the
time to have fun and be wild, without regret. According to one partier, getting
drunk is "an experience that everybody needs, just let loose, have fun with my
friends." *Animal House* is the model.

What happens in emerging adulthood and college, the assumption is, stays in
emerging adulthood and college. The experiences and influences can be hermet-
ically sealed off from later life, many suppose, when emerging adulthood is over
and real life begins. It is as if partiers picture themselves as tree saplings that,
when caught in a strong wind, bend in a particular direction for a time; but once
the wind stops, they are confident that they will spring back into an upright pos-
ture and continue to grow strong and tall with no damage done. Even karma
(discussed in chapter 1) will not carry over into real life after emerging adulthood, many seem to think. Later, when partiers are older, that will be the time
for them to settle down, work a real job, get married, and have children. The
success of a respectable, bourgeois lifestyle will come then. Meanwhile, it's time
to party wildly, to be a consumerist-bohemian of sorts. One expressed this outlook, and a few other themes noted above, in this way:

When I drink, you go to these parties and everyone is just drinking and it's just sort of like it almost has become a little bit socialized. It's sad to say but it really is. It's like you're not going to really make friends with a bunch of drunk people when you're sober. It's always like, you're not endangering your own life, it just sort of becomes a lifestyle in a way. I think the key is understanding that it's not permanent. That way, you grow up eventually and that life kind of becomes an old style of things, you know?

Not many partiers realize, however, that some of them will not exit the temporary party lifestyle so easily—as certain emerging adults, discussed below, have already learned the hard way.[24]

While the nonusers and occasional users mentioned above express concerns about losing control of themselves, partiers are confident that they have total control.[25] As one told us, "I got to college and I was like, ah, I'll try drinking, it can't really hurt me, and I tried it and from there I started buying into it and it didn't really change me at all, I'm still the same person." Another told of being determined when younger not to do drugs, because she had a friend who was sent away to "some special school" for doing drugs. Then her sister starting smoking pot and pushing her to smoke too, and she eventually gave in:

Freshman year [of high school] I just tried it, and realized that it didn't negatively affect me in any way, didn't make my grades drop, wasn't a gateway to other drugs. I've never really felt bad about it because it hasn't negatively influenced me or anyone else. I don't drive while I do it. Marijuana is less bad than alcohol, which is legal.[26]

Many partiers believe that their heavy substance use is perfectly safe and "mature":

When you're a teenager you experiment with things, you get bored and start experimenting. I think every teenager does and should experiment to a safe level, a mature, safe level. I'd say [for me the start of partying] it was just experimenting, and you know, I had fun doing it, so I continued to do it. I just don't smoke much pot anymore because I get really antisocial on it and I don't like being antisocial, I smoke it more when I'm drinking, because it evens it out. I drink every weekend pretty much.

Thus, the health risks of heavy drinking seem worth the social lubricant that alcohol provides most partiers, as this one explains:

It's a good time, people open up when they drink, you know, I'm a pretty shy person but when I drink I don't really have a problem going up and having random conversations with people. So that's something that I use to open myself up a little bit more. And, you know, I know the health effects, that if you binge drink every day and become an alcoholic, are bad. But most people drink in college and they're fine now, so I don't really think it's as much of a big deal. And I'll be 21 in a year anyway.

That, however, continues to raise the question: why can't emerging adults feel comfortable in social interactions without being buzzed or drunk?

Partiers often point to addicts and people with real substance abuse problems, whom they see themselves as differing from, as a way to affirm their own self-control and ability to eventually cut out partying when the time comes. As one put it, "My parents know that I'm going to make the right decision [despite doing some cocaine, acid, marijuana, and psychoactive mushrooms (sometimes called "magic mushrooms" or "shrooms")] because I have a good idea of what I want at the end of the day. I think my friends who don't have a good idea of what they want, they're the continuous users." Establishing clear boundaries between their own more self-regulated ways and the ways of "continuous users" seems to help many partiers feel more in control of their lives than some of them actually are. Some partiers in fact talk as if they are invincible. Said one, for example, whose father is an alcoholic:

I know the statistics, that I'm probably more likely to be one, and I think alcohol can control me, it's a drug, I'm sure as hell it could control me someday, but I'm like so independent that I catch myself. I've been in a lot of situations where I'm almost there [i.e., become an alcoholic] and I always catch myself. So I'm counting on myself to catch myself.

Partiers are particularly vague, open, and unclear about moral standards in general. On most matters they go particularly out of their way to avoid stepping on anyone else's toes. When they sometimes do offer clear moral statements, these only apply to themselves; nobody else is ever implicated. In our view, this vague and tacit tolerance of many attitudes and all social behaviors likely makes it more difficult for partiers to develop many substantive positions on real issues. And that in turn likely hinders the development of deeper, more complex friendships and healthy romantic relationships. There are real limits to relationships between people who have few definite beliefs, boundaries, or (nonsexual) passions. If so, alcohol and drugs may be used to further avoid challenges that come up in real relationships, while still allowing people the comfort of being part of some kind of community (the party crowd). If being a person with convictions, thoughts, and a vision for the world is too difficult to manage, a long evening of intoxication can take care of that problem. As one said, "I believe in just having fun and living in the moment, you know, doing something with you, it's not like conformity, it's just okay, let's have some fun, let's be dumb." Another, a very heavy partier, observed: "Technology-wise, we're just advancing so quick and everything's changing so rapidly, it's just snowballing. So I want to say that makes us less active, more lazy, makes people not as sociable, I think. I mean, you are socializing [during parties], but not like personal interaction necessarily all the time."

Some partiers we interviewed did appear to be beginning to phase out of this wild stage. They are thinking about wanting better grades, a stable job, or just some peace and quiet. They said things like "I felt like I just need to grow up, and alcohol's been fun enough for me," and "When you're sober, you know, you think a lot more clearly and it's a heck of a lot easier to get a job when you can pass the drug test." Having a baby also usually, though not always, has a big impact on partying: "Since I had my daughter, I cut back, I tried to be just like [better]. Before I had my daughter, I was turning into mud," one new mother said, laughing. Most partiers, however, are not having babies. And for most of these who seem to be considering cutting back, their party days are far from over. Some have picked up more responsibilities, but not enough to convince them that partying is no longer fulfilling.

Some of these possibly transitional cases had recently experienced a lousy romantic relationship or a bad breakup that had caused a spike in their substance use; then, when the relationship or mourning over the relationship ended, the heavy partying began to calm down. These kind of experiences seem built into emerging adult culture. By postponing marriage commitments and yet still yearning to have close, bonded relationships, many emerging adults find themselves in situations, as one put it, of having "everything but the ring." That is another, often awkward disconnect between the now and later in emerging adulthood. Yet the lack of commitment and the ability to end such relationships at any time, which happens frequently, sets up emerging adults for recurring emotional wallops, which the booze and drugs of parties are often used to help anesthetize. One guy told us:

> It's like a stress thing. Like recently, I broke up with the girl. I wasn't smoking [pot], I told myself and my friends I wasn't smoking as long as I was with the girl. Right after we broke up I was like, "Yeah, I'll smoke again."

Another we interviewed told us that, just after her boyfriend had cheated on her, the relationship became "toxic," they broke up, and she took psychoactive mushrooms: "It was a great experience. I can definitely say it was something that I'm really glad I did, because, I don't know, the fact that it's a drug, it makes you feel as though you're on a completely new sense of awareness to everything and every, the whole world made sense for about twelve hours—but um . . ." But she then said she would never do it again. Why? "Because the next day was just awful. I took them around 11:00 at night, I literally could not shut my eyes until 9:00 the next morning, and I just, the aftermath of it was just death. I felt terrible for two days and I will never do that again to myself." Partying to anesthetize bad feelings thus has its problems.

Recovering partiers. The next major type of emerging adult substance users—representing about one in five (21 percent) of those we interviewed—are what we call recovering partiers. These are people who not long ago belonged to the partier crowd and engaged in the full partying lifestyle. But something more recently had moved them to moderate or to stop their frequent alcohol and drug consumption. Recovering partiers tend to be older, are slightly more likely to be male, and were especially likely to have begun drinking in high school (rather than in middle school or college). Many of these are in the process of shifting or have already shifted from being binge drinkers to the kind of occasional users described above.

For many, this change was prompted by realizing how crazy and out of control their partying lives were. These emerging adults often regretted their recent partying phase, looking back with some remorse or disgust. One told us, "I drank for so many years and it wasn't doing anything but harming me, so I had my experience with it and it was fun but something that I don't see benefiting me in the future or helping me in my goals. And it costs money, too!" Another reported, "It's not worth it, I wake up and I feel like crap the next morning and got to worry about whether I made a fool of myself [*laughs*], and my girlfriend says I'm a real jackass, so yeah, it's worth avoiding the fights, and I feel better too!" Yet another recounted:

> I started drinking a lot and partying and being reckless in my late teens. A month after my 18th birthday I got a DUI, crashed my car into a pole. I was extremely intoxicated and I don't remember anything and I went to jail. So I guess I just figured out that. I didn't have a license for a year, so it wasn't like I could drink and drive, but do I think I would have if I could have? Maybe. It took me a while to figure out what I needed to do.

Still another told us, "In high school I was [drinking] a lot more, more easily influenced by everyone else doing it. So it would be Friday and Saturday night, and everyone is having a party in someone else's house so everyone is drinking there. But now, once you have a couple of hangovers, then it's like, no more."

For others, the transition out of heavy partying was provoked by the more pragmatic realization that new or impending life responsibilities would be compromised by continued partying. These often said that it is fine to be an "idiot," "a little bit crazy," or "immature" for a while, as long as one eventually moves beyond the "superficial" partying stage. These recent partiers realized that binge drinking and drugs did not serve their real personal interests and could not help them adjust to their future lives. One, for instance, explained, "I wanted to actually join the FBI, and you had to stop doing stuff like three years before you applied, and plus I just thought I didn't want to do it, I had no interest in it. I know friends who do it every day. I don't think starting [drugs] affected my life at all. It was just something I had to try, an experiment, that's it." Another agreed:

> Obviously you can't get a job [not passing a drug test]. I don't feel marijuana should be illegal. It's not a drug, it's an herb. If it was legal, would I smoke it? Maybe. I stopped just to get a job, and now I'm in the Coast Guard and it's really illegal. I really would get in a lot of trouble.

The kind of reasons offered in retrospect by recovering partiers for becoming partiers in the first place are mostly the same as those offered by the continuing partiers described above, with perhaps somewhat more emphasis on partying as simply being "part of the college experience." The first year or two of college seems for many to have been a time when they were particularly vulnerable to being sucked into partying in problematic ways. As one told us, "Freshman year it was definitely a little bit more on the abusive side, because I was just down in the dumps and after one particularly unpleasant experience I was like, not like that again, ow!" Another observed, "The first couple years of college was rough [*laughs*], living in dorms. But then in the last two or three years, I had my own apartment, just didn't do it. You weren't really subjected to all the parties that you were when you lived on campus." Another explained in greater depth:

> In the last few years my drinking has definitely gone up, because my parents were so strict, I really didn't do it a lot then [in high school] because I was afraid of getting in trouble, I usually did. In college I probably went a little bit crazy my freshman year because I was like, "Oh my God, I can do everything." And then I got sick a couple times and toned it down. Since living up here [at college now] and all my friends being 21, we go to the bars a lot more. But not always, like in [high] school people binge drink a lot more than here. Sometimes now we'll just go out for a drink with dinner.

Another described the kind of change that can happen for some over the college years: "I think that when you're younger in college, friends are more willing to go out every night even if you have a test [to study for] or something ridiculous like that. But when you're older, you realize it's important to stay home and study and concentrate more on the things that are going to get you far in life and not worry about where everyone's going this night."

Recovering partiers offered a number of more specific reasons for wanting to leave the party scene and moderate their substance abuse. The most frequently mentioned reason was wanting to take on more responsibility and gain control in their lives. "I thought if I'm going to really try and get a business going," one said, "and actually be able to go to college, if I'm paying for it, I want to be able to actually learn something from it and not just forget it the next day." Another told us, "Now that I've got everything on track and everything's being a lot busier, you can't do certain things, so you just say, oh, that's worth giving up anyways. I've had my fun."

A second common reason given for recovering from the partier lifestyle was concern about the possible damage that partying was doing to mental health and intelligence. One told us simply, "I'll never do [it] again because I know how dangerous it is." Another described the longer-term effects that partying has had on his body and mind:

> I still have trouble remembering things. I don't remember really talking to people that often. I'll talk to someone and then maybe an hour later I'll completely forget that I even talked to them. That affects your life too. And when I'm just relaxed, sitting around, driving, and I'll just like have like a twitch. It's really kinda annoying. And I can't really focus on anything. I mean I couldn't focus on things before. I think now it's worse. It's not really anything that's fun. I didn't even like the physical effects of it, but I don't know, just the mental state of mind, it kinda makes you feel depressed about a lot of things. It gives you a fake feeling of happiness.

Recovering partiers sometimes told stories of realizing with surprise just how heavy their consumption of alcohol and drugs had become, which woke them up to the need for change. For example:

> I used alcohol quite heavily for a time, to the point where me and my friends would go to a bar on campus, and we would go drink beer during lunch. We would go have a drink with our professors, then go out at night and drink. It was too often happening where I was waking up and not remembering the previous night. After quite awhile I quit

doing that, tapered down to the point where it is social. If I am at a bar with friends I will have a few drinks. At parties I am no longer the one stumbling around. I am the one cleaning up after everybody now.[27]

Another common reason for backing away from partying was a life-course transition that marked a noted stage in growing up, such as graduating from college or turning 21 and no longer finding partying to be attractively rebellious. For many, this was accompanied by the growing realization that partying was actually boring and unfulfilling. "I just realized how immature people were doing it," one told us. "Just the people I hung out with, a lot of friends, they liked to party and have a crazy time, stuff like that. Plus it costs money." Another reported:

I went through that whole phase when I was younger and drugs were the cool thing to do. And now when I see people my age doing that I'm like, "Wow, that's really sad that you're stoned on a Wednesday night." There's people that I do hang out with that still do stuff like that, but I feel like there's more [to life] than sitting around and eating Cheetos and watching TV all day. I have more things to do.

Simply growing weary of partying was a definite theme among the recovering partiers: "When I first started drinking, it was cool, the thing to do on weekends. After a while you just got tired of it. You get tired of making an idiot out of yourself because you're drunk, and it's expensive." Another agreed: "As I get older, there's no way I'm drinking, because there is such bullshit around thinking you're super cool for drinking, you know."

Others reported having problems driving under the influence of alcohol, which forced them to cut back. "I'm not trying to get drunk and I'm driving everywhere," one told us, for example, "driving to college campus, so I have [only] one beer with my dinner. I'm just over it, you know, things have changed." Yet others changed their attitudes and behaviors as a result of seeing the damage partying has done to friends or family members. One related this story, for example: "There was a friend that I had to cut out of my life because he was using every day and dropped out of college and was living out of his parents' trust fund and barely even working. I was like, wow, you had a house and two cars given to you and you can't even hold it together. This is bad and not for me." Another said, "I have friends who have problems with alcohol and drugs, and it's never gonna become a problem in my life. I see it as, I mean, it's something you do when you get together with people." Some described changes in romantic relationships or friendships associated with backing out of the partying world. One, for example, explained:

I was dating the guys that were drinking seven days a week and they had no goals. They weren't gonna [go anywhere], you know. I dated a guy that like dropped out of high school and did nothing all day, didn't work, didn't do anything. And my parents were like, "Really?" and I was like, "I love him so much," and they're like, "That's what you want to marry?" The more I thought about it, I was like, "Wow, maybe I should marry somebody that's educated. Maybe that's a good idea." So it's made me a lot more aware of how people really are when they're not drinking.

This same emerging adult mentioned her parents helping her to cut back:

It was like every Friday, Saturday, Sunday night in high school and that was really bad, when it was becoming an all-weekend thing. I'd go to school and be cool and then it was like Friday afternoon, I'd be like, "Let's do this" and would leave school and be drinking. Then finally my parents were like, "Wow, all the liquor in the cabinet's gone," and I was like, "I don't know where it is. Where did it go?" So they were like, "We're cutting it out right now. Today."

Others, such as this case, described becoming more comfortable in social relationships as a factor that helped limit their partying: "I see very few advantages of drinking, but you know I enjoy it now on a more limited basis in just a social setting than before. I think a lot of younger people, they're drinking more to feel more comfortable and at-ease in situations."

It is not the case that all recovering partiers have totally rejected their former outlooks on life or have settled down into a fully mature lifestyle. The last quote, for instance, was followed up with this comment: "Now I enjoy having a glass of wine with a meal or like that, but I don't go out and get drunk very often." He still goes out and gets drunk, just not very often. These recovering partiers mostly seem to be trying to negotiate a somewhat different microphase of emerging adult transition and learning. For many, it is a process, not a dramatic, one-time decision. And in that process it can be difficult to let go of the good old days, even when they also admit that they were or are not actually all that good:

We do occasionally still smoke pot, just from a feeling of nostalgia from back when we were sneaking around, that feeling like, man, we're doing something we shouldn't or we're buddies, you know, that's it. But I've grown out of it. I see myself becoming more and more responsible with drinking, so I'm not gonna need to do anything [bad], I'm going farther away from having problems.

Emerging adults thus sometimes do drugs more out of camaraderie or nostalgia than for the experience of taking drugs itself. Likewise, this emerging adult is in the midst of his transition, someone who still drinks a fifth of rum at a time, but who also, oddly, says he feels little need to drink anymore:

> I got the idea of tasting better types of beer and that got me into wanting to get into heavy alcohol, liquor, dark rum. And I smoked pot some. But I've noticed sometimes I literally have to drink most of or a whole bottle, a fifth, before anything will happen to me, like, where I'll start wobbling a little. I can still be here talking to you, maybe mumbling a little, but I can still stay there and understand exactly what you're saying. But I'm starting to get to a point where I don't even care to drink any-more, because it just doesn't really do much to me. After taking down my meds [for seizures] and I was starting to feel better, I've kinda real-ized I don't think I need it, so I stopped the pot.

Recovering partiers who have made dramatic changes in their alcohol and drug consumption usually reported positive effects in their lives, changes that they really like. "Since I stopped," one said, voicing this typical sentiment, "I definitely, without a doubt, I've definitely been doing a lot better in my school and I've been much more focused in everything. Working, grades are better, I'm consistent at work, just a lot more work output." Another said, "The change was just a happier outlook on life." Another told us, "Cutting back has made me a lot smarter, because I was making dumb decisions." Similarly, this one explained:

> Before, I would come home whenever I wanted, be home three or four nights out of the week for six hours, just sleep and go back to work, and then just party and stay at someone else's house. I'd say my life is pretty organized now because of not doing drugs. Stopping makes you able to focus clearer on things and makes you less irritable. It helps bring trust back and just makes your family [relationships] better.

Some recovering partiers explained that partying still helps define their lives socially, though in a relatively good way. "I'm still defined by drinking now," one reported, "because I'm being defined by the rejection of it, as opposed to by doing it. But if I have to be on one side of the fence, I'd rather be on the side of rejecting." There are some among recovering partiers who report having no bad feelings about their former partying lives, who—in keeping with the standard partier script of "party now, settle down later"—are simply ready to move on to the next thing. But they are the minority. Many if not most recovering partiers admit that there are real costs that partying exacted in their lives and give happy testimonies about the benefits of leaving the partying lifestyle.

Recovering partiers are an informative group. By showing us when and why emerging adults no longer find intoxication quite as appealing, they help us get closer to answering the initial question of why emerging adults find intoxication necessary in the first place. Because they are mostly on the far side of the partying life—having been there and done that, and are often sadder but wiser— they provide insights into the life of emerging adult partying that current partiers either do not seem to have the perspective to see or are too invested in alcohol and drugs for the moment to admit. They tell us, for instance, that a lot of partying is driven by questionable motives, such as personal insecurity, the need to conform socially, and the inability to relax and relate well to others without first having raised their blood alcohol level. They report that partying is also some-times associated with, if not driven by, problems in other parts of life, like depression, difficulties with school, and health problems. Recovering partiers tell us that it is easy to get in over one's head with partying, despite the assur-ances of partiers that they are in control of everything. They tell us that the party life involves a lot of idiocy, immaturity, "bullshit," and wasted time and money. They report that partying is often risky, dangerous, frightening, socially embar-rassing, and harmful to body, mind, and sometimes emotions. They say that par-tying interferes with performance at school and causes stupid decision making in relationships. And most tell us that they are very glad they have cut back or stopped consuming alcohol and drugs. Presumably, many current partiers will come to similar conclusions in due time. It seems regrettable that they cannot learn those lessons sooner in life. It is also regrettable that not all of them will in fact be able to recover from partying, as we see next.

Addicts. Not all emerging adult partiers come out of their "crazy" and "imma-ture phase" so easily, and some never do. Some emerging adults start with par-tying and eventually become not occasional users but addicts. They are alcoholics or are addicted to drugs, or both. We stretch the meaning of "addict" here for the sake of convenience to include steady, heavy users of marijuana.[28] These are also disproportionately likely to be cigarette smokers. Eight percent of all of the emerging adults we interviewed are addicts of one kind or another—by which we mean longer-term, consistent (often daily) users who experience difficulty in any attempt to stop their substance use, whether they themselves admit being an addict or not. They tend to be older males who initiated their substance use in middle and high school. They say they started drinking or doing drugs as a cure for stress or a response to a traumatic event, out of curiosity, or because they had a friend or close relative who also drank or did drugs. Four out of five of them (80 percent) report normally practicing their addiction with other people. One in four (25 percent) of the addicts we interviewed deny that their addiction is a major problem in their life, and only one in five (20 percent) expresses unhappiness about their addiction. Two (of 16 addicts interviewed) say that doing drugs helps them to make spiritual connections. Those who do regret their addictions say it consumes too much money and makes them irresponsible.

Many readers probably have particular images that come to mind when they think about drug addicts—likely involving crack-house vagrants and down-and-out homeless people who end up as unclaimed bodies in city morgues. But most emerging adult alcoholics and drug addicts do not resemble those images, at least not yet. Most currently hold down regular jobs or are college students passing their classes. Some are in denial about their own addictions and may look quite normal to most people around them. Nevertheless, they are addicts, saying things in interviews like "I smoke pot every day, wherever I want, whenever I can get it, if I got money I get it." Part of why they may often look like regular people in many settings is because the substances that they are addicted to help them to maintain their composure for a period of time. One, for example, told us:

> I smoke pot every day, multiple times a day. Steady, just stay high, got to be high. That's just it. After smoking for so long, it's just like, if I'm not high, if I haven't smoked at all, I'm just real on edge. You know what I'm saying? Shit bothers me more if I'm not high. You get a little delayed reaction [when high], so I get the little split second to think about it before I react. But if I'm sober and I hear something I don't want to hear, then I'm just gonna explode.

This same emerging adult also reported, "Cigarettes too, I guess [I smoke as] a stress reliever, you know what I'm saying? Basically it's addicting, cigarettes, after you eat. So it's just a habit, bad habit. I smoke all the time, pretty much go through like a pack of cigarettes a day." We do not have the data to establish a possible association between drug and alcohol addictions and problems with frustration and self-control ("I'm just gonna explode").[29] But anecdotally we did notice that theme among some of those we interviewed. For example, another emerging adult addict described in this way his experience being a person of his age in our culture and society today:

> It's tough because you have a bunch of people telling you that you need to grow up, you need to do this. But then on the other hand, they also teach you, like, you're too young to understand what's going on, which we really are. I'm 18 years old. [But] I understand. I've been through a lot. I know. And people don't understand that, and *it just makes me want to hit people* [emphasis added].

Many addicts seem to have started into their substance of choice as a response to life stress. One, for instance, spoke of a peak in drug consumption when his father died:

> I was doing more stuff the last time we spoke, three years ago, that's when my dad died. I was a little bit wilder then, I was doing a lot of mushrooms, popping like here and there, and I was much wilder. Now I'm just a lazy couch potato.

Another told us her addictions began when she had sexual intercourse for the first time and thought she got pregnant, in the context of social relationships lacking support: "I started smoking pot and cigarettes the night I lost my virginity and right after that, when I thought I was pregnant. So I started smoking the day I thought I was pregnant [*laughs*]. That night was the first night that I smoked pot, and I liked it." While she did not say so in so many words, the marijuana likely helped ease her into her encounter of first sexual intercourse. Pot then became a coping mechanism in handling her parents' reaction: "It helped me deal with my parents when I was home, because they were really strict." It also helped her deal with her sexual partner's lack of support and interest in her apparent predicament:

> It's the same guy who dumped me at prom. [I told him on the phone] I thought I was pregnant, and he said, "Well you better get an abortion because I won't help you take care of it," and then hung up. I had gotten to know him for six months before this all happened, and I thought I knew him really well, like the back of my hand, but I didn't know him at all.

(It turned out, however, that she was not pregnant after all; it was a false alarm.) Others talked about their drug addictions in explicitly therapeutic, comforting terms:

> Smoking pot makes me feel better the next day. Like this weekend I've been doing a lot of drinking, going out and stuff, my skin just gets awful and I feel like shit in the morning. I smoke a little pot, I feel better, hungry, and sleepy, that's it, and I wake up the next day fresh. So I would rather do that. I think it should be legal, personally.

Others hold a matter-of-fact, might-as-well-enjoy-yourself kind of attitude:

> It's [pot] just what I do now. I just chill at the house, watching movies, smoke. Every day, steady, probably like two years now, since college. It's

like they say in [the 1993 film] *Dazed and Confused*: I did the best I could while I was here, had the most fun I could do while I was here, banged the most broads I could do while I was here. That's what the world is. You just do what you do.

Another, affirming this go-for-it-with-all-the-gusto-you-can-get-while-you-can approach to life, told us, "I think when I'm 30, I will definitely have calmed down, or hopefully have calmed down on drinking and drugs, so this way I get all that garbage out of my system." So, we asked, if it is garbage, why not calm down now? He replied, "It's fun and all my other friends do it. I don't know. It's just that now, I'm 19, I finally have that ability to do what I kind of want to do, so I'm going to kind of push my limits, I think, just to see how far I can get."

Emerging adult addicts sometimes compare their dependent substance use to other forms of pleasure or consumption, in order, it seems, to help justify themselves, to make their addictions seem more natural and reasonable. One, for instance, compared his substance use to taking a relaxing bath:

> If I'm hanging out with someone, we're just drinking. If I'm going to a party and we're drinking, wherever, you wanna just have fun. I just wanna drink. And I use pot now to just relax myself. Like, people take long baths after they get back from a long day of work. I kinda use pot as like a remedy to make myself feel better.[30]

More typical, heavy pot smokers compare their addiction favorably to regular drinkers of alcohol: "Honestly, I'll never stop doing this, smoking pot," one told us; "I would rather come home from a long day at work, sit on the couch and smoke a half a joint and watch TV or play a video game than the guy who comes home and stops at the bar and has a few beers."

Many emerging adult addicts seem aware of some of the problems and dangers of their addictions. Some, for instance, know that the partying people who they associated with because of their addictions are not really good for them. One, for instance, told us, "I mean, not to sound weird or anything, but I just love smoking. I love the way it makes me feel. Like, the benefits of smoking, I guess, kinda outweighed the bad for me." So, we asked, what is the bad that needs to be outweighed? He replied: "Well, dealing with the people you surround yourself with when you're smoking isn't always the most ideal situation. They're not the best people to be around. I stopped [for a while] because of that. And then I started up, because I just didn't think, like, that was holding me back anymore." The thing about addicts is they always seem able to start up again, often even when they try to stop. Another told us:

I've been putting myself at risk since forever. Since I can remember, I've been putting myself at risk. At any given moment I could end up in jail because I'm just doing stupid shit and I just really need to cut that shit out. If I get put in jail now, it's gonna, I have a baby and everything, I'm saying now it makes a difference. Before, it really didn't make any difference.

Some hard core cases even appear highly aware of the illusory nature of the happiness they enjoy as drug users, yet still continue in their addictions, as is the nature with addicts. One, for example, began by telling us that his drug use is more limited by lack of money than personal self-regulation. "Money more than self-control, I would say based on money." How many drugs does he do? "Drugs in general, if you were to mix them all in one category, marijuana and all the psychedelics, everything together, painkillers, I would have to say one usage of whatever it might be once per day, every day, since I've been in college and kinda been more free with my time." What is it about college and drugs? "In college I feel that people should be able to do whatever they want to do, within the realms of their own house, as long as it's not hurting themselves or one another. But if you really want to hurt yourself by taking a specific drug, so be it, if you really want that, go for it. That's what I feel." So why does he take drugs? "I feel better about myself, basically, I'd be happier. The painkillers kind of make me interested in more things, like wanting to clean, whereas if I don't take 'em I just want to sleep." But then he immediately tells us this about his experience:

> Going to get a drug is sometimes more supplemental [i.e., effective] than having the drug itself. Like on the way to getting a bottle of painkillers, say, I think I'm happier, on the way to get 'em, than I am once I have them in my system. I don't know why or if I ever will know why. I've definitely talked to many people and they say they experience the exact same thing. I do feel that, yeah, I'm happier knowing that I'm going to get it than once I have it, and I'm like "You know, this isn't that good, now I want something else."

But understanding that fact does not change the pattern of behavior:

> The problem is you want more and more and more, and I'm tired of wanting more. And once I have that idea in my mind, "Oh yeah, that's gonna do it for me, once I have that in me I'm gonna be great, I'm gonna be happy, I'm gonna be able to do this, do that," I'll drive myself into thinking, "Yep that's perfect." But then once you have it, you say, "It's not as good as I imagined."

Still, he takes various kinds of prescription medications illegally, as well as other drugs, every day. The amazing thing is that he actually stopped taking all drugs recently when he had to have surgery. Did that affect him in any way, we asked? "Yes, definitely," he said. "Stopping the [illegal use of] pain medication significantly increased the amount of energy I had, the amount of aspirations, motivation increases, getting a job." But then he immediately shifts back into the addict's view of things, like about getting a job, which he critiques: "While using drugs regularly," he observes, "getting a job does not seem a very important thing. It may just be because you want to financially fund the drug habit by the job, you know, you say, 'Gonna get a job so I can take more of this stuff.' And that'd be even worse." So, compared to addicts who work jobs to pay for their drugs, this guy is in a better position, apparently. "I'm kind of different in thinking," he explains, "in that I'd rather sit at home and get high than go to work and be paid so I can [afford to] get high. I'd rather sit home and do nothing and be mentally out of it than, I don't know."

People who are unrecovered addicts, when you hear their real stories, live sad and often pathetic lives—whether they are crack-house vagrants or seemingly successful college students. A lot of people do not think of there being 18- to 23-year-old drug addicts and alcoholics.[31] But they are out there, living out the more advanced stages of the emerging adult partying scene. Some know they are addicts. Others cannot admit that fact. But in either case they are compulsively captive to chemically induced intoxication. What, we continue to wonder, might that tell us, not only about the sad lives of some people but also about American culture and society?

Recovered addicts. Some emerging adults age 23 or younger are, amazingly, not just addicts but already *recovered* addicts. Again, it is typical to think of sobered-up alcoholics and recovered drug addicts as probably middle aged or older. So it was simply remarkable for us to interview 19- and 21-year-olds who have already in their short lives hit bottom with addictions and done the hard work to quit, recover, and piece their lives back together. Some of these young people were inexpressibly inspiring. Two of these recovered addict cases—a 21-year-old former heroin addict and a 19-year-old former alcoholic—we have described at length elsewhere and will not repeat their stories here, although they are well worth reading and definitely complement the stories below.[32]

Four percent of all of the emerging adults we interviewed were recovering drug addicts or sobered alcoholics. These tended to be both male and female, though slightly more often female, of varying ages, many of whom still smoke cigarettes. Many of them got a head start on addiction and recovery by initiating their substance use in middle school. They started into substance abuse, they said, because of particular traumatic events, difficult family lives, or sometimes through curiosity or a friend or relative who was a substance abuser. They had been addicted to alcohol, pot, or other drugs, or, very often, various combinations of those. Factors prompting their recoveries included facing up to their basic inability to function in life, becoming parents, checking into rehabilitation programs, and experiencing religious awakenings. Here are the voices of some of the recovered addicts we interviewed.

"I used to smoke marijuana pretty frequently," one guy told us, "but within the last month or so I have decided that it is not worth it. I don't like it anymore." What role, we asked, did smoking pot have in his life?

> I think for the last year or so when I did it, it wasn't peer pressure, but it just became habitual. It was an addiction. I think it really was. It wasn't physical. It was a mental addiction, just in the sense of accepting it and smoking it when it was offered. And it was such a routine that it became ingrained in me that I should accept it, that I enjoyed it. I think I was lying to myself and telling myself that I enjoyed it when I really didn't.

So what exactly caused him to stop smoking pot? "I have kind of outgrown it," he explained. "I don't like how it makes me feel."

> It makes me really kind of loopy. I can't focus on anything. It kind of makes me an idiot. It was fun for awhile, and I have a lot of friends that still do it. That is what made me decide to quit. I realized that I would always get high and then decide later on the next day that I shouldn't have done it. I started feeling guilty about doing it, so I knew I had to quit.

That was enough, in this easier case, to make him give it up.

Another recovering addict, a young woman, started smoking pot at age 17, out of curiosity, she insists, not because of peer pressure. Her father was an alcoholic and her ex-boyfriend, who, she hinted, may also have had major substance problems, had been killed in a motorcycle accident, that after having "totaled God knows how many cars, I think like five cars in three or four years."[33] Smoking pot became a regular thing in her late teenage years. At her peak, she was smoking pot five times a day. She fit that in between shifts at work and college classes. During that time, she enrolled in an online college and thus was able to smoke, she said, as soon as she woke up in the morning and while studying during the day. Plus, she said, "one of my roommates was my sorority sister and we would smoke a lot." Drinking a lot of alcohol was part of the mix as well. "When I was 18 and 19, it was out of control," she said. "I mean, we were going out drinking six nights a week, getting plastered." One and a half years before our interview, however, she quit smoking pot. The requirements for starting EMT school prompted that change. "I had to quit," she explained. "They drug test you to get into the paramedic program, so I actually stopped smoking, that was the last time I smoked pot." For three months she replaced her pot-smoking habit with cigarette smoking, something she had never done before. "Then," she said, "I learned in paramedic school the horrendous things that people do to themselves. I knew how bad smoking was for you, but once you just find out [like that], I stopped."

It was actually not only drug testing for EMT school that forced her to stop smoking pot. She also had a scary experience of memory loss at work that motivated her as well:

> More than that [the drug testing], there was actually one instance where I went to work and I picked up the phone, I talked to a customer, and when I hung up the phone I could not remember who I talked to, or what that conversation was about, and I said, "That's it." I cannot, you know, I cannot have my memory going like this, I have a job, I have responsibilities, things like that. So that was the main point where it kinda hit me, what the effects were, in terms of actually stopping and not picking it up ever again, because I was starting [to smoke again].

She did not tell us specifics about what was involved in quitting. But has stopping smoking affected her life, we asked? "Yeah, absolutely," she replied. "I'm so much more clear-minded, it's clearing out my mind. Now that I'm where I am [recovered], it kinda makes me feel like it was bringing me down. Stopping has definitely cleared up my mind on remembering things and just thinking." Even so, she refused to say that she regrets having been addicted to marijuana. "I don't regret it, I don't really regret it all. I think everything that you do makes you who you are, so I don't really regret it."[34] Furthermore, the immoderate alcohol consumption has not entirely gone away. She says that she still goes out two or three nights a week to drink: "I drink a lot of alcohol. Not often, but large amounts. When I do go out, if it's a huge occasion, I drink probably more than I should. Now I don't really have [much] time to go out. And when I go out, I'm not gonna get plastered. But I still probably drink more than I should."

The last case we will recount is more dramatic. This young woman started using hard drugs occasionally in high school. At age 19 she then went through a very rapid transition into marriage, to a man in the Army, and then they broke up the next year. After the divorce, she moved back to her home town to attend school in her state of residence, where she qualified for in-state financial aid. Here is her story in her own words, recounted at length:

> I moved down there and the first thing was like, "Man, I want to do some coke." I had a job in a restaurant, so, you know, of course the

restaurant industry is notorious for drugs, all the waitresses and waiters and the cooks, especially the cooks, the cooks are always the one who have all the drugs. So I just made friends and it was more than daily, it was multiple, I stayed high for about six to eight months.

"That," she notes, "is part of the reason why I'm in debt now, because I had student loans and a credit card and I would just go and borrow it all up, used all the money to buy coke. I'm still paying for that." She continues:

> Then several months after I moved, I started meth. I came back out to [my hometown] and ran into my old boyfriend, the same one who is the father of my child. You know, I had this on-and-off thing with him all through middle school and high school, first puppy love kind of deal. I ran into him, and he knew that I had done drugs in high school, and he was like, "Here, try this, it's way better, it's cheaper." When I started, it was like a daily thing, but it wasn't much, because meth is something that will kill you very quickly. You have to build tolerance. So I started with just a tiny bit and by the end of it I was using enough to have killed any other human if they just started.

Then, she said, "I had my religious awakening, and that was a pretty rough experience there in itself. But because of that, you know, I realized there really is a God, that I better get right and start doing right. I'm done with this mess, I'm not doing it anymore." What, we asked, was this awakening?

> In a nutshell, God just basically came down and said, "Boo!" you know, "Hi, Connie! I'm here, I'm real, and you better start realizing that if I'm real, the other half of me has to be real too. You can't have good if you don't have bad, there ain't no good without evil" kind of deal.[35] And so it started with I got stupid evil person like that,[36] it's just bad.

We asked her to explain in more depth what happened. She was reluctant: "I don't know how much I really want to get into that, but we'll go there a little bit." Then she gave some details:

> I was using amphetamines heavily for a long time. And I saw a friend of mine at the time and we had been friends all through middle school and high school and he grew up very religious. He very much believed in God and whatnot. Anyway, we're riding down the road, it's the middle of the night and the windows are down in the car, and I happened to look in the rearview mirror. At the same time I looked at the mirror, my

friend looked at the backseat. And I wouldn't have missed anything [that was there]. We just looked at each other, because the epitome of all evil and bad in the world was sitting in the backseat. There had been no one in my backseat [before], nobody. But there he sat, like the devil himself came up from hell and sat on my backseat and said, "Hey! You're mine. You're going to be mine."[37]

We asked her to continue, if she would.

You know, it was really scary. It terrified me. I mean, it terrified me to no [end], it was all-consuming. My friend looked at me and I looked at him and I said, "Did you see him?" He's like, "I don't want to talk about it. We can't talk about this." It still gives me heebie-jeebies. So we're still riding down the road, and I mean the whole car, it felt really hot, it's like something you've seen in some weird movie.

So what did they do then?

I don't really know a lot about religion or God or any things, but I do know the Lord's Prayer, so [I said] maybe we should say that. So we just started praying the Lord's Prayer over and over, riding down the road, and then we sang "Jesus Loves Me," and that just, you know, doing those little things made me feel better. And when we stopped [praying and singing], that God-awful feeling would just come back.

Then what happened? "So we made it to where we were going [Connie's home] and left [the car]." Connie's mother then took her to the hospital, where she was given, she said,

a couple of Valiums to calm me down, just because I couldn't, I was hyperventilating, freaking out. Then my friend just told me, he said, "You have to believe in this because you know what you just saw. You cannot hide from God anymore, because now you know." So I just sat there and bawled and cried and confessed every wrong thing I have ever done in my life from when I was like two.

She realized then, she said, that "you can be religious all your life, you can go to church every Sunday, every Wednesday, but still it doesn't mean it entails to it [i.e., it is real to you], [until] it becomes personal to you in a very real way." She says that was the only such experience she had ever had in her life. Later, she said, "my grandmother said that it was not the devil at all, she said that it was God who manifested himself as the devil to scare me, so that you know, people said they have the lights scared out, I feel why I have the lights scared *into* me. So that was it. That was, yeah."

"After that," she declared, "I swore never again would I touch that stuff, would I look at it, would I associate with people who did it." But how did that work practically? Did she have hard withdrawal symptoms? Not too many:

> I was pretty familiar with the concept of withdrawal, because I had done it a couple of times throughout my drug usage and found out that the best way to do it is just, you know, when you're going to start coming down, just eat a really big meal and then go to sleep, because you don't eat when you're doing that stuff. So you get really just not healthy. I just ate a really huge meal and went to sleep, and I slept for probably three or four days. I would just wake up and eat and go to the restroom and then [more sleep].

Her mother also arranged for her to spend time out of state in a drug recovery halfway house: "The reason I went there is because my mom wanted me to go. It made her feel better. She said, you know, 'I trust you, I believe that you're done [with drugs] because you say you're done. But for my appeasement will you go for just a couple of months?' For no other reason, than to get me away from what I was." And how was the halfway house?

> I didn't know anybody up there, I couldn't get on the phone and, you know, if I had a bad day or whatever. It was okay. There were a lot of people there that were much worse off than I was, and they didn't really want to stop doing anything that they were doing. They were just took there by their parents and forced to do better, so it was okay.

And how has kicking her drug addiction affected her? "Stopping has been nothing but good. I got to bring a beautiful girl in the world and make a family for somebody,[38] I have met my boyfriend, I have a good relationship with my mom, I set goals that I'm looking forward to, and life is good," she reports. Even so, her former life of drugs and encounter with Satan or God in the backseat sometimes still haunt her:

> I still, you know, I still think about that stuff sometimes, doing the drugs and whatnot. And it's so much fun to rehash what you did and how much fun you had. But when I start thinking about that [experience], I get the heebie-jeebies, it's like a reminder that it really wasn't fun: remember what happened and what was going to happen to you, I

would have died, I would have overdosed eventually, I would have killed myself. So you know, I still get the heebies sometimes. But then I just start talking to God, everything's okay.

This is the wildest addiction-recovery story we heard. Most others are tamer. But it is one story, something that seems really to have happened, that shows the range of experiences that emerging adults are capable of having. Sometimes, it seems, extreme measures are required to deal with extreme problems, interventions from completely outside of normal emerging adult culture. At the same time, the religion of most emerging adults is much more domesticated than the religious experience recounted here.[39] Next we engage in some more sociological reflection on the matter of intoxication among emerging adults—some ideas that are more prosaic than Satan in the backseat of the car, but we think are important nonetheless.

Sociological Reflections

The standard reaction by most Americans to many of the problems observed above is to focus on the individual bad choices made by intoxicated emerging adults. If the individuals did not make such bad choices, the standard thinking goes, then there would be no problem. Poor individual choices are of course involved in problems concerning emerging adult intoxication. Yet to suspend the analysis after highlighting individual choices only would miss the influence of the larger institutional and cultural contexts that in fact powerfully shape those choices. To adequately understand people's lives, we need to understand not only their decisions and actions but also the social contexts in which their lives and choices are embedded. We need to see, for example, how those individuals have been *socialized*—how their assumptions, beliefs, and aspirations have been formed and internalized. We need to understand the composition of their *social networks*, the significant social relationships that provide and constrain information, opportunities, and social pressures. We need to analyze how the *social institutions* in which people live their lives shape their expectations and resource flows, fostering and constraining certain forms of social action. And we need to understand how the larger *culture* in which people live defines the conceivable and legitimate cognitive categories, life-course scripts, and norms and justifying accounts that shape people's thinking, feeling, desiring, choosing, and living. Yes, individual people make real decisions that help determine the character and outcome of their lives. But they do not make decisions in a vacuum. People make their decisions in *social contexts* that powerfully influence the timing, direction, and impact of those choices. Thus if we want to understand

and explain things like emerging adulthood's culture of intoxication, we need to step back and consider some key features of the larger social context that forms that culture. Here we offer not a comprehensive analysis of those features—which would take an entire book itself—but a short list of a handful of relevant and suggestive possibilities.

Consider, for example, the influence of *normative culture*. By this we mean the cultural scripts that tell people who are playing specific social roles (such as "teenager" or "college student") how they should think, desire, feel, and behave. Somehow, for some reason, growing up in American culture usually entails being socialized into internalizing the cultural script that says that in middle-to-late adolescence one needs to experiment with drinking and smoking and possibly with drugs. That script says that once a person leaves home, they need to exercise their new freedom by partying, acting wild and crazy, perhaps idiotically, particularly by consuming large amounts of alcohol and maybe some drugs. (The script also prescribes certain sexual interests and behaviors, which closely relate to our observations in chapter 4 next.) The script also says that eventually, in one's late 20s or early 30s, one needs to stop this partying, settle down, and become a good, successful, financially secure family person. When I (Smith) teach Introduction to Sociology, I spend two classes discussing the question "Why Intoxication?" At first, most students cannot even imagine the justification for even asking the question at all. Isn't it obvious? But when I push them, they essentially conclude something like this: "The entire time we were growing up we were 'taught' that when you get to college you're *supposed* to party, be wild, get crazy, have fun, drink a lot." Their answer, in short, is: *we do exactly what we were told to do.* Note that these are otherwise bright people who profess to be, even insist that they are, autonomous and self-directing individuals, whom it can take a long time to convince sociologically that life is not simply about making individual choices. Yet many party like crazy—and suffer the associated hangovers, black-outs, injuries, risky and meaningless hook-ups, and sometimes substance addictions—because, they explain, it is what they have been taught to do in college. In some sense it is a version of Aristotle's "bovine existence"[40] being lived out by otherwise very smart and promising young people. Such is the power of cultural norms, socialization, and life-course scripting about people's "individual" choices.

But emerging adult intoxication is about far more than cultural norms. Those scripted norms, as powerful as they are, are also facilitated and promoted by a set of powerful *social institutions* that benefit financially from emerging adult intoxications. We must always pay attention to the power of social institutions. One, of course, is the global black-market industry of illegal drug production, transportation, and distribution. From poppy fields in Afghanistan to "jelly" labs in Russia,[41] from cannabis fields in Central America to meth labs in the American

Midwest, the global world trade in illegal drugs totals an estimated $320 billion.[42] That is nearly *1 percent* of *all* global commerce ($32 trillion world GDP). The United States is a leading consumer of those drugs.[43]

A few statistics are also telling. In 2005, about 800,000 teenagers (ages 12–17) *sold* illegal drugs; in that same year, about 25 percent of all U.S. middle and high school students had sold or been offered or given an illegal drug *on school property*.[44] About 1.5 million Americans are arrested each year for drug violations.[45] Emerging adults are of course not the only drug users in the United States. That is not the point. The point, rather, is that American children grow up through the teenage years and into emerging adulthood surrounded by a not-too-secret black-market industry supplying a plethora of illegal drugs. Many feel compelled to try those drugs. Some become regular or heavy users. Others become addicted. Of course, in the end, this black-market industry exists because an immense demand for drugs creates massive financial incentive for its bosses and workers to run the risks inherent in the industry. But supply and demand are always mutually reinforcing. Once established, the ready supply of drugs also facilitates and pushes the consumer demand that it greatly profits from by meeting. And American emerging adults are an important group of consumers both created and served by that illegal though institutionalized system of product production, distribution, and promotion.

Drugs, however, are only part of the story. When it comes to emerging adult intoxication, the entirely legal, culturally nondeviant U.S. alcohol industry is powerful and influential, too. Alcohol producers spend *billions* of dollars to advertise and promote alcohol consumption, the majority of which targets emerging adults, and some of which targets underage drinkers, including teenagers.[46] These billions of dollars are not wasted; they achieve their strategic effect—which is why the alcohol industry spends them. In 2009, for example, Anheuser-Busch alone spent $4.99 billion on marketing, advertising, and sales expenses. That "investment" represented 14 percent of its total $36.7 billion in revenues. Why does Anheuser-Busch spend so much money on advertising? Obviously because that is necessary for it to earn its $19.6 billion in gross (2009) profits.[47] Follow the money. If these sums had little effect in promoting drinking, then they would be wasted, and we can be sure that smart, rational, self-interested corporate leaders would not waste billions of dollars this way. They are not uselessly spent. They effectively promote drinking alcohol as an integral part of the normal emerging adult lifestyle, closely associating alcohol with sports, the camaraderie of friends, "funny" male idiocy, boosted male self-confidence, women's bodies, romance, and sex.

As part of the alcohol industry's larger marketing campaign, some alcohol producers engage in clearly irresponsible and predatory marketing, targeting underage youth, heavy drinkers, communities of racial minorities, and other vulnerable and at-risk populations.[48] One example: despite its many public reminders to drinkers to "Live Responsibly," Miller Brewing Company is reported to have attached its Miller Lite brand to some of Universal Studio's 2003 25th anniversary DVD re-release of the 1978 frat comedy *Animal House*. In this iconic film, "beer is portrayed as the fuel and lubricant of American fun,"[49] and college binge drinking is depicted positively; indeed, it is celebrated—as in the scene in which Bluto (played by John Belushi) chugs a bottle of Jack Daniels whiskey in less than a minute (it is worth noting that in 1982 Belushi died from a "speedball" shot, a combined injection of cocaine and heroin). One of the promotional posters for the DVD announced: "Miller Lite Celebrates the Release of Animal House—Double-Secret Probation Edition—Own It Now on DVD." In one of its advertising reports, Miller explicitly stated, "Our core age group is no longer compromised of Gen Xers. We are now dealing with Millennials, whom research shows appreciate bigger and better marketing."[50] Much more could be written about the influence of the alcohol industry in promoting heavy alcohol consumption among emerging adults. For present purposes, our point is this: that influence on youth is a fact. So the choices and behaviors of emerging adults, while they are their own individual choices and behaviors, must also be understood and explained in part by the social and cultural context fostered by the annual billions of dollars spent to influence emerging adult senses of normalcy, identities, choices, and behaviors.

These institutional analyses should not be difficult to understand and are hopefully not difficult to believe. But our sociological examination of intoxication can be expanded still further. We think that to get an adequate picture of the place of intoxication and addictions in American culture, it is necessary to shift up from specific institutions, like the alcohol industry, to the big-picture, macro level of the economy as well. We need to consider how intoxicating habits and addictions are possibly related to the kind of pervasive consumer culture and lifestyle systemically entailed by the American economy and actively promoted by its agents. Here we follow closely the argument of the late populist historian and social critic Christopher Lasch.

The United States' mass consumer capitalist economy thrives on the incessant production, consumption, and discarding of goods and services. The economy is undeniably a fantastic success in this regard. Such an economy requires that people purchase and consume vastly more than they need. The economy could not survive if most people lived moderate lifestyles that met their true needs and provided for only a moderate amount of additional pleasures and treats. That would generate a too limited demand for goods and services. This kind of economy must sustain continued growth at an acceptable rate or else it will contract and eventually collapse. Yet the growth needed to sustain the economy's health cannot be maintained on population growth alone. The economy needs to grow faster than the population grows. The economy therefore needs the limited number of its consumers themselves to *desire* to consume ever-increasing amounts of goods and services. And that has institutional and cultural consequences.

The systemic imperative of economic growth in early 20th-century America launched not only new methods of mass production on the assembly line, which brought the price of most goods down to popularly affordable levels, but also three other key economic institutions. The first was a new marketing and advertising industry, which learned to sell products based not on the actual features of products themselves but on the identities, emotions, aspirations they as advertisers could construct for consumers to (often arbitrarily) *associate with* the products.[51] Advertising thus became fundamentally irrational in the character of its appeal, making products desirable in ways often having nothing to do with their actual product characteristics. The second key institution generated by America's burgeoning mass consumer economy was "planned obsolescence," first experimented with in the 1920s and 1930s. In some cases, this meant intentionally designing products to have limited useful lives, so they would break or wear out and have to be replaced. In other cases, this meant purposefully changing products' visual styles and fashions, in order to make still-functioning products unwanted by consumers seeking to stay fashionable and "with the style." Thus, the former CEO of General Motors, Alfred P. Sloan, who helped invent the automobile's annual model change, said in 1941, "Today the *appearance* of a motorcar is a most important factor in the selling end of the business—perhaps the most important factor—because everyone knows the car will run."[52] The third institution invented to meet the systemic requisites of the rapidly expanding mass consumer economy was consumer credit. Until the early twentieth century, when the economy shifted from being production-oriented to consumption-oriented, most Americans called borrowing money to pay for consumer items "debt" and considered it moral vice and practical foolishness. Good, smart people only bought what they could afford and saved up the money before purchasing new goods. In order to create a new consumer mentality that would encourage people to buy all they could afford and more, therefore, financial leaders replaced the old term "debt" with the new term "credit" and promoted credit-buying as a consumer right and moral good.[53] In addition to these three new institutions, of course, the dissemination of radio and television and other communication technologies would later play a major role in advancing America's new mass consumer economy and society through role-modeling and advertising.

The history of twentieth-century American culture and society can be well read through the lens of the dramatic transformation these institutional inventions wrought in the American people's expectations, values, lifestyles, and identities, all of which mass consumerism came to dominate. In short, the massive economic success of the American economy in the twentieth century gave rise early on to *a new vision of the good life*, of a life well lived. According to Lasch,

> The good life [became] conceived as endless novelty, change, and excitement, as the titillation of the senses by every available stimulant, as unlimited possibility. "Make it new" is the message not just of modern art but of modern consumerism, of which modern art, indeed— even when it claims to side with the social revolution—is largely a mirror image. We are all revolutionaries now, addicts of change.[54]

Ownership and consumption in such an economic and social context naturally fosters a basic orientation toward "addiction," broadly speaking: "The model of ownership, in a society organized around mass consumption, is addiction. The need for novelty and fresh stimulation become ever more intense, intervening interludes of boredom increasingly intolerable. It is with good reason that William Burroughs refers to the modern consumer as an 'image junkie.'" By addictive substances, Lasch meant "commodities that alleviate boredom and satisfy the socially stimulated desire for novelty and excitement." On this point, Lasch—writing here during the 1980s, at the height of the "Reagan revolution" and a high point of the Christian Right's influence[55]—turned the tables on so-called neoconservatives, revealing how destructive to the "traditional morality" that they purport to cherish is the very neoliberal, free-market economy which they also champion:

> The effect of the mass media is not to elicit belief but to maintain the apparatus of addiction. Drugs are merely the most obvious form of addiction in our society. It is true that drug addiction is one of the things that undermines "traditional values," but the need for drugs— that is, for commodities that alleviate boredom and satisfy the socially stimulated desire for novelty and excitement—grows out of the very nature of a consumerist economy.

Here is the explicit connection between the imperatives of the mass consumerist economy and drug addiction. Drugs and alcohol are merely two specific types, we see, of a much larger, systemic problem of addiction, understood broadly. The American economy's survival and thriving depends upon consumerist addiction to an endless stream of stimulating goods and services that the economy churns out, most of which consumers do not actually need yet cannot do without. So American society itself has been transformed in myriad ways to serve the national imperative of addiction in multiple forms.[56] Most Americans are not drug addicts or alcoholics. But most, having bought into the narrative that a life without continual socially stimulated novelty is boring, *are* addicted to expanding material expectations, the mass media, shopping, and ever-entertaining recreation.[57] Increasingly, ordinary sex with real people, for example, seems inadequate for a growing number of Americans, who now also "need" the extra stimulation of pornography provided by the market. Few Americans anymore seem able to tolerate the apparent boredom of life without cable or satellite television or the constant stimulation of all of the new digital-media communications and social networking.[58] We are all addicts now—some people's addictions are simply more common and acceptable than others'. Until we put the common emerging adult quest for recurrent intoxication into this perspective, we believe, we will never adequately understand its cause and meaning.

Conclusion

Becoming intoxicated is a central part of emerging adult culture and of the lives of many individual emerging adults. We began in this chapter by asking why. That led us to a variety of types of emerging adults' relationships to alcohol and drugs, which in turn exposed us to a number of explanations offered by emerging adults to explain their common quest for intoxication. Exploring those explanations then led us back to a variety of basic commitments, values, and practices of mainstream American culture and institutions. The common emerging adult quest for intoxication is not an anomaly inexplicable in terms of the larger adult world. It is rooted in, derived from, and reinforced by many aspects of mainstream American society. If we hope to address the problem of intoxication in emerging adulthood, therefore, we will need to understand its roots in the larger social order from which it grows.

The Shadow Side of Sexual Liberation

It is not possible to devalue the body and value the soul. The body, cast loose from the soul, is on its own. Devalued ... the body ... sets up a counterpart economy of its own, based also on the laws of competition, in which it de-values and exploits the spirit. These two economies maintain themselves at each other's expense, living upon the other's loss, collaborating without ceasing in mutual futility and absurdity. You cannot devalue the body and value the soul—or value anything else.

—Wendell Berry

Today's emerging adults have grown up in a culture that is two generations on from the sexual revolution of the 1960s and '70s. What were once daring and rebellious acts of "love" outside of committed relationships have now for many emerging adults become routine, almost pedestrian. Emerging adults today in-herit and help to perpetuate a culture that is highly sexualized, in a casual and sometimes chaotic way. Some commentators bemoan this fact, while others cele-brate it.[1] Our concern here is not to take sides in these partisan debates. Rather, we seek to help inform such larger discussions by offering insights into some of the complexities and difficulties involved in contemporary emerging adult deal-ings with romance, physical intimacy, and sexuality.

In this chapter, we first briefly review research findings describing the preva-lence of emerging adult sexual behaviors. We then describe some cultural themes in emerging adult life that we think are important to understand for what fol-lows. The bulk of the chapter then focuses on emerging adults' evaluations of their own sexual experiences.[2] We find a lot of variance among emerging adults in these matters. They can have very different experiences and viewpoints on the subject. But amid those differences we note an important theme that most aca-demic studies and cultural commentaries miss. That is that for a significant number of emerging adults—especially but not exclusively women—sexual freedom is accompanied by real hurt, confusion, grief, anger, and regrets. This is the darker side of American culture's sexual freedom that we think is far too often hidden and ignored. Our aim here is to bring it to light.

Adolescent and emerging adult culture encourages casual sex in the context of often amorphous and transient relationships among people who often by their own subsequent admission are too young to make wise decisions or to know how their lives are going to change. This is compounded by the fact that more than a few of them have different kinds of family, emotional, and psychological problems that complicate issues. And this causes many emerging adults a lot of pain and regret, if not serious suffering and long-term damage. All is not well, as we will see, in today's sexual order among emerging adults. We think this darker side of sexual liberation is well worth seeing and understanding, as we as a society reflect on what to make of our shared norms, values, and practices when it comes to sex, romance, and growing up.

In order to put the question into larger perspective, consider some nationally representative statistics on the matter. According to our NSYR survey data, 85 percent of never-married 18- to 23-year-old Americans have (in the words of the survey question) "willingly touched another person's private areas or willingly been touched by another person in their private areas under their clothes." Among that same age group, 71 percent have had oral sex and 73 percent have had sexual intercourse. The average age for both first oral sex and first sexual intercourse is 16 years old. One-quarter of the 71 percent of all never-married 18- to 23-year-olds who have had oral sex have had it only once or a few times; one-quarter have had oral sex several times; and half have had oral sex many times. Of the 73 percent of never-married 18- to 23-year-olds who have had sexual intercourse, 13 percent have had it once or only a few times; 21 percent have had sexual intercourse several times; and 65 percent have had intercourse many times. The typical never-married American 18- to 23-year-old has had an average (median) of 3 oral sex partners and 3 sexual intercourse partners. In short, the vast majority of never-married emerging adults ages 18 to 23 have been physically intimate with at least one other person. The typical one started at age 16. And half of the sexually initiated have had a good deal of sexual experience with more than one or two partners.

Some recent accounts of young adult sexual behaviors seem to want to suggest, in contrast to our story, that all is indeed well. Some writers celebrate young women's sexual license as a way to cheer on the alleged evening of the old double standard for men and women when it comes to sexual adventuring. Others, in documenting the sex lives of youth, hardly veil their enthusiasm for the spread of serious sexual activity among them. As long as sex is "safe" and consensual, these writers seem happy to expand sexual freedom to larger segments of youth and to increasingly lower ages.[3] We are less upbeat. To be clear, we do not raise doubts about these optimistic viewpoints because we are puritanical prudes intent on eliminating pleasure from young people's lives. We raise doubts because we have heard too much directly from the mouths of emerging adults themselves about the major pain and damage that their free pursuit of sexual pleasure has often caused in their lives.

This is not about ideology or perpetuating the rebellion of a prior generation. The central questions that, in our view, should guide our thoughts concerning all of these matters are: What is genuinely *good* for emerging adults? What will promote their true well-being? What kinds of lifestyles will foster their own health and happiness? We do not claim to have all of the answers—far from it. But we do believe that what many sadder but wiser emerging adults have reported to us about their own experiences should be taken into consideration in larger public discussions about sexual norms and practices in American culture.

Background Cultural Context

Before jumping into examining emerging adults' reflections on and evaluations of their sexual experiences, it is worth setting them in context by noting a few more general themes that define emerging adult culture and are relevant to their outlook on sexual behaviors. In another book on emerging adults, two of us (Smith and Snell) described many aspects of the common emerging adult outlook on life. Five aspects—which are somewhat contradictory—we recount here.

The first is a *tremendous optimism among emerging adults about their personal futures*. The emerging adults we interviewed are, as a whole, some of the most optimistic people we have ever encountered or studied when it comes to their own personal lives and futures. Their eyes are firmly set on the future, which they look to with great hope and assurance. Some emerging adults are indeed beset with fear or despair about what awaits them. But these are relatively few. For most, their hopes run high, their anticipated prospects in life are bright, and they expect good things in the years to come. If severe personal limitations, misfortunes, and failures at some point impinge on people's lives, that has not yet happened in the lives of most of America's 18- to 23-year-old emerging adults, at least not that they will admit. Even many of those whose lives are in desperate shape, beset by serious troubles or hampered as a result of terrible decisions or awful circumstances, tend nevertheless to fortify themselves with optimism and assurances that things will get better, that their personal future will be bright. Even many young men and women enslaved to addictions or debilitated by severe depression insist that things can and will only get better, that they are on the road to good things, that life will turn out well.

Few emerging adults in America are cynical, weary, jaded, despondent, or defeated—at least usually not for more than a day or two. Rather, they say things like "This is my optimal path, what I've always wanted. You know, I really think where I'm going is exactly where I wanted to go in high school and the beginning of college." And, "Right now I'm headed into finding my first, real, year-round job, and that's very exciting to me. A lot of changes have happened but they're positive changes." Or, "I think I'm making a turnaround, like before I was going down, things that were going on in my life or whatever I was doing was wrong. But now I think I'm going in the right direction." And, "My son's made me the happiest I've ever been in my life. Everything's not where I want it to be, but I think with time it will be where I want it to be, because like I said, I'm very determined, I'm absolutely sure of myself." Even this single mother who was homeless with her children reported to us, "I'm still lost, still lost, just taking it one day at a time and God's gonna show me which way he wants me to go, because right now I am lost. I need to change, I am so lost, I haven't found my purpose, but that doesn't really affect me. One day he gonna show me, one day he gonna show me, I just haven't found that one day, but he gonna show me."

A second relevant theme in emerging adult culture is emerging adults *smarting from hard lessons learned.* The prevalent emerging adult optimism about their futures does not mean that they have not suffered hard knocks in the past. Many have. Already by age 18 to 23, many emerging adults have endured their own or others' drug addictions, alcoholism, divorces, arrests, relational betrayals, frightening accidents, academic failures, job disappointments, parental abandonment, racism, and deaths of friends. Many have suffered from the consequences of risky behaviors and self-described poor choices. Many emerging adults are stinging from the wounds of living troubled lives in what seems a broken world and are still working on recovering. For some, that sounds like this: Man, I was so stupid and, god, did I pay a price for those idiotic decisions! I will never do that again. For others, the litany of problems and hurts seems endless and irresolvable. It is true that some emerging adults have lived fairly simple and easy lives, and most are coping more or less well overall. But many have definitely suffered some of life's bruisings, are beginning to accumulate scars, and now grimace as they look back and try to make sense of the hurt and mistakes.

A third relevant theme in emerging adult culture is that they very much *want to profess to have no regrets about their lives.* Despite often hurting from hard lessons learned, most of the emerging adults we interviewed initially denied feeling any regrets about any of their past decisions, behaviors, or problems, at least explicitly so. In keeping with their widespread optimism about the future, most who we spoke with, including those with serious problems, insisted that the past was the past, that they had learned their lessons, that they would not change a thing they had done even if they could, that what's happened is part of who they have become, and that they have no regrets about anything at all.

In reality, many emerging adults appeared to us to harbor regrets about the past and sometimes expressed them—as we will see below—even as they often denied that they were doing so. Most emerging adults simply do not want to see themselves as having regrets, even though they also get angry with themselves about mistakes and continue sometimes to be haunted by problems from the past. So, for example, after a lengthy explanation by one girl about how she invested so much into advancing her boyfriend's career that she herself never finished more than one semester of college, she concluded, "I put aside my dreams to try and help him follow his, for him to become a cop, but I feel like if I was just a little more selfish, I could have advanced myself a little bit more. It's a lesson learned. I don't really regret it at all." Likewise, addressing whether quitting drugs had an impact on his life, one guy said, "Yeah, absolutely, I'm so much more clear-minded. Now that I'm where I am it kinda makes me see it was bringing me down, even though I don't regret it, I don't really regret it all. I think everything that you do makes you who you are, so I don't really regret it."

Their thoughts and feelings on this matter, however, are inconsistent. It appears to us that overtly admitting regrets would somehow be capitulating to a self-doubt or compromise or nascent discouragement against which they are holding out at all costs through the power of positive thinking. It seems as if many of these emerging adults are too young to name and own their unalterable disappointments with life by admitting regrets. Instead, saying "no regrets" puts a good face on matters that are in fact obviously problematic, optimistically reframes the difficulties of the past, and keeps all of life's concerns moving forward in a positive, constructive direction. Denying regrets also appears to protect a sense of personal self—which, in a world in which the self is central, seems *sacred* to emerging adults—against threats to the ultimate good of "being yourself." That is because actually expressing regrets suggests that the self that one has become embodies something that is wrong or unwanted. When one's life is essentially about "being who I am," one must try to negate the existence of genuinely regrettable choices and experiences, since even the worst and hardest have contributed to making oneself who one is. The very idea of regrets also presupposes a clear view of good and bad, right and wrong by which to judge past decisions, which many emerging adults lack, as we have seen in a previous chapter. In any case, we will see below that many emerging adults do in fact have regrets, despite what they say to the contrary, and those regrets are often about problematic experiences related to sexual relationships.

A fourth general feature of emerging adult culture, which we need to account for in order to set a helpful general context for this chapter, is the fact that "*hooking up" is common among emerging adults.* One routinely named category of relationship that has become commonplace in the last decade or two, different from friendship and dating, is "hooking up."[4] Most emerging adults have heard of

hooking up, have friends who regularly hook up, and many in fact hook up themselves. At the same time, most acknowledge that they are not quite sure exactly
what "hooking up" really means. The ambiguity and vagueness of the term itself
seems to be part of the nature of the relational and physical encounters to which
it refers. For some emerging adults, hooking up means hanging out and drinking
at a party with a new acquaintance. For many, however, it also means heavy kissing and "messing around" with somebody one just met. For a lot, it also means
having sexual intercourse with someone one does not know. That may happen
only once per unfamiliar person met and slept with or repeatedly over a period
of time with the same person. But in any case the encounter happens between
two people who are essentially strangers or "kind of friends." A lot of emerging
adults suspect that hooking up means any and all of the above, depending on
what those hooking up want it to mean.

One emerging adult told us, "You know, it just depends, anything from casual
sex or just making out. It all just depends. I mean you can say, 'Oh, I hooked up
with her,' and that could mean from just making out to getting laid. Everyone has
their own definition." Another explained, "Different occasions, different things.
Hooking up can mean, yeah, I think for some people it means you have sex, and
for others it means you've made out. To me, it just means making out. Something sexual happens, but it usually doesn't entail sex." And a third reported, "Literally, like a random guy at the party will say, 'Yeah, you're like pretty cute,' and
you start talking and the next thing you know you're making out. And then it's
like, 'Alright, bye.'" In any case, hooking up is clearly distinct from dating, as one
emerging adult woman explained: "Having expectations that dating will come
out of hooking up will only get you screwed."

Whatever hooking up entails, it is clearly not uncommon in the lives of many
emerging adults. It carries almost no connotation of audacity, daring, or wild-
ness. In most cases, even if a particular person has not hooked up, their friends
have or do. It's not a big deal. Some emerging adults hook up as much as they are
able, for their own entertainment or their friends', with whom they will share
their tales of "conquest." Others do not believe in hooking up but have found
themselves doing it anyway, particularly, it seems, when "on the rebound" after a
romantic breakup—often with the consequence of feeling frustrated and angry
with themselves, sometimes even feeling dirty. In any case, the key point is that,
whether any particular emerging adult hooks up or not, hooking up as a phe-
nomenon is an ordinary part of the worlds in which they live. It does not raise
eyebrows. It generally passes as routine, as reflected in this emerging adult's
musing about motivations for hooking up: "There are all sorts of reasons people
hook up—I've had some who I really had strong feelings for and sometimes
you're just glad that it happens, you just feel like it. You're like, 'Yeah, well we're
here, I guess just go for it.' I don't know."

Finally, the hooking-up culture has produced its own vocabulary, particularly among college students. "Sexiled," for instance, means being sent out from one's room by a roommate so he or she can have sex. A "booty call" is a telephone call or other communication or visitation made for the purpose of having sex (although that term seems to be going out of fashion). "Sexts" are text messages that contain sexually suggestive communications, often as invitations for sexual encounters. Sometimes people in such relationships are called "friends with benefits." And "walk of shame" refers to college students having to walk back to their dorm room across campus with messed-up clothes and hair after hooking up with someone elsewhere the night before.

An additional fact of emerging adult culture about which we should be aware is that *devastating romantic breakups happen.* A significant number of emerging adults appear to have suffered hurtful if not devastating breakups involving romantic partners with whom they thought they were very seriously involved, and often, they assumed, on the road to marriage. Usually, but not always, the most damaged party is the woman involved, not the man. We were struck by the number of very traumatic breakups that we heard described in interviews, since we assumed that emerging adults generally want to hold off on seriously com-mitted relationships. But the truth is that, while most emerging adults do want to hold off on marriage, many of them—again, particularly women, it appears—also long for the kind of intimacy, loyalty, and security that only committed rela-tionships can deliver. So in the ill-defined world of romantic relationships that they inhabit, some emerging adults, who think that they have found "the right" partner who feels the same way that they do, jump in with heart, soul, mind, and body. Later, when they are betrayed or dumped, they often discover that their partner did not in fact share their understandings or expectations, or maybe that their partner's feelings or interests gradually changed without them bothering to talk about it.

Many of these emerging adult breakups are not the standard middle school and high school splits that sweep through the local rumor mill, create a lot of drama, and leave somebody crying for a day or two. Rather, the breakups that many emerging adults recount sound more serious. They frequently involved couples who are sexually involved and who are cohabitating or semicohabitat-ing.[5] They often resulted in real emotional and physical trauma. Some dumped partners, as we will hear below, told stories about days spent sleeping and crying or lying in bed immobilized with depression, of the anguish of being cheated on or otherwise betrayed. They spoke of profound struggles with self-doubt, self-criticism, and hopelessness lasting for months, of uncertainty about being able to trust another man or woman who they may love in the future. Some had to work very hard in their interviews to keep or stop themselves from weeping. Their accounts seemed analogous to the experience of going through a difficult divorce, though without ever even having gotten married. For many, the pain and fear linger even as they try to pick up the pieces and move on with their lives.

In sum, many if not most emerging adults work to hold together bundles of cultural and personal contradictions and tensions. They are highly optimistic about their personal futures. But many have also suffered some hard knocks and are still bewildered and nursing their bruises. In romantic and physical relationships, they often proceed with amorphous definitions and unclear boundaries, including those involved in hooking up. But then they are sometimes devastated when what they thought were serious, committed relationships end in breakups. And throughout all of this, even as they may discuss all of the bad decisions and difficult circumstances of their lives, most emerging adults work desperately hard to deny that they have any regrets about anything. They very much want everything to be okay and to assert that their future is bright—including when it comes to sex. This is the context within which we must evaluate—as we shall below—what can come tumbling out of emerging adults about more serious confusions, hurts, problems, and, yes, definite regrets, when they reflect on their romantic and sexual histories and experiences.

No Problems

To begin, the central theme of this chapter—that much of emerging adult sexual freedom has a dark side—needs to be balanced by recognition of the fact that many sexually experienced emerging adults today who are never married profess to have no regrets, hurts, or problems as a result of being sexually active. There is no denying that fact—at least as far as sociological surveys and interviews are able to determine. Only half or less—depending on how it is measured—of never-married, sexually experienced emerging adults report grief and regrets stemming from their sexual activity. To be sure, that itself does not entail that all is well in these emerging adults' lives. Real problems related to sex may exist now that some emerging adults are ignoring. And problems may arise in the future, including after they have "settled down," problems about which they are currently oblivious.[6] Then again, a certain proportion of emerging adults may simply hook up, have some unhappy breakups, perhaps engage in serial monogamous relationships without suffering any apparent significant repercussions. That is possible. In any case, at least during the years we studied, a large group of unmarried and sexually experienced emerging adults appear to have little to no current angst, pains, or regret about their sexual histories and experiences.

One emerging adult woman, for instance, told us, "There's really no good reason why I started having sex, but it didn't really bother me. It wasn't something that I held in high regard, it just wasn't that big a deal to me. Just happened. I'm fine with it, it's not something I regret." Another related, "I definitely don't think that people, people need to rush into it, so I don't think really young people should have sex. I was 16 when I lost my virginity, and that was young in some senses, though some people lose their virginity when they're 13 or 14, but for me, it was okay because it ended up working out." One young woman told us this story:

> The first time just sort of happened. I had always said that I didn't want to lose my virginity to somebody that I was really involved with. I know that sounds weird, but I didn't wanna be romantically attached to that person. So the first person I actually ever slept with was my neighbor, and I was just like, "Okay, well, this is happening," like, "I'll just, you know, let's just get it over with" kinda thing. But I'm happy with the way that it was.

Some, such as this young woman, attribute their drive to have sex to hormones:

> In eighth grade I took an abstinence pledge. I was thinking, I'm not saying I'm gonna stick to this but I'll make a pledge. [Now] I feel like girls are gonna do whatever they want no matter if they made a pledge to anybody, God, school, parents, work. You can't control a girl and her hormones. About sex myself, I have no regrets whatsoever.

Others, such as this young woman, more or less laugh off the complications that their crazy behaviors have caused:

> At this one party, it's probably the drunkest I've ever been in my life, beyond anything that I ever experienced before or since, and I just kinda went crazy and made out with three different people, just to do it, for no other reason except that. So after that the boy I was seeing said, "Um, yeah, you kind of acted like a skank a little bit." He was totally justified in saying that. But we still hung out together and I was like, "Ok, that's totally fine with me 'cause . . . whatever."

Because she was drunk, she says, "I wouldn't remember everything that I did, at least not in details. A couple of times I've seen on friends' [Facebook] profiles some really not-flattering video footage. Well, I brought that on myself." Others' not very negative outlooks on their sexual experiences, as with this young man's, cast these experiences as opportunities to learn more about their own interests and tastes: "I think experiencing different people sexually can help you, not necessarily to know what you're looking for sexually, but in a romantic way to see, because everybody has their own different thing. But if you experience more people, you may be able to know what you like when it comes to romance, if it comes to sex, things like that." This emerging adult woman also talked about her boyfriend and hooking-up experiences as a learning situation:

> I've had my long-term relationships, but when those were cut off, I was hooking up. I think it's okay. It's a learning process. You want to learn, go out there and learn things. When you meet somebody, at school, parties, through friends, just whatever, you get their number, maybe talk a little bit on the phone, see if there's any chemistry, just different things, I don't know. I may have waited a little longer, but no, I think the person I lost my virginity to was the right person, in terms of that. So no, I wouldn't really change too much. No regrets.

In expressing unhappiness about her first sexual experience, one emerging adult woman likewise brought up learning: "I'm not happy about it. I wish I would have waited later and maybe got with a person that I knew better, because I thought I knew him really well but I ended up not. But I don't regret it because I learned from it." Another spoke about the same topic in this way: "I was fifteen. It just happened. I mean, we had been dating for a long time, but I don't regret it. Even though it just happened, I don't regret it." Yet others, including this young man, have found their sexual experiences to be so uneventful that they were not worth discussing much: "Sex is really just overdiscussed. Sex is just sex."

At the same time, even in these cases of emerging adults who profess no regrets about their sexual histories, one can sometimes detect a slight ambivalence in their stories. One sexually active young man, for instance, almost seems to regret that he will not enter marriage with both him and his wife being virgins:

> I started young and everything, I know what I like and what I don't like. I think it would be a different experience if you wait, you can have two people that are married, inexperienced together, it's cool, on the one hand. Like, that y'all are each other's first, learn from each other and grow with each other. But I don't know. I guess it's hard for me to see it that way, because it didn't happen to me.

This young woman expressed similar sentiments:

> At my age it's going to happen, definitely going to happen. It would be better if it didn't, if we all waited until we were married, because that's just good. It just makes it more special for both people to wait till you're married. That person is getting something special, something that no one ever had. People [now] look at it like they're feeling old at 13, like

growing up. "I'm almost an adult"—that's how people look at it. No-body looks at it like, oh, wait, I'm not going to have sex until seven more years when I get married, when I'm 20, or something. People are not looking at it like that.

Another sign of slight ambivalence among the otherwise "no regrets" emerging adults has to do with the number of sexual partners they have accumulated, as with this young woman:

I have had sex in different kinds of situations. When I was in a relation-ship I had sex a lot. I think that for every time I've done it in a relation-ship, I've also done it outside of one [*laughs*]. Yes, I counted the other day and it made me nauseous. Ten [different sex partners]. [It is fine though], because, although I think that you're still too young to be able to handle the consequences in high school, I do believe that you learn so much about yourself through that experience. When I lost my vir-ginity, it was because I wanted to know what this was like. It wasn't for anybody else, not because I loved him, unfortunately. It wasn't anything else other than the fact that I wanted to do it for me.

This woman is made "nauseous" by the number of men with whom she has had sex—which potentially puts her in the category of a "slut," a role traditionally assigned in our double-standards culture to those woman who are "too easy."[7] She also appears to wish that she had actually loved the man with whom she had her first sexual experience. There apparently was something "unfortunate" about the fact that she did not, that she was having sex for self-centered reasons. So even in cases when all appears to be well among sexually active emerging adults, there may actually be hints of bad consciences or nagging unhappiness. Still, in many cases, emerging adults will say, "Sex is fun, just fine if you want to, I'm happy with it," and that is the end of that.

Definite Hurt and Regrets

Even though most emerging adults would like to deny that they have regrets about their lives thus far, many actually do have real regrets—including regrets about their sexual experiences. Our nationally representative telephone survey of emerging adults, which also asked about regrets, provides us some revealing data on the matter. The specific question that the survey asked was: "Looking back to evaluate your sexual or physically intimate experiences overall, how many regrets would you say you now have about those experiences? Would you say you have . . . no regrets? A few regrets? Some regrets? A lot of regrets? Or very many regrets?" More than half—57 percent—of all emerging adults in the United States expressed having at least a few regrets. Thirty-four percent have only a few regrets, and 12 percent have some regrets. Almost one in ten emerging adults (9.7 percent) reported having a lot or very many regrets about their sexual or physically intimate experiences.[8] Women were more likely than men, by a 9 percent margin, to express some, a lot, or many regrets.

If anything, however, it is worth noting that these responses may very well underestimate the extent of actual sexual regrets among emerging adults, given their general reluctance to admit any regrets about anything, as noted above, and given possible "social desirability effects" sometimes operating in survey responses (in which respondents may be biased toward providing positive or happy answers to what they perceive as uncomfortable or evaluative questions). It is not unlikely that more emerging adults struggle with more regrets about their sexual histories than they are willing to admit to themselves and others.

In face-to-face, personal interviews, it can be even more difficult for emerging adults to talk about such personal matters. Even so, nearly 40 percent of all of those we interviewed who were never married and had been sexually active expressed some level of regret about their sexual experiences. The likelihood of interview respondents having, or at least expressing, regrets varied by gender. Three-quarters of those who had no regrets were male, and two-thirds of those who expressed regrets were female. At least in terms of self-evaluations of experiences with sex, then, men and women do not appear to be equal. Among those who profess no regrets, almost one-quarter are in long-term relationships or are engaged—these we would expect to be the least likely to profess regrets. And about one in ten has had sexual contact but not sexual intercourse. The remainder have engaged in hook-up sex or have had longer-term sexual relationships.

"Objective" causes of regret. For those emerging adults who do have regrets, what are their regrets about? Various things, as we might expect. Some emerging adults regret having become parents at such young ages. One emerging adult woman with two children, for instance, replied to our question about whether people should wait to have sex until they are married by saying, "Young women, I would advise that they do. Because it's not worth it, but to each his own. But I say it's not worth it. It's really not worth it. It's not worth it. You're not missing anything." Another young woman, who had slept one last time with her ex-boyfriend—who she left because he was abusing and neglecting her—and had gotten pregnant, said this:

> I think I did wrong and I wish I hadn't slept with my ex, but we were together for a little over three years. But I do regret doing that. Of course I have a child now, and, god, I don't regret having my son, but it would

be a lot different if I didn't have a kid and I would be somewhere else today. But there's really nothing I can do about it now. I have to deal with it and go on with life.

What, then, we asked, would she recommend to teenage girls whose boyfriends were pressuring them to have sex? "Don't do it," she replied, "nuh-uh." Why not? we asked.

> Well, it's stupid. And they're young and don't need to be doing it until they're really mature enough to realize, I'd say when you're an adult. I mean as a teenager you're not sure what you want. I know several people from school who would go out and have sex and thought that was love. And they really messed up a lot and, like me, ended up with a kid. And they regretted it.

Yet another told us: "I was feeling guilty, feeling dirty and 'easy,' all of those things. I used to worry about getting a disease, used to get checked up about every six months." Then she got pregnant and changed her behavior. "I've learned not to be stupid, to make the right choices" she continued,

> I've made enough mistakes. I wish I would have waited until I was older, not gotten myself into a lot of crap. But I was hard-headed. I should have just listened to people but [I didn't]. I have a lot of regrets.

As in the following case involving a breakup, regrets over becoming pregnant are made worse in situations of betrayal or abandonment by the other parent:

> My children's father, it was totally like [*becoming nervous and teary*], I lost him in a week. Girls tell him he looks cute. He met a girl and basically left me for her, and that's it. They're getting married. They can go to hell. You reap what you sow. So the same thing is eventually gonna come back, slowly but surely it's gonna be coming back on him.

Another reason why some emerging adults have regrets about their sexual experiences is the abortions that have resulted. In 2005, American women between the ages of 15 and 19 had 118,131 abortions, and women ages 20 to 24 had another 234,747. That total of 352,878 represented half of all 719,415 abortions in 2005. All told, about 2 percent of women ages 15 to 24 have had at least one abortion.[9] Most, though not all, of those who were willing to talk about their abortion experiences in our interviews expressed sadness, struggle, and regret. One young woman, for example, told us:

I had the abortion last summer. It still affects me in so many ways, emotionally, physically. God, I've been thinking about it. I didn't want to do it, but I felt desperate. I think it was needed, I felt like I couldn't handle a child. I don't believe in abortion at all. I think that's wrong, but it's a decision I made.

One young man recounted his difficulties involving his girlfriend's abortion:

We had an abortion in January, right after I took my senior comp exams. That was probably the most stressful time in my entire life. I feel pretty strange about it now because at that point I had so much going on, comprehensive exams and things, and the stress placed on her, and then all this other stuff for the abortion and everything after that, and then it was back to school. So we had this thing and never got a time to just recover and take in what had happened, and we were both still kind of scared about it. We talk about it now, but not a lot. But I'm not done thinking about that, I don't think. It's something that I'm gonna have to think about and deal with for a while.

This woman describes the fear, shame, and broken relationships stemming from her abortion:

I was 15. So I was definitely scared. He was 18. I ended up getting an abortion. He knew about it, but he wasn't really there. I just remember one time he said he wasn't ready to have a baby and I just based my decision off of that. My mom was involved, more than anybody else. But I was really ashamed at that time, so nobody was really there for me. Not even my boyfriend, because he was scared, so he separated himself from me.

In many cases, having abortions strains family relationships. One woman who was living in her mostly absent father's house at the time of our interview, for example, told us with sadness and apprehension that she was scheduled to have an abortion three days after our interview with her:

I'm tiptoeing against my pregnancy. I made an appointment Friday morning for an abortion, but that was before a cousin of mine told my parents, because she didn't want me to do that by myself. She said, "A lot of things could go wrong having an abortion." Her conscience wouldn't be clear if something happened to me and only she knew about it. I'm just nervous right now, like I'm here, and it's my safe haven away from [my mother's] home, and I really don't want to go home [and face my mom].

When the interview was completed, she was still not certain whether she was going to have the abortion or not. Like some quoted above, many others, such as this young woman, talk about the feelings of strangeness and guilt involved in choosing to have an abortion for practical reasons when they are personally morally opposed to abortion:

> My period didn't come, so I took a test and was pregnant. I didn't want an abortion, but my boyfriend wanted it, and I feel weird. He'd never support me and I couldn't support a child on my own. I felt bad about having my abortion because I've always been so against it. If you ask anybody that knows me how I feel about abortion, they'd say, "Oh, she would never, ever." But what are you gonna do? I couldn't afford a child.

In that particular case, events around the abortion resulted in this couple later breaking off their engagement. In some cases, the boyfriends of pregnant emerging adult women do not find out about their girlfriends' abortions until afterward, which causes them a different kind of distress, as with this young man:

> I was really shocked when she told me that she had an abortion. I had no idea. We were talking one night, sitting in my car outside my house, and she just started crying. I was like, "What's wrong?" and she said, "I can't tell you, I have done something horrible." I told her she could tell me, it's okay. Back and forth like that. And she finally told me. Then my mind raced, because I was stupid enough to be having unprotected sex. That was just a stupid decision on my part. My immediate reaction was that I caused this, and "What was I thinking?!" I asked when, where, who, anything about it. To this day I know no details at all. She just didn't tell me, and that makes me wonder. I hate to think about it.

Numerous emerging adults also recounted similar stories of stress, conflict, and regret over "pregnancy scares" that in the end proved not to be pregnancies and so did not have to raise the question of abortion. One, for example, related this story:

> I've had two "scares" in my life and they were horrible. The first time was with my steady boyfriend. I was horrified but it wasn't as bad 'cause I had a support system. The next time it was another boyfriend, after

we'd broken up, but we were still hooking up, just 'cause we're idiots. I was almost two weeks late. I was completely and totally having a meltdown, because he wasn't somebody that I could count on and I knew that. If I had been pregnant, I would've owned up to him. But just to paint a lovely picture of the kind of person he is, he would've been like, "How do I know it's mine?" So I wouldn't have gotten any support there. I would've had to go to my family and that would've been horrible.

Such experiences are not uncommon among emerging adults.

Another likely reason why some emerging adults have regrets about their sexual histories is because they have contracted a sexually transmitted disease. Every year about 9.5 million 15- to 24-year-olds are infected with STDs. That represents about half of all STD infections in the United States in any given year.[10] Emerging adults obviously contract and live with STDs. However, few of the emerging adults we interviewed spoke to us about their own STDs. It simply seemed to be too personal or taboo a subject to bring up and admit in that context. A few were willing to talk about their fears of *contracting* STDs. One, for example, shared this:

> I was really stressed out about STDs for a while after my whole one-night-stand thing. I was like, "Oh my god, I don't know anything about him!" And that was the third [previously unknown] person I'd slept with at that point. So I was like, "Oh my god, this is just not good, we are on a bad path here." I got checked out and am okay. But what is it—one in five people have a sexually transmitted disease? I got lucky. I slept with five people, one of them should've had something.

Another told us, "I have high blood sugar, close to diabetes, and sometimes when you have that it gives you fever blisters, so the first time I had sex, actually, the next day I had a fever blister, I was like, 'I have herpes, oh my god.' I went to the doctors, like, 'I'm never doing it again, please tell me I don't have herpes.' The doctor was, like, 'You don't have herpes.'"

A few others spoke with us about their friends' STDs. One young woman, for instance, reported, "My friend, her first time she had sex, she actually got an STD. Thankfully it was one that could be cured with antibiotics, but it's just amazing, like wow, your first time—and she has to go to the gynecologist undercover, her parents not knowing, it was a big ordeal. I've just been with one person but [it is worrisome because] sex was so prevalent in college." A young guy reported, "One of my friends got his girlfriend pregnant and someone else got an STD. And I think, like, if you weren't doing that [having sex] to begin with, then your life would be a lot better off. You just have to have patience in my opinion."

Besides these, only a few spoke of their own STDs. One young woman told us, "I had a STD once. One time, and that came and I was devastated. But I didn't tell anybody, I just took the medicine and it was over with, and I just knew that I had to be more careful." A young man said, "I am very conscientious about wearing a condom because there is a lot of nasty stuff out there, a lot more than people realize especially among people my age. It is kind of disgusting, so I try to protect myself as much as possible. I have had an STD before, it was something that was asymptomatic among men but that can be passed on to women, and that scared the daylights out of me." Finally, this emerging adult woman described at length the complications and pain that STDs have caused:

> My guy used to cheat and lie about it. I used to always talk, "Hey, if you mess with anybody." But I don't know what he's doing when he's out there. All I know is I had feelings for him, so when he comes back, we probably will end up doing something, even if it's two weeks later, three weeks later. It's going to happen one day. So I say to him, "If you are doing something, at least use protection. Be safe about it." My city has the highest AIDS rate, different things, STDs left and right. I'm in the group home and my boyfriend's locked up [in prison] by then. All he did was write me two- and three-page letters expressing his feelings: "Oh, no more soul searching, I want to be with you."

But her warnings to him did not help:

> Then when I got locked up, I found out I got chlamydia from him, my first STD ever. So that hurt a lot. I was like, I'm never messing with him again. I'm having his baby, still got feelings for him, but we're never going to be together. That's how it was. When he got out, I'm telling him I want to be abstinent. And he's like, I respect that, we can do that. The second week of weekend leave, he starts wanting to have sex. Didn't do it. The third weekend, I come home and I do end up messing with him. I didn't have sex with him, but oral sex. And he gave me head and was rough, so he left a little cut. The next week, from that cut, a herpes blister blew. The next week! In three days! I was traumatized. I was so hurt, crying, I was calling him from the group home, "You cheated on me! How could you do that? I have herpes. How could you do that?" And he's on the phone, sounding sad, "I swear to God, I put on our daughter's life, I did not cheat on you." I'm like, "How could you sit there and put it on our daughter's life and we both know it's a lie? How else? I'm not messing with nobody else." And so I go home again that weekend and show him. He's at my mother's house, and he just hits the wall and

slides down. That let me know what he does. So he lies anyway and says he just got some head from a girl. So she must have had herpes in the mouth and gave me. Whatever.

In addition to the difficulties of living with herpes, she also suffers from knowing how she contracted it:

> I finally got the truth about a month later. He finally told me everything. He didn't even know the girl, she just helped him make some calls from prison. The lady was 26 years old, he's 20. When he got out, she said she was going to help him out and everything, give him some money, help him get back on his feet. So he went down there, he's getting money from her, coming back and giving me money. I'm like, where is he getting this money from? Giving me $100 this weekend and $60 this weekend and buying me shoes and an iPod. I'm wondering where he's getting all this stuff from. So that's not the only thing she gave him. She gave us all a lot of things. And that just hurt me, because I thought our baby girl was going to have herpes. I thought I was going to have to have a C-section. But thank God. I haven't had another outbreak since the first one. It's just knowing that you have it. That's what hurts, and knowing who gave it to me. I would feel a lot better knowing that I slipped up, got drunk one night and had sex with somebody like that.

Besides these cases, other emerging adults said little about STDs. But emerging adults' inability or unwillingness to talk about contracting STDs does not make those diseases less difficult to deal with or reduce the sufferers' regrets about having contracted them. If anything, it reveals how much shame is involved in the matter. Most of the public discourse surrounding STDs related to adolescents and emerging adults focuses on prevention. But that does not address the fact that for many millions of emerging adults it is too late for prevention. They are infected; they have diseases. And those are realities that many deeply regret, so much so that they apparently do not want to discuss the matter.

Something similar is the case with persistent unwanted sexual advances, sexual coercion, and date rape. The sexual climate in emerging adult culture leaves many feeling entitled to act aggressively in pursuing sexual encounters. Especially when alcohol or drugs are involved, and with people with emotional and psychological problems, this situation can lead to life-scarring misconduct. Seemingly nice guys—it is usually men—can quickly turn into sexual predators. Women—again, especially when alcohol is involved, or when they are too naive or trusting—can end up overpowered on a dorm couch in the wee hours of the morning by someone they hardly know, or wake up to find themselves half undressed on someone else's bathroom floor.

Studies suggest that between 20 and 25 percent of all college women in the United States experience attempted or complete rape during their college career. More specifically, about 42 percent of college women have experienced some type of coerced or forced kissing or fondling, 23 percent experienced vaginal or anal intercourse as a result of continuous arguments or pressure, 22 percent experienced some type of coerced or forced oral-genital contact, 6 percent experienced attempted vaginal or anal intercourse by use of threat or some degree of force, and another 9 percent actually had anal or vaginal intercourse under those same conditions. Furthermore, two-thirds of all female rape victims between the age of 18 and 29 had a prior relationship with the rapist.[11] We also know from studies and, indeed, from the personal stories of some of our own students that these kinds of violations happen more than their victims publicly admit or report.

We did not ask in our interviews explicitly about rape, so reports of being raped or of friends being raped were sporadic. But they were heartbreaking when they did come up. One told of a friend's sister who committed suicide: "She was 26. She went through bulimia, was raped, and went through a lot of horrible stuff and just sort of shut down, was hospitalized a few times. Killed herself with a shotgun." Another told us, "My sister was raped three years ago. It . . . I . . . none of us are anywhere nearly the same people we were before. I can't even imagine my family without that. It's like that drastic." Still another answered our question about the age of her first sexual experience this way:

> I'm not sure which answer to give for that one. I have several different answers that are all true. It's possible my first experience was when I was nine and ten, unwillingly. It's kind of hard to remember. Willingly with females, sometime in middle school, 12 or 13 maybe. Unwillingly with males was when I was 14, I definitely remember. And then willingly with males I was 16. So I have four different answers.

Regarding those experiences, she says, "I couldn't report them. I have moved on. I do feel bad for the people who are around them, anybody else they might come in contact with in a bad way." But, she says, "They need to deal with themselves. I don't need to deal with them. It's not my life to live, I have my own." Another reported, "My first sex, I was a rape victim, when I was 12. The first time that I actually consented to it I was 16." Another young women spoke of her first sex in a way revealing the murky grayness between rape and consenting sex:

> I would've preferred that it would've been different, but it's too late now. I did kinda get a little pressured into it, like I wanted to, but didn't want it to happen that soon, and it was also, I don't know, I didn't really

know what happened. I was just kinda like, whatever. I would've rather it had been a little bit of a different circumstance because it honestly was not that special, was just kinda like, "Oh, okay, cool." So yeah. Sex until recently was not that enjoyable, honestly. It was like one of those things that I did for somebody else, like my way of helping my boyfriend out. He really wanted it and I didn't as much, but it wasn't like to the point where I was like, "No." I was just kind of in between, so I decided for him I would do it, because I wasn't like uncomfortable enough about it to the point where I was being pressured into it, or like even like rape or anything like that. It wasn't like that, I was like, "I guess." So at first it was not that enjoyable for me because I was doing it for him.[12]

The rape of young women certainly happened well before the expansion of sexual freedom in the last four decades. But many of the particular expectations and practices of emerging adult life today—the normalcy of hooking up, amorphous romantic relationships, abundant alcohol, easily available drugs, widespread partying, lack of clear personal boundaries, little older adult involvements, and the general wish to be free and crazy before settling down later on—readily lend themselves to creating tricky situations that easily lead to unwanted, coerced, and forced sex. And that typically leaves at least some of those involved with long-lasting pain and regrets.

"Subjective" causes of regret. In addition to more objective concerns about sex—pregnancy, STDs, sexual coercion, date rape, abortions, and so on—some emerging adults also have more "subjective" problems and regrets regarding their sexual experience. Some, for instance, look back and see that they simply did not enjoy sex at the young ages they were when they started, did not have the maturity at the time to make wise decisions about sex, and now cannot regain the virginity they lost at such early ages. One, for instance, told us, "I was a dumb little girl, dumb. If I could go back to when I was 14, I would never have lost my virginity that young, cause that's awful, 14 is awful. I cannot tell you how many people I should have told, 'No,' but [instead] I was like 'Uh-huh, okay.' Just stupid decisions I made." Another reported, "I had sex one time in ninth grade, so like [age] 13. It just happened. I'd known the guy for four years. It was an off-and-on thing." Looking back, she was not happy about when it happened. "No, not at all, because I was still a kid at that age. You're not ready to make that kind of a decision to give your body to somebody else." Another, a man, reported, "My first time, me and my girl, we was virgins. But it was, like, an awful experience, the worst." Still another similarly told us, "I definitely have more regrets about it [starting sex] and I'm sure I could have waited longer maybe. It was with my first boyfriend, my first love, my first time, whatever, high school romance. But I don't think I needed to have sex then at all, you

know what I mean? I don't know why we needed that to be part of our relationship." Yet another explained to us, "The first time, I was a freshman in high school, and I dated him for seven or eight months, not very long, but it was like my first true love. Then we actually broke up about a month after we had sex." And how does she evaluate that in retrospect? "Looking back, it sucked, it totally did not live up to what it was supposed to be, which ruined it, because it was supposed to be special. We were riding the train and it was just not emotional whatsoever. It was like, let's get this done and over with. It wasn't special." Many emerging adults like this look back and kick themselves for having had their first sexual experience so young, with someone they soon came not to care for, or when they did not really know what they were doing. Some remain quite bothered by that, others say that nothing can be done, so they have decided to get over it.

A sizeable number of emerging adults realize through their personal experiences about the undesirable emotional complications that physical involvements bring. One young man, for example, explained the difficulties arising from the different interests that men and women bring to relationships they are trying to build:

> I [have come to] really think sex is a problem. It makes things a lot more complicated. Because if you're trying to have a relationship with someone, trying to get to know that person, and when guys start doing this [physical] stuff, it makes things a lot complicated. Because with guys, they're physically attracted most of the time. Guys are physical. Girls, they're emotional, they get emotionally attached. So when guys get that physical part, they don't want to get the emotional part. They just get what they want, they get what they ask for, or what they need, I guess.

Similarly, another young woman, who described herself as "currently in the no-sex-before-marriage camp," explained, "I am there at *this* point. Last year, when I wasn't caring [*laughs*], trust me. But now I'm back to that camp." Why? "Well, there's the obvious reasons, the unprepared pregnancies, diseases. And then there's the level of emotional complications that comes with sleeping around. I mean, it's just really complicated." What, we asked, about people who say they are "emotionally ready" for sex? "I don't think there's anything such as emotionally ready," she replied. "If you're emotionally ready, then how many partners are you emotionally ready to have sex with? And are you willing to say, 'Okay, I'm going to have sex with this person knowing full well that you might be broken up in six months, and that's okay with me?'" She didn't think so. Similarly, a young woman who has had sex with 20 guys, 18 of whom were hook-ups, told us this:

I didn't really want to have sex the first time, was just influenced by friends around me. I knew him but was not in a relationship. Not at all happy about how it happened. When you get intimate with someone you kind of give yourself to them. And that's why people say wait until marriage. If you're not ready for it and it doesn't turn out to be the way you expected, I mean, like if the guy's not willing to be with you, I think girls have emotional problems. You can be really hurt, because you kind of gave yourself to them and then you're left empty. The best thing would be waiting for marriage and not going and having sex with everybody.

Another young woman told us that through "personal experience" she has come to realize the valid reasons for her religion's teachings about sex:

God says not to have sex until you get married, and now I know why. My religious beliefs affect me now. Sex makes things a lot complicated. It makes you not want to get to know the person when you do that. Because you're supposed to do it out of love, to do it because you want to have kids with that person. But when you use sex, that's what messes the relationship up. It really does.

This young man explains how his sexual involvements created relationship problems and difficulties for him at school:

I have a couple of regrets. There were a couple girlfriends that I went farther with than I should have. You know, while I didn't have sex with them, I got too close and was just barely able to get myself out of the situation. And I do regret that. I kinda wish I'd been in better control. At the same time, I was like 17, so, you know, to some extent it's excusable. But on the other hand I could have been a lot more careful.

So what specifically did he regret?

Well, because with one girl in particular, I broke up with her because of it, 'cause I thought that I'd made something clear and I apparently hadn't. And it ruined our friendship, like destroyed it entirely. It also made her angry enough that she went to school the next fall and told everyone in school that we'd had sex and I'd broken up with her the next day, which I was dealing with for the rest of my senior year. That was pretty tough. You know, there were some difficulties like that. I just wish I hadn't done it, gotten that far involved with a girl in the first place.

A key theme here concerns the emotional problems caused when two people are bonded in sexual intimacy and then one ends their relationship. An emerging adult woman we interviewed, for example, recently broke up with a guy with whom she had sex for the first time at age 18. "It was very planned out," she recalls. She thought they were serious and heading toward marriage. Looking back now, however, she says: "I don't want to regret it. I mean, I kind of do at this point, I regret a lot of our relationship, though, just because it's too fresh. I think at the time sex seemed like a very logical, well-thought-out plan. But, you know, it sucks when you have to be the one to say, 'Oh yeah, life does change.' And I was wrong." Another young woman told us about splitting up with her boyfriend with whom she was cohabiting. "We were going to go to the same college and were looking at apartments closer to on campus, since we were both moving." After finding an apartment and moving in together, she came home one day to find her boyfriend in bed with another woman. "I walked in and, yeah, it was pretty bad. Still, it wasn't an immediate break up, because we worked a couple things out. I don't even know why I went back, but it lasted for like four more months after that." But then, when the other woman told her boyfriend that she was pregnant with his child, "we just ended it. It was really bad, a real bad break up."

Yet another young woman related the damaging impact that being left by a man with whom she was emotionally and physically deeply involved has had on her:

> I'm scared. I'm damaged. I'm scared of having those kind of feelings for someone until feeling like there's someone that I have [a better relationship with]. And I don't like feeling like I'm out of control. I didn't feel like I was in control at the end of that relationship. And I'm too scared to feel that way again.

So what, we asked, is she doing with those difficult feelings?

> I think time heals a lot. I know my friends would say, "You're just growing up, you just need some variety [of other dating relationships], just get it off your mind." But I don't think it's like that. When you're on a different emotional level with someone, you don't just go and hook up with someone else. That's not gonna make me feel better about my last relationship, not gonna get me over it. I was truly and honestly and unfortunately in love with this one person.

Sometimes, as with this young man, the hurt person seems as much bewildered as crushed:

I didn't get hurt [in my life] until this last time. I've never been hurt before in my life. [But this time] it broke me. [Before] I always got exactly what I wanted, whoever I was interested in always was talking to me and interested in me—that would always last until I got bored. I was lucky then and I don't know why this happened, and I guess that's why I got hurt, because I was so naïve.

At times, the results of bad breakups of intimate relationships—especially when they involve betrayals, which are far from uncommon among emerging adults— are devastating. One young woman, for instance, told this story about a crushing event that happened while she was drunk and had fallen asleep in the bedroom in which she, her boyfriend, and a close girlfriend were "crashing" for the night:

My boyfriend, he had sex with my best girlfriend, best friend since I was 11 years old. I had known her my whole life. Happened in the same room I was sleeping in, and I did not handle it at all, in any way, shape, or form. The first week after it happened, I was so depressed, I didn't get out of bed, I just didn't go to class, I didn't do anything. Well, I'd go to my two choir classes in the morning, which I liked, and then leave school and I would go to my friend's house, her parents worked so they weren't there, and I would sleep in her bed all day long. That's all I did for a week. I really struggled with it for a really long time, and I honestly would say am just recently getting totally just okay with the whole situation.

Sometimes even emerging adults who are very cautious about sex get badly burned, despite their carefulness. Consider this woman's story, for instance:

Everyone around me was already starting [to have sex], but I didn't want to. I was being really cautious and didn't want another complication in my life to have to think about. And my boyfriend and I had been together so long, but I didn't want him to think of me like that, like, "This is fine, then when we break up it will be somebody else, and then later somebody else." I wanted to make sure that he had respect for me and I had respect for him. I didn't want him to think that I was cheap or all that other stuff.

Nevertheless, she explains, she and her boyfriend did end up having sex. "I didn't regret it while we were still together," she reported, "but as soon as we broke up, I wished we never did. Because, great! Now the next person I am with I am probably going to [have sex with], and then what happens if we break up, then is it going to be a new person? The numbers are just going to add up if that happens, and I don't want that to happen." Looking back, then, this young woman observes with remorse:

At the time you think really weird things. You don't realize how young 17 is. You are really young compared to a lot of things, like the rest of your life. We had been together four or five years and that seemed so long, like half of my life. He loved me and I love him, there was no doubt that I loved him. I still have love for him. I think if I was put back in the same situation, I would probably do it again, just because of the way I felt for him and the way we were together. But looking back, if I hadn't [had sex], then I wouldn't feel now like, "Well great, it is overwith and I gave him everything and I have nothing that I held back from." I have nothing that I could say that was still mine when I left.

This theme of regretting irretrievably giving an essential part of oneself away in sexual and physical intimacy came up in many of our interviews, especially with women. Consider, for instance, this case:

I gave away a lot more of my heart just because I trusted him completely, because he said he loved me, so I didn't question as much where to draw that line of physical touch. I learned the hard way that there's plenty of [emotional] baggage that goes along with that. We were so distracted [by physical intimacy] towards the end, just to cover our relationship. We drifted apart, and some of the reason we were dragging it out was because of the physical touch. I think that I would have been thinking a lot more clearly without that. We would have done better if we hadn't gone so far. We were making out pretty heavily and spending a lot of time, and weren't really talking together, so much as just like, "Well, we've gotta go make out."[13]

Still another woman, who now regrets dating and having sex, describes her experiences of that as "negative" for the same reason of having irretrievably given part of herself away, which hurts, she says, when the relationship ends:

I didn't really like [dating]. I think you are hurting yourself when you date a lot, because you give little pieces [of yourself] and take pieces of other people, you know. Because if they really start to care for you and you don't necessarily care for them a lot, you are hurting them. I see now that my attitude has changed in the past couple of years just dating and learning all this stuff. There really is no point in dating someone if you don't see yourself with them long term, because then you are just hurting everyone.

Not all felt regrets are this strong. Some of the regrets that emerging adults expressed in their interviews are comparatively bland. For instance, some emerging adults who profess regrets about past sexual experiences chalk them up to good learning experiences, which they say mostly no longer bother them any more. One young woman, for example, told us:

> I have regrets, yeah. I think sometimes I have had the tendency to move too quickly, you know? And that's meant certain things, like I used to confuse sex for love, and that would mess me up a lot. [But] that was a long, long time ago, and I'm kind of grateful that I went through it then, so I don't have to deal with it now or in the future when I'm older. So I'm okay that I went through all of that.

This young man said he lost his virginity because he was pressured by his peers to do so, and when he saw an opportunity with a girl that he did not know, he went for it. "It wasn't really sentimental or romantic or anything like that," he recalls. He then dated her for a while, but they soon went their separate ways. Looking back now, he says:

> I am not devastated over it and I don't think about it very much, it doesn't really matter to me. But if I could do it all over again I guess I would wait. If I could go back in time, I would wait until I had the opportunity to lose my virginity with somebody I knew a little better, got to know the person a little more. I think I would have liked to be a little more intimate or a little more meaningful than just the physical act itself of just having sex.

One young woman told us that:

> It didn't feel like I thought through my decision [to start having sex], just a little bit. I had been dating the guy for a while. Looking back I probably wouldn't have had sex with him, but oh well. It happened. I guess I'm not unhappy, but I'm also not happy about it. I'm kind of indifferent to it. If I could go back I probably would change it, but it's not something I'm unhappy about.

Another reported:

> There was a guy I met through a friend, who I hung out with a couple times and then we sort of hooked up and I slept over at his house, but it was just making out and then I saw him a couple more times and we had sex once, that was that. I never wanted to date him and he never wanted to date me. He was definitely a rebound, but it was kind of a poor

decision, in the sense that it's just, it's not that I regret it, but just, why did I do it?

And this young man told us: "I wish that with some of the girls I would have waited a little longer, known them a little longer. You know them and are cool, and then you have sex and it changes the relationship. It makes it a little bit more awkward when you see each other, you know, it's different, you see them and expect, I don't know."

In some cases, then, guilt and regrets come not from the emotional complications of relationships or bad breakups of serious relationships, but rather from the complete *lack* of emotional or relational meaning in the sexual encounter, as explained, for instance, by this young woman: "Hooking up is the one thing in my life I would definitely take back if I could. 'Cause sleeping with someone you don't know is so sleazy, and it's just so not good. It's one of those things where you convince yourself that you're okay with it, but you're not, not at all. But I did it." Sometimes the pursuit of multiple sexual partners has nothing to do with seeking to build relationships but rather the perceived need to alleviate personal insecurity through conquest. One young woman, for example, told us, "There were times I went a little wild. After my second time, when I felt a little more comfortable, there were four or five more guys I did it with." But as she talks, it becomes clear that at least some of her sexual involvements were not pursued from a position of strength and self-confidence but rather from insecurity:

> I did hooking up in between dating. It was totally for my self-esteem. If I saw someone that I thought was absolutely gorgeous, it would be my goal to be able to [get him], like a fun game thing. Conquering, that's exactly what it was. And knowing deep down that they didn't really like me and that it wouldn't mean anything afterwards, that didn't matter, because it was ahold of me and I was conquering that person to boost my self-esteem. When you have low self-esteem that's what you do. I don't think it's good, for your daughter or anything, but it's natural, and guys do it too, it's not just women.

Another theme, one that seems particularly associated with the mixing of sex, drugs, and alcohol, is some adolescents' and emerging adults' personal detachment from the emotions and relationships involved in sex. Sex literally becomes meaningless. One emerging adult woman, for instance, who as a young teenager with almost no adult supervision started drinking heavily, doing drugs, and having sex with a variety of fellow drug users, told us this: "When I was on drugs and alcohol, it just happened. I didn't care too much about sex. I didn't think about it, what I had done, that some people [I had sex with] weren't anything that meant anything to me, I just didn't care all that much then." Since then, she has gone through drug rehab and gotten clean, has become involved in the outreach ministry of a local church, and has settled down with a man she intends to marry, with whom she says sex is now special and meaningful. When we asked whether there was anything she wished she would have known earlier about sex, she replied: "I just wish that it had been pounded more into my head when I was younger, that sex is something that's special. I think it would have made a difference." As to regrets, she says, "I used to have them, but I've come to peace with it. It's not who I am anymore." At the same time, drugs and alcohol seem for at least some emerging adults to function as rationalizations for some of their casual sex, as this young man observes:

> Sometimes, after hooking up, you can feel real lucky, and sometimes you can feel like you wish you could go back and prevent it from happening. There is usually alcohol involved, which I think is an excuse— nobody wants to say they just hooked up with somebody to have sex out of the blue without having alcohol as an excuse. Or maybe alcohol plays a real role facilitating these hook-ups, I don't know, but it is usually something that happens between two people who have been drinking.

Finally, another young woman explained how hurts in the past continue to affect her today, though partly in a good way, having made her stronger and more willing to stick up for herself. "I'm huge on commitment," she begins, explaining, "Pretty much every man in my extended family has walked out on the female figure. Most of my aunts are divorced, my dad walked out on our family, so I, not that I need somebody, but I have commitment to others, and that actually has gotten me into trouble." How so? "I was in a relationship where the guy knew I was so committed that I would pretty much take anything and he could basically do anything and, yeah, take advantage of me. He would say anything, and it was six years of that, pretty bad." As to evaluating her dating relationships since that abusive boyfriend, she reports:

> Positive and negative, because there are still parts of me that are hurt. So, my current boyfriend might accidentally do something similar to something that somebody else did and I'll have an initial reaction like, "Whoa, back away," to protect myself. But it'll be an honest mistake, not deliberate. I *have* been deliberately hurt before, and he will accidentally, you know, in life, you get accidentally hurt. He didn't know it was going to hurt me. So, because [before] it was negative, I had a lot of trouble opening up to my current boyfriend on certain levels. But it's [also] made me stronger, so [now] I won't let anybody take advantage of me.

Even my boyfriend has learned that if you're gonna do something and it's gonna hurt me, I'm not gonna let you.

In sum, many emerging adults have tested the waters of permissive sexual activity in uncommitted relationships and have, to their surprise, found those waters to be deep and turbulent. More than a few have foundered and struggled to make it back to safety. Their hurt and regrets vary in intensity and longevity. But although their unhappy experiences vary, we can at least say with confidence that the idea that the sexual revolution's promise of easy, safe, uncomplicated, fulfilling, casual sex is being happily lived out by emerging adults today is misleading. Many, in fact, come to grief and thus learn the hard way that sex is more powerful and potentially problematic than they had ever imagined or been warned.

Young women take the brunt. Both young men and women get burned by the kind of negative experiences we have recounted above. But women usually take the brunt of it. That is evident in the proportion of stories being told by women in this chapter. Men are more likely than women to say and even believe that casual sex is fine and nobody gets hurt. In other words, "his" and "her" approaches to and experiences of the same relationship can often be quite different. So it is not difficult to surmise that guys' happy-go-lucky sexual experiences sometimes also have less happy counterparts—the hurting, confused, disappointed, and regretful young women they leave behind. Not infrequently, when the party is over, there is a mess to clean up. And, more often than not, the cleanup work is left to the women.

Consider, to begin, the outlook of many emerging adult men about girls and sex. One young man we interviewed reflected on his doubts about being interested in a girlfriend this way: "I just don't know, I mean, first of all I'd have to find someone who was worthwhile, but not that, obviously I'm trying to [get involved] physically, obviously, I'm always searching, 'cause that's what men do. But emotionally, like for a connection, I don't think so." Another, who we consider after three interviews to be a borderline psychopath, told us his view of the game:

If you're a guy, get as much as you can. If you're a girl, don't be a slut—no one likes a chick who's been ran through. Don't screw men into triple digits. There's a different standard for men and women. That's the way the world is, and that's about it. There is a double standard. Go into a crowded bar and most of the guys there are trying to get some. But you don't want your girlfriend to suck five cocks the night before you met her.

So, we asked him, are there any useful rules about dating and sex at all? "Nah, there's no rules. It's all bullshit." Another young man told us: "I've hooked up, basically, one night stands, that's about it. Just meeting girls, everybody being drunk and just having sex." Why, we asked, did he do that? "Lust. Just alcohol and fucking boredom." And how does he feel about it now? "I still don't see anything wrong with it if that's what they want. I mean for guys I obviously don't see anything wrong with it. But for females, I think it's degrading." He explains:

> A lot of females who hook up think that they can just act like a guy. But, you know, certain things are different because you're a female. For guys, it's just different. Like females shouldn't be letting multiple guys run up in them. It's just not the way it should be, I don't think. Granted, guys shouldn't be doing it either, if they're in a committed relationship, but other than that, I don't see anything wrong with a guy doing it because I guess we plant the seed, like they need us. You know what I'm saying? I just don't think that women should be sleeping around and presenting themselves as sluts or whatever.

Clearly the old double standard is alive and well. Many guys act like women are different, they cannot understand them, and it is not their responsibility to try to. But some young men can notice the kind of negative feelings that their approaches can create in woman. One, for instance, who told us, with regard to picking up girls, "I kind of got it down to a science," after recounting how he got a "gorgeous" young woman's phone number only the day before, also mentioned this: "But I mean, a lot of them [females] have feelings harbored against men for whatever reason, they're angry or they just don't, even though they're feeling you, they don't want to seem like they thirsty and stuff, so. There's a lot of ego with them, too." Another observed, "It might be harder for women to be ready for sex. From my experience, all my girl friends consider sex to be a lot more serious than do the guys I know."

To better understand what this can look like, consider a young man who we will call "Reggie," who well conveys the point of view of many guys his age about these matters. Reggie attends the local state university, where he is working on a degree in business administration. He lives at home with his mother—his father has long since disappeared—and is paying his way through school by working part-time as a youth-program leader in the church in which he grew up. Reggie is not really sure he believes doctrinally what his church teaches, but he likes the community there and appreciates the job. When it comes to women, Reggie explains, "Right now I'm just being myself, just trying to have fun, as far as my social life, females and all, I'm just having fun. That means no commitment right now." So what specifically does that mean? "My thing is, my relationships right now begin and end with sex. If I'm going to take someone out, then more than likely we've already had sex." So how do the women feel about that? "It does create a problem," Reggie admits, "because a lot of females say, 'That's what you get *after* you've taken me out.' Yeah, they expect the dates and all that before you have sex." Reggie says he has had this kind of relationship with about ten different women, and has never been serious or steady with any woman.

> I'm avoiding it. I like to do my own thing when I want to do it. I don't want to have to answer to anyone, not right now. I'm 21. I'm not really wanting to answer to anyone right now.

It turns out that Reggie actually believes, largely as a result of his church's teachings, that having sex outside of marriage is morally wrong: "Having sex at my age, not being married, is wrong. It is, to me, it's wrong. I believe that it's wrong, I do, sincerely. You know, I believe, not giving excuses, it's wrong, period." How then does that belief square with Reggie's casual sexual relationships with women? "I feel like it's accepted," he explains. "Everyone was young, even if you're old, you were once young, and if you're young, you understand. So I think it's accepted, but it's not right." Part of why sex needs to be accepted, Reggie explains, is that "sex is something that really no one can control. A young person is going to do that regardless. If a girl wants to see a boy, she's going to do that, there's really no way around that." Reggie says that even in his church, sex is not exactly condoned but is still unofficially accepted. His mother knows he is having sex with different women, and the only thing she has to say is "Be careful."

How long do Reggie's relationships with women last? "Well, it depends. Mine are usually no longer than two months. The shortest relationship could be, you know, one time." Reggie gets the impression that women expect more from their relationships than he does. "For me, it's always a conflict. Right now in my life, women, they deal with me because they want to. But they don't really [deal with me]. I'm at the point where, you know, this is how I feel right now." In short, if women are interested in Reggie, they have to take him on his terms. If they don't want to, forget it. "I'm not trying to be changed [by someone else]. I am up front with them [about that]. And it can get real ugly if you're not upfront. It can get real ugly." One can only imagine the scenes of hurt and angry women that Reggie encountered before he learned that lesson.

At base, then, Reggie's perspective is that young people should not have sex. But young people are going to have sex anyway. That can't be helped. So people might as well just admit that they want to have fun, "be themselves," and "do their own thing." And that means sexual relationships with no commitment. Women should not expect to influence or change men. Women should also be prepared to give men sex before, not after, they have been taken out on a date. And they should not expect their relationship to last more than two months at most. Finally, as long as everyone in relationships has been "up front" about their expectations, then nobody has any reason to get upset.

Not all emerging adult men share this outlook—some really do want committed, long-term relationships. But many emerging adult men *do* share Reggie's basic outlook. In fact, the major difference between Reggie's perspective and those of very many emerging adult guys is that most of them do not share Reggie's theoretical belief that sex outside of marriage is morally wrong. Otherwise, the assumptions are pretty similar. Have fun. Don't commit. Don't get bogged down. Don't be changed. Don't get obligated. Avoid hassles. If someone else gets involved and upset, that's their problem. For a lot of guys, that approach seems to work pretty well. Another emerging adult man, for instance, who has had "kind of habitual hook-ups" with two women, told us:

> I have never really taken dating really seriously. I have had women in my life that I have felt comfortable calling my girlfriend, but I don't think I have ever been willing to put a romantic interest in front of myself. I don't think I have ever been able to dedicate myself that much, and there have been imbalances in how much we care about each other.

In general, he says, he prefers "just kind of having fun together I guess, just sex and nothing more, no real emotional connection—just having fun with each other, having sex, kind of the antithesis of dating, just kind of spontaneous."

By contrast, women seem to tend to expect more, as Reggie observed. Not all do. Some young women seem happy to play the game Reggie described. But many women either go into relationships knowing that they expect more of them or come to find out through conflict and disappointment that they were in fact expecting more than their guys were. We do not want to reinforce simplistic gender stereotypes here. But it seems fair to say, based on our evidence, that more emerging adult women want greater personal depth, wholeness, investment, and stability in their romantic and intimate relationships than emerging adult men do. In part as a result, young women seem prepared to work harder at their relationships, to adjust to them, and to invest more into them. Consider, for instance, the case of the young woman mentioned above who has had sex with four different guys, one of whom had sex with her best girl friend in the very same room in which she was asleep drunk. In reflecting on her intimate relationships, she concludes:

> Sex should be a big deal. Sex is not a big enough deal to enough people. It should mean something. It should mean that you are giving a part of yourself to someone else and you are trusting them with that, and you should know them well enough to know that they're gonna treat that with respect and hold it as the sacred thing that it is. I personally feel that when you're that intimate with someone, you are giving something of yourself, something that only they get to be a part of.

She continues: "You don't know that [they will treat you with respect] after going on a couple dates with someone. And I really don't think you should waste sex on people who you're going nowhere with." Speaking more broadly about emerging adult culture, she observes, "I think that [the acceptability of recreational sex] is far too prevalent a belief. If a girl says [she wants] that, I would kind of say that she's a liar, that she's trying to put a good face on decisions she's not proud of." Then she returns to what woman want from men: "Guys should wanna take care of you, at least coming from a female perspective, that it is a more emotional thing for them, and they should understand that, and that they should understand that that is a big deal, and you are gonna require some extra care, some extra comfort, something that makes it special."

Another young woman spoke similarly:

> I think obviously sex is no longer sacred, and people are just giving it away like they're animals, so sex has lost its just value and sacredness. Just because our society is selfish—you know, men get what they want with women, which generally speaking is physical fulfillment, and women think they're gonna get what they want, which is commitment. And people just go from one person to the next.

And what effect does she think this has on young adults?

> I don't think women realize like how destructive it is to our core, and who we are, and how we were raised for loyalty, devotion, and commitment and nurturing. It's the way our bodies and minds are designed— like after sex, a hormone is released in women that's like an attachment hormone, and that just goes to show that there's supposed to be commitment with your sexuality. And our society has just lost that for the most part.

Our observation from the interviews, however, is that young women often do not make their hopes and expectations explicitly clear to men. They hope that they will not have to say it in so many words. They hope that guys will simply know and understand. But those hopes are often disappointed. Many guys are simply not tuned in to women's needs, desires, and expectations. The title of the 2005 book (made into a movie in 2009) *He's Just Not That Into You* captures the idea fairly well. This imbalance of expectations, desires, and investments tends to result in women doing more of the relational work than guys and being more hurt when the relationships do not work out. Thus, the fires of sex that can burn in passion can and often do also badly burn the passionate. And typically those who are most invested—again, often the women—end up getting burned the worst.

One of the ways this difference is manifested is in the observation that women seem to work harder after breakups to try to make sense of why the men they loved hurt them. The imbalance in relational work can continue after the relationship is over. Devastated women, partly in their attempts to get over their own grief, try hard to understand matters not only from their own perspectives but also from guys' perspectives. And in the process, they can essentially let the untrustworthy guys off the hook for causing their suffering. One young woman, for instance, told us that when her boyfriend suddenly dumped her after they had been physically intimate, it "broke her heart, oh yeah, it was crushing, really disappointing." But then she reflected on the painful experience in this way:

> I think a lot of it is a maturity thing, for me probably so, because he was younger than me, and guys mature less [quickly], so it [maturity] was bigger there. Girls commit their heart a lot quicker when the guys say stuff to them like, "I love you," and they believe that totally, 100 percent. Like, "Oh, really, that's what I've always wanted to hear, therefore I trust you completely because you want to marry me." But they have no commitment. That's what I believe. Guys, I think, they're a lot more black and white, guys don't think about it that much. So they say "I love you," and that means, "I love you right there." And that's not necessarily, "Yes, I choose you," even though it's hard some days and some days it's easy.

Here a serious boyfriend proved flakey and hurtful, first leading this young woman down the primrose path and then ditching her with little explanation. Yet somehow in her mind, through her effort to make sense of it all, the painful outcome has become *her* fault—because she was too mature, too ready to commit, too gullible, too interested in getting married, too aware of the gray areas of life and the need to take the hard with the easy. Guys, by contrast, are just immature, they "say stuff" that means little, they just don't know how to commit. How can anyone blame them?

Similarly, consider the case of this emerging adult woman who was having sex with one guy in an apartment and messing around with several of the four other guys living in the same apartment. "I slept with this guy and then a couple of his other roommates were like sort of hookups but not really, and it kinda just depended on whatever. This all happened in the same house with the same group of five guys, and so I mean it was just not a good situation." She got a "wake-up call" when one of the guys called her a "party favor" in public:

> When one of the roommates called me a "party favor," I couldn't dispute it. I think that that's finally what snapped me out of it a little bit. That was right after New Year's and I had promised myself that I was

gonna start over and do better. And we were all just sitting around, and he said, "Oh yeah, well she's still a party favor." I couldn't say anything. I couldn't defend myself, because he was right.

Looking back, what does she think about having sex with the first guy and then messing around later with his roommates? "I definitely [regret that]. It was just a really bad call—I didn't care about him, he did not care about me, and I hurt myself a lot more than I helped myself by doing that. I didn't feel that liberation or freedom that supposedly comes from that." So how did that experience affect her?

> For a while after that I just didn't feel like I deserved to have any self-re-spect. I completely and totally disregarded one of my own core beliefs just to have fun, and that's never [good]. You should always look past the moment, and I totally didn't. So then, when you have no respect for yourself over something like that, it doesn't bother you as much when people don't have respect for you, because you know they're right.

What this woman says is understandable. She clearly played a willing role in passing her body around like a plaything among this group of guys. But the bottom line, according to her, is that the men involved have no responsibility in the matter. What happened is essentially her fault. She did not stick with her New Year's resolution. She made a really bad call. She behaved in a way that did not deserve respect. She violated one of her core beliefs. She affirms the guy's assessment of her as just a "party favor." By implication, it is normal and acceptable for male roommates to engage in serial hook-ups with the same woman, to pass her around, and then to call her a "party favor" as a joke. Nobody expects better of them. Rather, it is the *woman's* responsibility to make sure that she behaves prop-erly. And if she doesn't, she deserves no respect and has no defense against being trivialized. Something more than the mature taking of responsibility for her ac-tions seems to be going on here. What is also going on is the perpetuation of an old double standard that puts all of the burden to behave responsibly on women and authorizes men to take as much from women as they can get.

One of the results of this kind of patterned situation is that many young women eventually come to believe—though too late for themselves—that it would have been wiser to wait longer before becoming sexually active. Consider, for instance, the advice that this emerging adult woman volunteered to younger girls:

> I would honestly say to hold off from sex as long as you possibly can. The first time, it only comes around once, and it only gets easier to do them with more people the more that you do it. It's like anything else:

you see it all the time, you're completely desensitized to it. Once my first boyfriend and I started having sex we pretty much did it all the time. Since then, I have done it with three other guys. But I would really hope that younger girls would not go that far with a lot of people, at that age. I would seriously advise against it. 'Cause I was happier before having sex. I didn't have sex until I was eighteen, and I was probably happier before it, before I knew what I was missing.[14]

What about intimate sexual involvements other than sexual intercourse? "Things like oral sex are sex, people who say that they're not, they're up in the freakin' night [i.e., are crazy]. The only difference is you can't get pregnant from them, but I mean they are just as intimate, if not more so." Having passed the threshold of first sex, however, this woman explains how difficult it is to exercise the kind of self-control she wishes she had:

> I have a lot of trouble looking past the moment. Because you know exactly where it can go and how great it can be, and both people have already been there. Before either of you have ever done it, it's so easy to not do it, because you don't know, it's such a big deal because it's the first time. And now that you've been there, it's there and it's available.

But continuing to have sex with different guys does not make her happier. "Do I really feel that great, the fact that I did start having sex? Not really. Again, I felt like at this point I'm rebuilding my self-respect, just because I do have these core beliefs that are so easy to say. But then when I'm actually faced with it, I have a lot of trouble [sticking to them]. I really do. I have a big problem." In retrospect, this young woman realizes that she was not in a good position to make informed judgments about the guys she was interested in. By jumping into heavy relationships too fast, she lacked the perspective to see these guys for what they really were:

> With my last two boyfriends we definitely felt like we were going somewhere in our relationship. With one I was very misguided, but we really thought that we were building something amazing. And with the other, it was just that he was this really great guy, how could I not fall in love with him, real love will come later, right? But it was definitely misguided, even though it was a conscious choice, as misguided as it was. See, that's the problem with calling the shots so early in a relationship, is that you have no idea. When you're past puppy love, there's no telling. That's why I say what I do about waiting [to start having sex], because I've been there and I've made the wrong choice.

Another told us:

> I wish there were more controls on certain people, because especially
> girls will talk a really big game. [Comparatively] I really think boys
> don't care, on a way bigger level, they don't care, they can sleep with the
> whole freaking town and it's just like, "OK, fine, whatever." I don't know
> why that is. I honestly would love to understand why it is that sex is so
> much more emotional for girls than boys. Now see, the boy isn't emo-
> tional there, they get that all, their own [pleasure] whatever, I'm totally
> all for it. But I feel like especially girls hurt themselves a lot more than is
> actually necessary, just to prove that, oh, they don't care, they can just
> do whatever.

Why do girls want to prove that? "I don't know! 'Cause even when I was more of
that mindset, I don't even know why." So she has no idea?

> Partially wanting to be adult, definitely partially this is the world. That's
> just the social system that we live in, especially for people my age. But I
> hate saying peer pressure, because honestly everything I've done, it's
> here [*points at herself*], these decisions were made here, no one made
> me do anything I didn't wanna do. And so that would be unfair. But I
> feel like it's a social pressure. Not an individual pressure from anyone I
> know, but it's just there, it's out there, that you should. And it's never
> said in so many words, it's just there, you just know it. See, there's this
> huge group out there that is like, "Well, it should just be kind of a free-
> for-all."

Can she describe a little bit more what "it's there" means? "Just that you should be
OK with sleeping around, partying a lot, and I don't know where it came from. I
was blissfully unaware of it until I was eighteen years old." Still, she says, how
much pressure is out there "depends on the social circle a person is in, because I
was definitely that [innocent] girl when I was 16, 17. And I would still really like
to consider myself that girl, I really would. I've just made some bad calls."

As a result, many young women struggle with how to make sense of their pasts,
how they should have behaved differently, and why it is that women so often
seem to end up the losers. To get a better sense for this kind of struggling, consider this extended conversation that I (Smith) had with a young woman who has
had sex with a number of guys and been badly hurt in the process. In the course
of a three-and-a-half-hour interview, in which she described her experiences, I
threw out the observation that it almost seems that the rules of the game serve the
guys and that women often just go along and try to convince themselves that they

like the rules when they really don't. "Yeah, it's totally true, but I always hate just blaming guys. I really do. But if I explained it, I would put it a lot the same way, 'cause I felt during my whole dating career that the boys had all the cards. They've always had all the cards." But why, I asked, do boys "hold the cards," if girls possess the bodies that the guys want? "I don't know," she replied. "I wish that I could . . . again, because I would say that I'm passive." She tries to explain:

> It's like you [as a female] want guys to think that you don't care, because you've been told your whole life, "If you try to catch your shadow, you're never gonna catch it, but it's gonna follow you if you run away from it." So people told us our whole life, and maybe not in so many words, but that's exactly it, socially, girls my age, this kind of thing— who knows where we got this information?—but if you do that to a guy, then you're gonna get what you want. "If you act like you don't care about them, then they're just gonna want you more," right? So I think it's just gotten to be a huge thing [among girls] that, yeah, I can sleep with you and not talk to you for three days, and I don't even care.

But why, I ask, don't girls hold out for a "higher price" from guys to get more of what they want in exchange for their bodies? Are they afraid that no one will be interested in them? "There's that, there's definitely that, because I think girls really are not hard to come by. I don't know, I do know some very moral, very stand-up guys, I do. But I feel like they are serious anomalies." Then she ups the ante: "Well, I really feel like most guys my age are pigs. Guys between the age of 18 and 23 are a waste of time as far as that is concerned because, again, sorry for the crudeness, but they think with their penis, that's all, I feel like." She says she knows guys who will tell her outright, "'Oh yeah, totally, I like to drink and I like to bang girls.' They will totally tell you that, they're pretty honest about it." Most guys she knows who are her age, she says, floor her sometimes, and she realizes, "'You just really don't care, do you? You don't care! It wouldn't even occur to you to care.' It's not even that they're bad guys, I'd never say, 'Well he's a horrible person.' It just isn't the same, sex doesn't mean the same things to them."

One time, she explained, when she had just been in a fight with a guy she was dating, a male teacher in her school sat down next to her:

> I was just crying and crying, just bawling, it was so embarrassing, and he's probably mid-fifties, and he just sits down next to me, doesn't even ask me why I'm crying, but he just says, "Men are scum." He's like, "I'm just gonna tell you that. Men are scum. And you were born into the wrong era, because that's all you are ever gonna find." He's like, "I don't know what's happened to men. If I had a son, honestly I would hit him

upside the head, because when I was young, you picked up the girl, you paid for the movie, you took her to dinner, and you took her home, and you didn't expect any more out of it than that. You dated people and you courted and met their family and . . ." He kinda went on, like, "And now you guys are all into, all you ever do is hang out." Which is totally true, we don't date anymore. We hang out. It's really strange when you meet a boy who's like, "I'm gonna take you to dinner and a movie and then I'm gonna take you home." Instead of, "We're gonna hit this party and then we can go back to my place or whatever, blah blah blah."

So the double standard comes up again.

Yeah, there's a double standard. I know that's horribly crude but we call it a roster [of people with whom someone has had sex], and if you compare a boy's roster to a girl's roster, and even if there's the same amount of people on it, the girl's a slut and the boy gets a high five. It's still not equal and I don't think it ever will be. Because guys wanna be with girls who have definitely done less with less people. And I don't know why, I don't know why that's in their head, except they want to be men of conquest. I will never understand.

She continues: "I think it's sad. I think that it's a lot of people selling themselves short. I was talking about this with my friend, 'cause I don't like her boyfriend, which she knows. I just think that girls settle, I know a lot of girls who settle for less than they ever wanted." Why do they do that, I asked?

I don't know, I'm just like, "Do you really think that this is the best that it's ever gonna be? Do you really think that there's nothing better out there?" Or are we all just so afraid of being alone? 'Cause I hate being single. But I would rather be single than put up with a lot of the shit that I have—sorry, excuse my language. And I feel like a lot of girls do it constantly. It's not even that every little thing you ever wanted needs to be met, that's not fair. But how about 75 percent? That's a C in high school, it's not even worth your, I don't know, to me it doesn't seem like that much to expect from another person.

We see, then, that the sexual norms and practices of contemporary emerging adult culture are a minefield of potential injury to those involved. But for various reasons young woman seem to suffer more damage trying to navigate that minefield than young men. According to what their own self-reflective accounts suggest, to use a different metaphor, women are more often the emotional losers of the sexual games of their generation. They tend to have higher expectations and investments than young men and so are more easily disappointed and hurt. The rules of the sexual games that emerging adult men and women play—particularly about sex being casual, as necessary to winning guys' attention and affection, as predictable in romantic encounters, and as legitimately pursued in short serial relationships—are tilted mostly to favor the assumptions, preferences, and interests of the guys involved. Gender equality has never really been a central commitment of the sexual revolution. And when "equality" appears to be at play, it has primarily meant women having to accept terms that mostly serve men. Are young women actually the beneficiaries of a culture of "girls gone wild?"[15]

Some women eventually come to sense that the rules—to the extent that they can even recognize the rules as operative—do not serve their own genuine interests. But few can conceive of actually changing the rules, and most do not know how to work around them. Many seem to know, and a few actually come out in discussions and say, that young women who do not play by the standard rules tend to be ignored by guys and not included in valued social groups (such as high-status cliques). In an effort to avoid such an outcome, many woman acquiesce to playing by the rules and often as a result are hurt and sometimes damaged in the process. The guys remain in control and largely benefit from the game.

One qualification must be offered, however: most young men also in fact have deep feelings, both positive and negative. And some young men are hurt and damaged in their romantic and sexual relationships, including by women who treat them badly. But many young men have been socialized to channel and express their feelings differently than women. Some men simply squelch their negative feelings, not knowing what else to do with them. Such repressing and denying of intense negative feelings only damages men in different ways. Repression and denial likely also lead at least some young men to become more detached and unfeeling with regard to women, and perhaps even predatory of them. The emotional dynamics and relational consequences in all of this are clearly complicated. But complications notwithstanding, the central theme here still always emerges from the data: young women can pay a heavy price for engaging in romance and sex, given the normative rules that govern those activities in contemporary emerging adult culture.

Men and pornography. A good deal, though hardly all, of the focus of our analysis thus far has concentrated on the frustration, hurts, and regrets of many emerging adult women who wish they could go back and erase some of their troubling sexual experiences. It appears that young women are more vulnerable than young men to being hurt in various ways by casual sexual involvements. It might be that women are simply more likely to be hurt than men by the kind of troubles that beset many emerging adult sexual relationships. It is also probable that young women are better than young men at recognizing their own emotional hurts and are more willing to talk about them. But there is at least one significant way that America's relatively permissive—and sometimes aggressive—sexual culture can create immediate emotional and relationship troubles for young men in particular, troubles that seem less directly challenging or difficult for young women. That is the ready availability of pornography. Pornography can hurt women in a variety of ways, as we will suggest, but the more immediate problem of addiction seems to be a particularly male issue.

Pornography use is difficult to study, because people who view pornography are often reluctant to admit it or talk about it. Viewing porn is something most prefer to keep secret. Therefore, in our study, not many young men proved willing to discuss the topic in our interviews, although merely the raising of the subject made some guys uncomfortable. Still, a few were willing to address the matter, though usually by talking about others. One Christian young man, for example, mentioned the problem of pornography among guys his age while discussing his Bible study:

> My Bible study is very important to me, because I get to talk with a bunch of Christian guys who are my age and have so much in common, and we can relate it all back to the Word [Bible] and what's going on in our lives. Like one of the guys is like, "You know what? Hey, I'm struggling with porn," you know, something like that, and we can understand where he's at, because we're at that age.

If young men can wrestle with pornography in an immediate sense, the emerging adult women in their lives can also suffer in different ways as a result. One woman told us that among the things in life that make her sad or depressed has been

> my boyfriend's struggles with looking at pornography, that's really been hard for us and for him. He has a lot of people who are holding him accountable and he's started going to a counselor. But that's just really been strange on me, and you know, all those things that have [raised issues for me of] self-image, and it's made me really mad at him a lot of times. That's like the only struggle in our relationship, so that's been tough.

Another similarly told us about having a boyfriend break up with her twice, at least in part, she is certain, because of his pornography addiction:

> The first time he broke up with me, he had some personal problems, he was addicted to pornography, actually, and I think he felt guilty with

everything and he knew he couldn't get married with that problem. He said he had a habit for 13 years that he has been trying to break, was going to counseling and support groups for it. I can almost be 100 percent sure from all the guys I have talked to that it was pornography.

After the first breakup, her former boyfriend later called her back and said he had broken his habit and wanted to get back together. But after one month he broke off the relationship again. In her interview, she wondered apprehensively about how, as someone addicted to porn, her boyfriend had "looked at" her: "He took care of that and then came back and, I don't know, I wonder if he even just missed the relationship or even looked at me as . . . I don't know, just how I looked with him. Does that make sense?" The breakups themselves, she said, were traumatic. "Yeah, actually I was in counseling [as a result]. I can be pretty emotional and take things really hard, so I get attached to people pretty easily."

Besides these few comments, one young man was willing to talk about pornography, and we recount his story in more depth here. To keep this young man's identity anonymous, let us call him "Alex." We do not suggest that Alex is representative of all men or even of all who view pornography. Nobody really knows enough to say. But his case does at least reveal some of the difficulties that easy access to pornography can help cause in the lives of some emerging adult men, particularly those with other personal troubles.

Alex is a member of a very conservative religious denomination. Until the previous year, Alex had been attending a college sponsored by his denomination, where he had a girlfriend who we will call "Laura." Alex firmly believes that all sexual activity beyond kissing that takes place outside of marriage is morally wrong. At the time of our interview, however, Alex had been expelled from college for disciplinary reasons, had separated from Laura, was living at home with his parents, was under the disciplinary watch of his church leaders, who had placed him on probation, and was in counseling with an expensive behavioral therapist to try to sort out his life. Alex's main problem is that he is addicted to pornography. He was first exposed to porn as a curious 11-year-old, he recounts, and quickly "got hooked." Some years later, Alex also became addicted to masturbating. Alex was able to cover up these sexual addictions until he got to college. Within two weeks of college orientation, Alex started "dating" someone online, although he had never met this "girlfriend." (They have since remained "friends," Alex reports, although he still had not met her in person at the time of our interview.) Alex soon also met Laura on campus, and they "got pretty physical pretty fast, because that is how I am," Alex said. In due time, Alex and Laura were having sex, even though that was strictly prohibited by their college. When their illicit activities became known, they were disciplined and Alex was sent home.

Since then, Alex has been doing computer-based work part-time at home for a relative and going to counseling. Laura remained interested in Alex but had broken off their relationship until Alex overcame his problems. That, Alex reports, is not easy. "I am still struggling," he says. "It has been really tough." In the past, Alex has gone to a number of different church-sponsored, residential pornography-addict therapy groups that are modeled on Alcoholics Anonymous, each for "twelve weeks, and there were like twenty guys in the group. The majority of them were married with kids and they had been battling it for ten or fifteen years." Alex himself struggles mightily every day to make any headway in gaining control over his addictions. He says that he and his current behavioral therapist "associate 'sobriety' [i.e., abstention from porn use] with being clean and not having acted out."

> I actually met with him yesterday morning and then two weeks before that. I hadn't been "sober" when I talked to him at the two-weeks-previous meeting. He was like, "Alright you are going to be sober," and I was like, "Yeah," but I wasn't. I told him that I did a stupid thing the previous night, that I was working late on the computer and I was tired. It was right at my finger tips. My eyes were tired and I went down a bad path and acted out.

Counseling has led Alex to the realization, he says, that he has overpowering emotional needs for physical connection and affirmation:

> I have come to the conclusion, though I have pretty much known it all my life, that I have a real need for physical touch and intimacy of some kind, whether my hand on her foot while we are sitting watching a movie or whatever, just something. If I don't have that or know in my mind that it is available—that somebody is there, whoever it is, that we are connected and we love each other and are friends and we care about and trust each other—then it is really hard for me.

So far, Alex's work on his problems has enabled him to go "clean" for only a few days at a time:

> I will have a period of three or four days of sobriety and then I am like, "This is good, I am doing really good," and then I will act out and then be like, "What am I doing, why did I do this?" I will just get mad at myself. I get to a point where I would beat myself up enough to act out again, and then it would just be a vicious cycle. That doesn't last as long [now] as it used to. I am at a better point in a lot of ways. I do pretty

good at not beating myself up after I've acted out, but a lot of the time I just can't help it.

Alex's struggles have extended to his use of the social networking site, Facebook:

> I go and find people that are hot and add them, and they add me for whatever reason. A lot of the people are from other countries, they just don't know any better or they want friends or I don't know what their reasoning is. And there are a lot of people who have really, really sexually explicit pictures, just right up front, which I wanted to see, so I would add them as a friend. Then I would have these stints where I would sit on Facebook and just be going and going and adding people and adding and adding and adding. I was actually approaching my friend-request limit, adding probably 75 or 80 people at that one time. Then I would come back to reality and ask myself, "What am I doing? What is the reason?" It's because I want to look at their pictures and masturbate. It's pointless. It is completely destructive to my spiritual self and my way of life.

Alex's goal is to beat his sexual addictions. That is because doing so is the precondition for what he says matters most to him: "growing up," being responsible, getting Laura back, being reinstated in his church, perhaps being readmitted to college, and serving in his church's overseas ministry. Yet, for whatever reasons, Alex also seems unwilling or unable to achieve his goal. Near the end of the interview, Alex admitted the following rather matter-of-factly:

> This is probably really stupid and I am not sure what to do, but I have gotten involved with this woman on Facebook who is like 40 and married, and we've been verbally involved romantically and intimately. She and her family invited me over to Europe, she is like, "If you ever want to come over," she says, "we have to make it happen, to come over to visit"—she wants to show me her country and everything.

And what do the people helping him with his problems think of this idea? "When I talked to my therapist, he said that is probably not wise. I talked to my parents about it and I explained that this family has invited me over to Europe and they said that sounds really fun, a little summer escapade." Then Alex admits, "I mean, this wouldn't be the whole reason I would be going over, but she and I would also be going to a hotel room to make love."

Alex is clearly an extreme case. We are, again, not suggesting that Alex is typical of all sexually involved young men, or even those who regularly view pornography. Available empirical evidence, scanty as it is, suggests a wide range and intensity of emerging adult men's use of and struggles with pornography.[16] Some have no interest in it. Others, like Alex, are badly addicted. And many others find themselves somewhere in between. To be sure, not all emerging adult men see viewing porn as a problem. One, for example, told us that one of the things making him most happy and excited in life now is "getting a job recently in a porn store, just making more money than I've ever had." Another— who believes that any sexual activity is fine for young people as along as it is "private, alone, away from everyone else"—also told us that he has learned his own ideas and attitudes about sex from "friends and porn." Exactly how problematic pornography is in young men's lives we cannot quantify here, because, again, most we interviewed were reluctant to discuss the matter. In any case, our point here is not about Alex's representativeness of any population. Our point, rather, is that, among the many and diverse cultural consequences of the sexual revolution of the 1960s and '70s, at least one of them—the pervasiveness of online and DVD pornography—creates conditions that cause real and sometimes debilitating and destructive problems for some men. That itself does not of course condemn the sexual revolution and its consequences per se. It only contributes a bit more to the larger picture we are painting here, namely, that there exists a dark side to the sexual freedom available to emerging adults, which, at least for some, results in real trouble, grief, brokenness, and regrets.

Conclusion

Emerging adults today are all over the map when it comes to their feelings and evaluations of their sexual histories and experiences. Some, we have seen, appear happy and at ease about their sexual histories. Others, as we saw above, harbor some hurts and regrets, but none too intense. But then there are other emerging adults—those who we think are too often hidden from view and neglected in discussions on these matters—who have not found all of their sexual encounters to be pleasant and free of negative consequences. Some have contracted diseases or had abortions. Others have babies who they often love but did not want to have. Others have been victims of sexual force or coercion, including rape or attempted rape. Some have been deeply hurt emotionally in various ways and bear the scars to show it. Some feel that they have irretrievably lost an essential part of their own personhood to others who do not care for them and perhaps who they do not even know. Some are ashamed of themselves for the dumb choices they have made, which they wish they could take back but know they cannot. Others are angry at former partners with whom they were once intimate, for proving to be uncaring and unfaithful. Then again, some just yearn for intimate relationships with greater depths of understanding, loyalty, love, and commitment than those for which they too often settle.

Thus, all is not well among the emerging adults who inherited the sexual revolution launched by their parents and grandparents in the 1960s and '70s. A lot, though not all, of emerging adults today are confused, hurting, and sometimes ashamed because of their sexual experiences played out in a culture that told them simply to go for it and feel good.

The truth that emerging adults in the current cultural regime of easy sex within fluid and amorphous relationships do not seem to grasp is that sex is not only often pleasurable, sex is also definitely *powerful*—often in ways beyond individual control. Whether youth and emerging adults realize or accept it, sexual intimacy has an immense power to bond, to make vulnerable, to complicate, to bind. Failing to see this, two young lives can, without quite realizing it, quickly be bonded together so intimately and profoundly that the wrenching that happens when they pull apart is more distressing, difficult, and debilitating than either ever expected. Emerging adults can jump into intimate relationships assuming that sex is just another consumer item, recreational thrill, or lifestyle commodity. But many of them soon discover the hard way that sex is much more profound and precious than that. But then it is too late. They feel they have lost a part of themselves that they cannot recover. They nurse wounds that are slow to heal. Some have difficulty trusting in new relationships. Others become indifferent or hardened to their own feelings or those of others.

Historically, human societies and cultures have known that sex is both powerful and potentially destructive. So every one has devised ways to regulate sex. Typically, the social regulation of sex throughout human history has involved the exercise of patriarchy, repression, domination, coercion, and exploitation. The social control of sexuality has not always or even often benefitted the individuals involved. The sexual revolution of the 1960s and '70s was in part an attempt to remedy some of those problems, to lift former restrictions on sexual expression and leave more up to individual choice and happiness. The sexual revolution has been facilitated by and promoted the growth of liberal individualism, technological change, and other institutional transformations that have reduced the authority of family elders and increased individual autonomy. Of course, fully evaluating anything as complex as the sexual revolution's consequences requires a depth and complexity that is beyond our capacity in this chapter. Here we have only one central point that we wish to contribute to the larger, public, collective sense-making about the sexual revolution. That is that *not far beneath the surface appearance of happy, liberated emerging adult sexual adventure and pleasure lies a world of hurt, insecurity, confusion, inequality, shame, and regret.*

In this more shadowy world, emerging adults confess things like "I didn't feel that liberation or freedom that supposedly comes from casual sex," "It sucked, it totally did not live up to what it was supposed to be, which ruined it, because it was supposed to be special," and "I just wish that it had been pounded more into my head when I was younger, that sex is something that's special."[17] This is not quite what the leaders of the sexual revolution expected. Furthermore, this world is particularly, though not exclusively, the realm of emerging adult women. In this underworld that hides the darker sides of sexual liberation, the line between victims and perpetrators is sometimes blurry. Most participating are direct agents in their own hurting. Few confess the reality of their own confusion and pain. To do so would almost seem to admit personal failure at a game that nearly everyone else *appears*—especially in television shows and movies—to be playing with success. Instead, many emerging adults blame themselves as individuals, for exercising poor judgment, for acting naively, for trusting too much.

But to focus only on individual choices is to miss the all-important larger social and cultural context. Here again the sociological imagination comes into play. Each emerging adult who faces the darker side of liberation does so within a dominant culture and social structures that set up expectations, offer promises, reinforce identities, and encourage scripted behaviors that often lead to the predictably problematic outcomes we have documented in this chapter. If there is something to be done about all of this, surely individuals will have to learn to make better choices. But just as surely, we as a society have some hard thinking to do about our institutionally reinforced expectations, values, and scripted ways of life when it comes to youth, romance, gender relations, power, self-gratification, and sex.

We are not suggesting that American culture's ever-advancing sexual revolution is somehow directly and solely responsible for the date rapes, sexual harassment, unwanted pregnancies, abortions, sexually transmitted infections, relational disappointments, damaging betrayals, and vague sense of emptiness and longing that we have observed among many emerging adults. Social and personal dynamics never work that simply. And people have always had such problems in more sexually restrictive societies. However, it would also be folly to deny that the sexual revolution has helped to generate a larger climate of norms, assumptions, expectations, interests, and practices that create conditions that often increase the probability of emerging adults suffering those negative experiences and problems.[18] Different cultural approaches to emerging adult sexual relations would not necessarily produce the same outcomes that we have observed in this chapter.

Civic and Political Disengagement

There is, in practice, no such thing as autonomy. Practically, there is only a
distinction between responsible and irresponsible dependence.
                                                            —Wendell Berry

As record numbers of emerging adults turned out to participate in the 2008 U.S. presidential campaign and election, there was a buzz in the media and popular culture that a new page was being written in the history of youth political and civic involvement.[1] The many young voters who showed up on election day to cast their ballot prompted some observers to conclude that the former era of civic apathy and disengagement on the part of youths might be coming to a close. Many have grown hopeful that young adults today, who are said to be entering the political scene with a renewed vigor, are turning over a new leaf of hope and involvement. If true, such a change would indeed mark a break with years of social science research findings that suggest that today's emerging adults will not easily become highly engaged civically and politically.[2]

Recent research, however, shows that adolescents and emerging adults today tend to be less involved in various forms of overt political activity and are less reliably and consistently involved in politics than previous cohorts of young citizens.[3] To further explore these discrepant claims and expectations, this chapter explores the extent and character of contemporary emerging adults' political interests and civic engagements. We conducted our interviews during the summer of 2008, exactly when emerging adults would have had reason and opportunity to become politically and civically active. What we find, however, is that any heightened interest among emerging adults in politics and civic life evident in the 2008 presidential campaign, as reported by journalists, must have been a temporary blip or mere media hype. The vast majority of the emerging

adults we interviewed remain highly civically and politically disengaged, uninformed, and distrustful. Most in fact feel disempowered, apathetic, and sometimes even despairing when it comes to the larger social, civic, and political world
beyond their own private lives.

Varieties of Disengagement

Are emerging adults "political?" We begin our analysis with that simple question
to get our exploration started. In our interviews with emerging adults around
the country, we asked them, "Do you consider yourself to be a very 'political'
person?" and "How do you feel about politics in general?" The majority—69
percent—told us outright that they were not political in any way.

Considering that their offering *any* evidence of being political—however
minimal it was—was counted as a "yes," that they were political, this number
actually *under*estimates the extent of political detachment among emerging
adults. For what often counted as being political was very little. For instance, the
most frequent proof of "being political" offered by emerging adults who said that
they were so was that they watched the news on television. Similarly, other
emerging adults explained that they considered themselves political simply
because they read the news on a regular basis. As one said, "I get what I get from
the news." In response to our question "Why do you consider yourself to be a
political person?" one emerging adult told us, "Because I'm always watching the
news or reading a news story and paying attention to what's going on." Another
similarly said, "I'm always watching the news or reading a news story." Following
the news seems to be less intense for some than for others, as is evident in this
exchange:

  I: How do you feel about politics in general? Are you a very "political" person?
  R: Sort of. Not really.
  I: Do politics or world or national events interest you?
  R: Like, elections do. Sort of, I guess, sort of.
  I: Other than that, do you pay attention to politics?
  R: I watch debates and stuff like that.

Other emerging adults, when asked if they were interested in politics, simply
said "sure," "sort of," "they interest me at times," "kinda interesting," or "I guess."
One said, "I think I'm sort of in-between. I have my opinions, but I'm not super
into everything." Other examples of responses substantiating that the emerging
adults we interviewed were "political" included "I'm informed" and "Sure, I discuss it with my friends sometimes." Thus, most of the 31 percent of interviewed

emerging adults who counted themselves as "political" relied on very minimal standards by which to make that judgment—hardly the kind of activity that one imagines to constitute being "politically involved."

By taking a closer look at the substance of emerging adult discussions about civic and political interests and activities, we are able to tease out a more nuanced understanding of where they actually stand than the simple 31 vs. 69 percent yes-no divide just noted. Our analysis reveals six distinct types of emerging adult orientations to civic and political life, which we call the apathetic, the uninformed, the distrustful, the disempowered, the marginally political, and the genuinely political.

The apathetic. The first type of emerging adults consists of those who are politically apathetic, that is, those who are completely uninterested in politics. The apathetic, totaling 27 percent of the emerging adults we interviewed, represent the largest single share of the politically disengaged. They were slightly more likely to be female (54 percent). Politically apathetic emerging adults express a nearly perfect indifference to political issues and no motivation to become involved in civic life. They give short responses throughout our interview's section of political questions and respond to our political identity question by saying things like "I don't pay attention to politics at all," "I don't keep up with politics at all," "I ain't interested in politics," or "I don't really follow the politics deal." One emerging adult typified the group in the following exchange:

I: How do you feel about politics in general? Are you a very political person?
R: Naw.
I: Do you pay attention to politics and world and national events?
R: No.
I: No? What would you say your own political position is?
R: You say what again?
I: What would you say your own political position is?
R: I don't have one.
I: You don't have one? So you wouldn't consider yourself to be Republican or Democrat, conservative, liberal?
R: Naw.
I: Are there any social, political issues you especially care about?
R: No.

These emerging adults seemed to want to move away from the topic of politics as quickly as possible. Another interview exchange, for example, went as follows:

I: So how do you feel about politics in general? Are you a very political person?
R: No, not really.

I: So do politics or world or national events interest you?

R: That's the same answer still.

I: Does it interest you?

R: No, not at all.

I: So what would you say your own political position or view is?

R: I don't really care about it.

I: So would you consider yourself to be more conservative or more liberal? Or nothing?

R: Nothing.

I: Nothing. Are there any social or political issues that you especially care about?

R: No.

Interviews with other politically apathetic emerging adults tended to follow this exact pattern. The only variations heard within this group were occasional minor elaborations about why they do not care about politics, as in the following:

I: How do you feel about politics in general? Are you a very political person?

R: Not really.

I: Do national or world events or anything interest you?

R: No, not really. I just don't really have a huge sense about the world activities at all, but world events don't really interest me. I'd say I watched the world's stock market more than I do the world events.

Another explained that he is not interested in politics because "it's basically like a circle of the same thing happens every year, over and over and over."

This apathy did not extend to other topics. These were not consistently apathetic people. They could and did articulate interests in other topics we asked about, elaborating a great deal when we addressed other, nonpolitical issues. But when it came to politics, they simply did not care about world and national events. They described politics as unimportant, repeatedly saying "I don't care" and "it's boring." At most, when prodded, a few might say something like "I mean, not really, like I mean I care about ones that involve humans, more or less." Another stated, "Nothing really affects me. I mean I have got it pretty good." Others told us things like "I just do not care, got no care in the world for it," "It's just not really something I find important," and "A waste of time for me, don't have no impact on me, not important to me." Thus, one after another of this apathetic type—which, again, we estimate to represent a bit more than one-quarter of emerging adults—said things like "It don't interest me. I guess it should, but it just don't," and "I don't really have any opinions." Others said similarly, "It doesn't matter who our president is going to be next, you know," "It's not really something I'm passionate about or love," and "It's not in my high priority list."

On occasion, some apathetic emerging adults expressed mild regret for not being more concerned and active. One, for instance, said, "I wish I could be pro somebody. I would be so passionately pro somebody if they were worth it, if they were worth my while." But then they said it was just not worth the investment. Another told us:

> I feel like I should [be more political]. I don't know, that I'm lucky enough to live in a system where I, to at least some extent, get a say in what happens and what gets to be okay and what's not, and those kind of things. And that, especially things that I have an opinion on, I should go out and do something about it. But I don't.

"Why not?" we asked. "I don't know," she answered; "I'm really bad at having a really invested forethought to things that aren't happening around me. I think that it's horribly bad that I tend to just talk about myself, and there are other people my age that are in a war [in Iraq]. And it doesn't affect us at all." Thus, at times, even some politically apathetic emerging adults might wish that they were more invested in the world beyond their personal lives. But that wish does not translate into any change of thinking or behavior.

The uninformed. A slightly different group of emerging adults we interviewed were not so much politically apathetic as politically uninformed. These shared many commonalities with the apathetic interview responses. They tended, for instance, to give short responses to our questions about politics. They also said they did not really care about anything political. The one significant difference in this group of uninformed emerging adults, however, was that they said explicitly that their lack of political interest and involvement was a result of the fact that they did not know enough about politics to be engaged. They explained their political apathy as being caused by a lack of information. These uninformed emerging adults made up 13 percent of our interviewed emerging adults, of whom 61 percent were female and 39 percent male. Their responses usually sounded like the ones in the following exchange:

I: How do you feel about politics in general?
R: I really don't know that much about it.
I: Are you a very political person or not really?
R: Not really.
I: Do you pay attention to politics and that kind of thing?
R: No.

I: What would you say your own political position is? Do you think you're conservative, liberal, something else?

R: I don't know.

The emphasis here is on a lack of information, leading to disconnection. Other typical responses to our questions about politics from this type of emerging adult sounded like this: "I don't watch much TV, so I don't know very much about political stuff." Responding to our question about liberal vs. conservative political stance, one woman replied, "I don't even know." When we asked, "Are there any social or political issues that you especially care about or pay attention to?" she answered: "Social issues like in the world? I don't know." These uninformed emerging adults repeatedly told us, "I don't know nothing about it"; "I don't even know what that means really"; "I don't know. It's one thing I've never really put a lot of emphasis into learning about"; "Honestly, I don't know. I'm not sure"; "I don't really keep enough eye on them to know or say anything about that"; and "I really don't know that much about it." When asked what his own political position is, one emerging adult said, "I don't know. I just don't go that far into politics to know. I don't have much knowledge really to say anything about it." Another said she was not politically involved "because I don't really understand it." She reported that she took a political science class in college that she did not understand, explaining, "So, with me, not understanding it, and taking so many classes, trying to understand, I just don't pay attention to it." Another emerging adult similarly described her lack of political involvement by saying, "I have no idea. I tried really hard to listen to it all, but it wasn't enough inside my head, but now I just couldn't understand." Yet another explained that she does not know much politically, although that did not prevent her from having ill-informed opinions:

I: Are you a very political person?

R: I'm politically opinionated, but not well politically educated. I'm one of those annoying people that like has an opinion before I know anything or everything, so I'm not gonna lie.

I: What would you say about politics? Like do you consider yourself a political person?

R: No.

I: No? Okay, do politics interest you at all?

R: No. I kind of watch it. If there's nothing [else] on, I look at it.

Politically uninformed emerging adults, as we have seen, particularly repeated the words "I don't know." Sometimes they said that they thought they should be more politically involved but did not know how to find out more information about it. One, for example, told us, "I wish I knew." Then, when asked if he had any particular social or political issues that he cared about especially, he replied:

> Not really. Again, maybe I should. I don't know. I haven't really followed anything. I am not even registered to vote yet. I should be, but I am not. I just haven't gotten registered yet.

Another said, "I'm not as educated on all the issues as I could be." And another stated, "I should be more involved in it, only because I should know more about our country. But I'm not very involved at all."[4]

Many of these politically uninformed cases did strike us as entailing a genuine lack of political knowledge. These emerging adults did not seem to be making dishonest or evasive excuses. But it is unclear to what extent emerging adults do not care about politics because they do not know about politics or whether they do not know about politics because they do not care enough to become informed. On the one hand, very many Americans do live their lives focused mostly on their own private concerns inside fairly parochial worlds with limited horizons. On the other hand, there is arguably more information available today about local, state, national, and world politics through various media than there has ever been before in human history. Thus, many of today's emerging adults not being informed about political life may reflect a failure of our educational system. But we also think it reveals deeper cultural problems concerning the relations of individuals to public life, as well as simple individual lack of responsibility—which of course is also related to the larger cultural problems—as we explain below. Whether increased access to information about politics would help spur these uninformed emerging adults to greater political concern and involvement we cannot say. But we think that the problems involved run much deeper than just a supposed lack of information, media, and education.

The distrustful. Nineteen percent of the emerging adults we interviewed fall into a type we call the distrustful. This group is evenly split between men and women. Those in this group tended to give more elaborate answers to our political questions and often seemed to know a reasonable amount about politics. But they still remain disengaged from political or civic life. Their reason for this lack of participation, they say, is their distrust of the political system or politicians. One respondent expressed this view by saying:

> I mean, I pay attention. I watch the news sometimes and just basically see what's going on. But I just think a lot of them, the majority of them, are just corrupt. They're just out there trying to make as much [money] as they can as quick as they can and completely care less about the whole situation.

The following is a typical exchange with emerging adults of this type:

> I: How do you feel about politics? Do you think of yourself as being a very political person?
>
> R: Oh, no. I hate politics.
>
> I: Is there any particular reason why you hate politics?
>
> R: I hate it because I don't like how they put people in power. I don't feel like a person like that should have power over a whole community, like the mayor had power over a whole community. I don't like any of that. Even with the president, I don't like it. The president has the power to send people to Iraq to fight, but nobody in your [i.e., his] family goes to Iraq. Everyone's safe. You're sending other people. We're all equal. We're all humans. I don't like that, having someone above you. I don't like that.

Many in this group similarly expressed being particularly distrustful of politicians. As another emerging adult said, "I don't really see a lot of difference in people I would vote for, so it seems kinda the same. Seems like the past couple of years were actually okay. But most of the time when I would vote, it's for people who are arguing for control." Still another told this story: "Our Senator, when he first went into office, was talking about how he was gonna get us out of debt, this and that, and now we're twice in debt from then. The situation only got worse." This distrustful type of emerging adult seems to know more about political events and institutions than either the apathetic or the uninformed. They often gave passionate responses to interview questions and could easily describe specific features of the political system. Distrustful respondents seemed to know how to get politically involved and find information, if they wanted to, and seemed to care about the topic of politics generally. But despite their potential interest and knowledge, they described themselves as disliking or even hating politics. This disdain ranged from some responses focusing on disliking the idea of authority (which seems to them like authoritarianism) in general, as in some quotes above, to hating the U.S. political system and process specifically. But the main view shared across their responses is the expressed cynicism about political leaders working the political system. As another example, consider this answer to our question about political interests or identity:

> I'm not [interested]. I just try not to be too idealistic, because when it really comes down to it, probably most politicians are puppets for lobbying groups and special interest groups and stuff like that. Even who runs for president and stuff like that. And it's really just all a game. So it's hard to really be truly passionate about something that you know is rigged. Just puppets on strings.

Respondents of this distrustful type consistently made comments such as "I don't feel like any of them tell the truth," "I don't trust them, any of them," and "I think politicians are corrupt. They are like snakes, man. You have to sift through all the b.s. and take out what is really true, and it's awfully hard." One said, "I think a lot of it's just junk. I don't think they're honestly telling the truth about a lot of things, and I don't really try and follow their lingo or just get in the political sludge." Another stated, "I think there's a lot of things wrong with politicians. Like all the criticism that they have, that they're liars, that they cheat, they're corrupt. They're not really helping our society as much as they are putting a barrier between, like, corporate and blue-collar people." Another told us that he does not vote because he thinks politicians "just tell you what you want to hear."

Many politically distrustful emerging adults specifically stated that they thought politics was inherently about manipulation and deceit. One stated, "I feel that they are kind of corrupted. They're trying, but it's just that I feel, like any other system, it's just going to have corruption, and it does." Another said, "Politics is just a manipulative thing by the people in charge to distract you from the real issues at hand." Yet another said, "I think politics are just a lot of smoke and mirrors." One told us, "In the end, a lot of the time, politics are out of the hands of the everyday man." Emerging adults of this type often described themselves as doing all they could to steer clear of politics, saying things like "I try to avoid politics at all costs, actually." They sometimes described politics as ridiculous or stupid, something that disgusted them, as in the following exchange:

I: How do you feel about politics in general?

R: I think it's all a load of crap. I think that you pick the lesser of two evils. I don't think that any of them actually tell the truth, and even if they are telling the truth they can't back up what they say. They have no actual power to do the things they say they're going to do, on presidential levels. On local levels I think that the candidates have more of an impact.

I: How do you feel about politics in general? Are you a very political person? Like, do politics or world or national events interest you?

R: World events interest me. Politics do not interest me. I think that there's a lot of things wrong with politicians.

One bluntly expressed his distrust for other Americans for being politically gullible, stating: "We're too partisan, and then we're too fear-driven now. Also, people trust politicians, the American people, I just hate how they trust politicians." He summed up his own political "realism" by saying, "If they have *no* chance in hell [of winning], then that's probably because they're telling the truth. If they wanted to win, they would lie their asses off."

Politically distrustful emerging adults also typically express their dislike for the conflict and divisiveness that can result from politics. One, for instance, said, "I don't like a lot of the divisiveness that politics have to use." Another answered, "No. I try to stay out of the line of fire." And yet another told us, "Controversy is a good word, but I don't like confrontation. I don't get into debates about barely anything. I just don't like it. So when people talk politics, usually it's some sort of debate: 'I believe this.' 'This is right.' Or 'That person is right' or whatever. So I stay away from it." Another said, "I think it's ridiculous when some people have conflicts." Yet another explained why he is not involved in politics this way: "Probably the clash, people feuding and clashing over politics. I hate that." Thus, in an effort to avoid the conflict that occurs in politics, many emerging adults say they simply stay away from it altogether. Some emerging adults who chose this strategy likened their avoidance of politics to their avoidance of religion, saying things like "Politics are the same as religion to me. I don't, well, politics is how religion was to me. Politics and religion, I never bothered with them." Another described how she did not like to talk about religion or politics with people, saying, "I would never tell them, because you're not supposed to talk about that stuff. With religion or politics you can just start fights." For some, this approach also seemed to result from a belief that politics and religion are similar insofar as with both it is impossible to find out for certain what is actually true. As one said, "You never know the actual truth behind what you're seeing."

Politically distrustful emerging adults thus demonstrate suspicion and hostility with respect to politicians, the political system, and other people involved in politics—and say that this is the reason for their own lack of interest in being civically engaged. Though generally informed about political issues and even often passionate about the topic generally, these emerging adults seem alienated from greater political involvement by their pervasive distrust.

The disempowered. The next type of apolitical emerging adult shares a number of similarities with their distrustful peers. Emerging adults in this category similarly seem to be generally informed about political issues and also frequently express themselves with fervor on the topic. The main difference is that they emphasize not believing that they can do anything to change the world—rather than distrusting politics—as their explanation for not being politically involved. The disempowered comprise 10 percent of the emerging adults we interviewed, and three out of four of them are male. "I used to be more interested in politics," one said, "but I didn't see much change or fruit coming that way." Rather than expressing distrust of politicians or the political system, these responses attest instead to a general sense of personal disempowerment. A typical exchange with someone of this disempowered type sounded like this:

I: How do you feel about politics in general? Are you a very political person?

R: I would like to be, but trying to get into all that politics is just something that I personally think that I can't change. I mean people say that if everyone voted we can make a difference, but then the problem is that everyone is not voting. It's hard to change something so big with so little people. And so I think politically, I'm really not into politics that much.

One said, "I'm very weakly political, for the same reasons that I don't volunteer. You could probably basically record and play back the same thing. Just because it takes a lot of effort, and it's something that you don't get the immediate feedback for being involved in." Another simply said, "One person wouldn't change anything." Yet another said, "At one point I kind of just felt like my opinion really didn't matter to an extent, so I kinda brushed it aside." Similarly, another stated, "I feel like even if I know about it, me knowing about something isn't gonna change anything anyway."

Emerging adults in this group often described politics or world or national events as "too big." They said they did not think one person could matter in a system that large. As one of this type said, "Politics, you could never cover all the bases, 'cause there are so many topics. It's unbelievable. You could never cover it all. It's insane." Disempowered respondents said that they did not think that they or anyone else could change anything about the political system. They described their opinion as not mattering or influencing them. "It doesn't affect me, I don't think," said one. Many emerging adults in this group, like the distrustful, also described staying out of politics as a way to avoid conflict. Not seeing the point in discussing or debating political matters, and assuming that no conversation about politics could exist without conflict, they described their lack of engagement as a way to avoid such negative interactions. This results in the kind of outlook expressed in this exchange:

I: How do you feel about politics in general?

R: I'm not a fan of politics, per se. I think it consumes too many people's lives, and I think there's a lot of negative energies put into it.

I: Are you a very political person?

R: No. I have my own views, and I respect everyone else's views. I'm closed-minded about politics, personally. That is one thing that I'm almost closed-minded about, I guess. I don't like to discuss them, I just have my own set of views, and that's the way that it is.

Politically disempowered emerging adults thus often seem to actually have political interests and convictions but choose not to act upon them or express them to others. Instead they tend to describe their political views as "personal" and say that they are best kept to themselves. Many explicitly state that they do not think they should talk to others about their political views. This stems from the beliefs that define this type of emerging adult—that talking about politics does not change anything, that the political system is too large and remote to participate in effectively, and that politics is too fruitless and conflict-ridden an endeavor to inspire their participation.

The marginally political. So far, the essentially apolitical types reviewed above represent 69 percent of the emerging adults we interviewed. Added to those, many of those who answered "yes" to our question about whether they were a political person also turned out, on a closer look, not to be nearly as political as their "yes" answer might suggest. Upon more careful inspection, these emerging adults fell into a type more accurately called the marginally political. We count 27 percent of all of our interviews—evenly split between men and women—in this category. Emerging adults of this type expressed some interest in politics, but it was far from clear how or even if they were actually civically or politically active. These emerging adults frequently use the word "somewhat" to describe their involvement and seem generally to be "on the fence" about wanting to be involved or not. A typical response to our political identity question was, "Sort of, not really," or "Yes and no." A more extended version of this kind of response is exemplified by one emerging adult who stated, "I always say I'm not political, but then when I talk to people about stuff I guess I'm more political than I think I am." Still, as noted above, in most instances it appears that their definition of being "involved" mostly means watching the news on television or reading the paper. That is, they describe themselves as "informed" because they follow the news at least somewhat regularly. For example, they frequently explain that they are "political" because they will stop to watch the news if they are flipping through channels and come across an interesting public policy debate. For a good number of these marginally political emerging adults, watching the television news or reading the newspaper appears to be their only political activity. Some describe themselves as "nosy" and say they are political because they like to know what is going on, in a way that is similar to reading magazines to keep up with the gossip on what is happening in celebrities' lives. As one said:

> I think they're very interesting. I wouldn't consider myself a political person. I'm not a political personality or anything. But it's always fun to talk over politics. There are so many different opinions.

Some emerging adults in this group say that they sometimes vote in elections. As one stated, "I do read the news on a very regular basis. I wouldn't say so much that I'm a very political person, but I do certainly vote every time I have the opportunity. I like to know what's going on." After describing himself as "somewhat" political and being asked what interested him politically, another stated simply, "I guess right now the presidential election." Another said, "I support a candidate, but I'm not an activist." Many of the emerging adults in this category also described their interest in politics as changing over time, and either described themselves as formerly more involved than they are now or becoming increasingly involved. One, for example, stated, "I try to be. I am less political now, as I lose free time, to keep up with it. I mean I try to stay on top of it. I catch some of the major headlines." Another only said, "I used to a pay a lot of attention." Conversely, another told us, "Politics interests me at times. I think I've gained some interest in it over the past couple of years. Before then I could care less. But now, I mean it's interesting, but I'm not hard-core about it."

A minority of this type of marginally political emerging adults tended to be fairly articulate about politics and sometimes named or explained a particular political issue in which they were interested. Although their actual personal political involvement is not as certain as with the clearly politically engaged group (described next), it did appear that at least some of them genuinely valued politics and saw being involved in political life as a worthwhile endeavor. Unlike the distrustful, many of these emerging adults seemed to think that it was possible to "make a difference," that being involved politically would matter in some significant way. Take, for example, this emerging adult woman's report:

> I would say I'm moderately political. I definitely take interest in politics, just because I feel like that's a good way to make a difference. You can really make a difference just by going out and voting. I mean it is up to you. Women have fought for the right to vote for so many years, and now that I have that right I'm not just going to give that up. That's not something I'm going to take for granted. I pay attention enough to know who I think is going to be a good leader. But I'm not one of those people who is constantly flipping through the channels, like, "Oh, what is the coverage now?" I just get online, I read current-events articles, I kind of sometimes watch debates on TV. So I'm moderately political.

Another said, "I think it can be a force that can hurt or help, and I also think it's something that hopefully everyone will get involved in. I know a lot of people are like, 'Oh my vote doesn't make a difference, "the man" is just gonna make the decision,'" but then went on to say, "Maybe my vote won't count, but at least I can say I went out and did everything I could to change what's going on now." Sometimes marginally political emerging adults state their support for political involvement by expressing dismay at others for not being involved politically. One, for instance, said, "I vote and stuff. I think that it's definitely our duty to vote," and then went on to observe: "We complain about politics all the time, but we don't even vote. We're too busy voting for *American Idol*. I think I heard—what did I hear?—97 million people voted for *American Idol*. [*Laughs.*] Oh my gosh! If politicians only sang."

In general, then, this type was not clearly politically active beyond some minimum level but did express at least some interest or the belief that people should be involved. And they did answer "yes" to the question of whether they thought of themselves as political. It seemed as though these marginally political emerging adults participate in some political activities—such as following the news and voting in elections—somewhat sporadically. But overall their commitment is low, and so it is less clear whether or not they will remain politically engaged once those specific events or interests subside.

The genuinely political. A handful of cases—*only 4 percent* of all the emerging adults we interviewed, almost all of whom were male—fell into this truly political category. Unlike the 96 percent of emerging adults represented by the five other types above, these emerging adults expressed substantive knowledge of political matters, genuine interest in participating in politics, and specific descriptions of meaningful ways that they are civically or politically engaged. They described themselves as "very political," "politically engaged," and "very interested in politics." One went so far as to say, "I love politics." Genuinely political emerging adults were atypical among their peers in being able clearly to articulate their interest and engagement in political matters. They named specific issues in which they were interested, such as "government spending," "social policies," "abortion," "poverty," "gay marriage," "renewable energy," "the war in Iraq," and so on. The following exchange demonstrates the outlook of this type:

I: Do you consider yourself a political person? How do you feel about politics in general?

R: I feel pretty political and informed and curious.

I: How would you define yourself politically if you had to? Would you say you're more conservative, liberal, something else?

R: Liberal.

I: What does that mean for you?

R: I'm more socially liberal in terms of wanting to distribute the wealth. Things like welfare and Medicaid. I think that if your needs are met that you should help others meet theirs. It's the taking from the rich and giving to the poor sort of thing. I think there's a lot of people who have a lot more than they'd ever need. With people starving, that's a travesty to me. I would define myself as liberal in terms of placing the good of the whole above the good of the individual sometimes.

I: Are there any social or political issues that you especially care about, either globally or in the U.S.?

R: Yeah, especially within the medical field, and things that affect people's ability to have general well being. The allocation of resources in that sense. And immigration.

Or consider this exchange:

I: Okay. How do you feel about politics in general? Are you a very political person?

R: Yeah, I mean, I definitely keep up with it. I used to volunteer for campaigns and stuff when, yeah, so.

I: So you said you are a conservative Republican?

R: Yeah. I mean, I always stay up, I always know what's going on, typically. Even my family, it's kind of funny, I make fun of my mom because she doesn't know people that represent us. She knows who the governor is, she knows who the president is. But she doesn't know cabinet members or anything like that, which to me is kind of funny because I know most of them.

I: Those people do a lot of important work.

R: Yeah, exactly. So I mean, people like always ask me questions, just knowledge-base stuff, so yeah, I mean, I keep pretty much on top of things, kind of.

I: Are there any social or political issues that you especially care about?

R: I guess, in some ways I care about issues a lot more than some people do, but there's no one that stands out. I mean, I just, I guess I have a pretty high, I guess I care about a lot of things.

When asked to describe what it is about politics that he likes, another said,

For me, it's being a voice. It's being that person that people count on to have, like, you being a voice for millions. I guess it's strange, but I like those odds, that responsibility. Someone has to do it. That's something I feel strongly about.

These few emerging adults tend to describe themselves as enjoying being "a part of" things, as believing that it is important to pay attention and have a voice in politics, and generally as staying informed about the main political issues of the day. Some also expressed being involved in politics because they were deeply concerned about the current state of affairs in the United States and wanted to help create change. As one explained, "I have serious worries. It scares the hell out of me." Another said:

I think I care about almost all political issues. Because it's my future, and the people here now, well my generation, we're the ones that have to really take over the world and whatever. And if it's not gonna be adequately prepared for us, then it's a lot. You have to worry about everything.

These appear to be the kind of emerging adults that various media observers have suggested are growing rapidly in number and transforming the political culture of American youth. Our research, however, shows that that is far from happening. Emerging adults who are truly politically engaged and active represent a very small minority among their peers, about one out of every 25 of them. The vast majority, instead, as shown above, are either politically apathetic, uninformed, distrustful, disempowered, or are only marginally politically aware and engaged.

Volunteering and Charitable Giving?

What about less politically focused kinds of civic engagement and public investment? What about, for example, volunteering and giving money to charitable organizations? Consistent with the theme developed in this chapter so far, the emerging adults studied in the interviews are not only not engaged in politics, they are also not big on volunteering and voluntary financial giving, at least at this point in their lives. They are so focused on their own personal lives, especially on trying to stand on their own two feet, that they seem incapable of thinking more broadly about community involvement, good citizenship, or even very modest levels of charitable giving. It is not that they are all apathetic—many do believe that dedicating time and money to helping others can be a good thing. They simply say that they do not think that they have the resources to be concerned with such matters at this point in their lives. For one thing, they think—whether or not it is true—that they have no money to give to any good causes, even if they wanted to. Thus, they feel no responsibility for voluntary financial giving of even the most moderate sums, because they consider themselves financially broke. As one said, "Somebody needs to give money to me!" They also view themselves as stretched thin when it comes to time, saying both that they have too many time commitments and obligations already to add anything else (especially something that doesn't pay), and that their schedules are too variable and unpredictable for them to responsibly commit to something like regular volunteering. Thus another said, "I actually don't have the time for it. I feel like if I'm going to do something good for the community I might as well do something good that I get paid for too. I mean like, uh-huh, but I don't have a lot of time."

So most emerging adults volunteer very little, if at all. They express only slight awareness that they may now even in small ways be establishing patterns and priorities concerning time and money that will continue through the rest of their lives. They also exhibit little appreciation for the fact that their time commitments and financial burdens will increase as their incomes and families grow, that the situation will not necessarily get much easier. Rather, nearly all assume that volunteering and financial giving are simply unrelated to their current existences but perhaps will become more important at some future time. Someday, when they have a lot more time and money than they do now, they may begin to volunteer and give money to good causes—that is, if as individuals they then so choose. Meanwhile, financial giving is something that extremely rich people, such as Bill Gates or Brad Pitt, should be doing. Meanwhile, any sense of, say, their dependence on a larger social infrastructure or on shared institutional goods that cannot be taken for granted but must be actively sustained, and to which they are thus obliged to contribute, if only in small ways, is in their minds nonexistent. Their view is essentially that they have grown up, have (more or less) played by the rules, and are now in the process of becoming fully independent. Whether they choose to volunteer or to give money away in due time—because they are "good people"—will be determined in the future. It does not concern them now.

When all is said and done, what emerged from our interviews with emerging adults is their extremely low estimations of anyone's ability to make a positive impact on the world, which we already heard about in quotes above. Contrary to some of the stories told in the popular media, most emerging adults in America have extremely modest hopes, if any, that they can change society or the world for the better, whether by volunteering or anything else. Very few are idealistic or activist when it comes to their making a mark on the world. Most, we have seen, are totally disconnected from politics, and countless others are only marginally aware of what today's pressing political issues might be. Furthermore, few of them are bothered by these disconnections and low expectations. Again, it is not that most emerging adults are totally apathetic or grossly cynical. Nor is it that emerging adults are generally vicious, "me first" social climbers and exploiters of opportunities for personal gain who do not care about others. They simply think of themselves as "realistic" about the likely influence they might have on the society and world around them. Helping to make positive changes happen, when possible, might be a good thing. But getting all idealistically worked up is naive, maybe even immature. "It's confusing," one respondent said,

> You have all these dreams when you are little. I am a big dreamer. Like if I wanted to sell lemonade, I thought I could sell a million of them. That is how I am. To save the world, you just start to realize that that stuff isn't necessarily possible. And it is just confusing because you have all the stuff you want to do, but how do you make it happen?

At bottom, then, when push comes to shove, it is very difficult for most emerging adults to imagine devoting any of their own resources—which they perceive to be quite limited—to the social, civic, public, or political world around them. They mostly think it would make no difference. They are also not entirely convinced, as we will see below, that they even have a moral obligation to help other people in such ways. They often think investing in public life is not their responsibility but rather those of wealthier, more famous, and more powerful people. And so most steer well clear of civic participation, public engagement, and political life.[5]

Some of this may reflect the fact that the political issue dominating the headlines during the five years prior to our interviews was the Bush administration's "war on terror," especially the bloody wars waged in Iraq and Afghanistan. Emerging adults were divided over the value of Bush's war, but nearly all viewed it (accurately) as a depressing affair well beyond their own influence to control or stop. Writ large, the world of politics and social activism more generally appears similarly remote and inaccessible to most emerging adults. They seem to feel rather powerless, in some cases hopeless, to influence the larger public world in which they live. In many cases, a strong sense of fatalism creeps into their attitude about the larger social and political world. So, while they are very optimistic about their own personal futures, they are hardly optimistic about the prospects of helping to make some aspect of the larger sociopolitical world a better place. At most, the "world around them," which they believe they stand a chance of influencing for the good, is very local: their families, careers, friends, and romantic interests.[6] The rest of the world will continue to have its good and bad sides. All one can do, from emerging adults' perspective, is live in it, such as it is, and make out personally as best you can.

To recap, many recent observers have suggested that the current generation of youth is more interested and actually engaged in political life and civic activism and optimistic about it than previous generations of youth, such as the so-called Generation X and Millennials. The apparent widespread interest among youth in the Obama campaign of 2008 and the reported uptick in their turnout on election day have encouraged many political and cultural observers to herald what they take to be an increasingly publicly aware, informed, and active cohort of young adults. The hope here is for some kind of a generational renewal of a rich civic life and political commitment, perhaps not unlike that said to have been inspired by President Kennedy in the early 1960s. But most of this positive commentary and hope has been based on anecdotal media evidence and on observations focused on very specific events, such as election-day turnouts. Contradicting this picture, our nationally representative social scientific research on the civic and political interests and engagements of emerging adults shows that such hopes have little basis in fact. The vast majority of emerging adults are either not at all politically hopeful or involved, or not politically active much beyond watching the nightly news on television and having occasional conversations about national or world events with friends and family. Only a small minority—about 4 percent, by our reckoning—actually cares much about politics and makes real efforts to be significantly involved in political life. Most emerging adults, by contrast, feel apathetic, uninformed, distrustful, or disempowered when it comes to politics and public life.

What Is Going On Here?

Democracy requires the active political participation of its people. A thriving republic depends upon its citizens becoming civically informed and active in order to exercise the informed public stewardship needed to sustain communities of responsibility and freedom. Effective government—to the extent that such a thing is possible—requires an attentive and informed public that can envision a common good, interact with the political system, and hold government officials accountable. Furthermore, any thriving human life by most accounts requires some participation in civic life, extending oneself beyond one's own private world to participate in broader communities and public institutions. By doing so, people have the chance to learn more about the larger world, connect relationally with different kinds of people, consider how to build shared lives together that benefit all, and personally contribute to the well-being of others. But little in the outlook on politics and public involvement among most emerging adults suggests that they have these interests, concerns, or experiences. Most are either alienated from or despairing of public life in various ways, or maintain only tenuous connections to actual civic and political involvements. Even for those emerging adults who have some interest in political issues, most of politics is mediated to them by the packaged, constrained programming of television news and expressed by them in the form of occasional statements of personal opinions in discussions with family and friends and perhaps voting in elections. Little of this makes for a robust, shared life of participation in the public square for the common good. What it mostly seems to lead to instead is indifference, focus on the self, and withdrawal into the narrower worlds of private concerns and comfortable personal relationships. And that seems healthy neither for the emerging adults involved nor for American society, culture, and public life generally.

What, then, explains this dearth of public-mindedness and civic and political interest and engagement among emerging adults? The full answer, of course, is very complicated—so complicated, in fact, that it would require an entire book to explain. Social science can identify a lot of factors that associate statistically with higher levels of civic engagement among young people.[7] But often that itself does not answer the deeper questions that have to do with cultural meanings and life priorities. For present purposes, then, we will focus in the remainder of this chapter on a handful of factors, sometimes connected to the concerns observed in previous chapters, that we think tell part of the story of the social causes and deeper cultural and moral meanings of most emerging adults' disengagement from public life.

To begin, we must remind ourselves that some of the civic and political disengagement we observed above is a well-known age effect—that is, it is due to their particular place in life as emerging adults. So, one of the likely reasons that so few emerging adults consider making change in the world to be a real possibility is that many of them feel nearly overwhelmed with the single challenge of standing on their own two feet. Anything much beyond keeping money in the checking account, getting the GED or finishing up college, and keeping up with important relationships seems unmanageable.[8] To some extent, we think that it is reasonable for emerging adults to spend some time concentrating on getting their adult lives in order before "going public" with things like volunteering, financial giving, and involvement in civic and political life —much like newlyweds withdrawing from normal life on honeymoons to focus on the very start of their married lives. At the same time, emerging adulthood spans many years, during which people are forming their identities, commitments, habits, and lifestyles. If emerging adults do not begin to learn the practices of public giving and participation early enough, at least by the time they are settling down, we do not have good reasons to believe they will learn them any better later.

We would also be unfair if we failed to recognize the truth in much of emerging adults' assessment of the state of the world and individuals' ability to influence politics and civic life. Emerging adults have grown up in a world of seemingly endless scandals, corruption, unfaithfulness, and exposés in the White House, on Capitol Hill, in governors' offices, on Wall Street, in corporate America, in the United Nations, and well beyond. They know that presidents lie—whether about their sexual indiscretions or reasons for starting wars. They know that senators and governors cheat—on their spouses and on their constituents. They see high-powered CEOs and investment executives who are selfish and dishonest— sometimes in their irresponsibility ruining the entire futures of employees, families, and other investing organizations. Emerging adults accurately sense that while the routines of electoral politics sometimes move officials in and out of office, the bureaucratic machinery of the nonelected state continues to rumble along beyond their influence and for interests that are not theirs. They point out quite accurately that government very easily breaks down into partisan gridlock and bickering, that many in political life seem more interested in playing "gotcha" games and in career-damaging investigations of opponents than in effective governance. They are also correct in seeing so much of government as driven and controlled by well-financed lobbyists and interest groups operating through extensive public-private "revolving doors."

So in many ways, we think emerging adults are clearly right about public life and politics. The views described above are not mere immature complaining, but in fact rebuke older adults and our larger society for serious problems we have in our public institutions. Democratic governance by, for, and of the people has grown pretty thin. Much of politics has degenerated into competing interest groups fighting for bigger pieces of the pie. Most public policies are made regardless of what emerging adults think or believe. It is far from clear who in public life is honest enough to trust with one's vote, ideals, or money. The world in which a news anchorman like Walter Cronkite could say "And that's the way it is" is gone. Emerging adults realize that they do not know "the way it is," and they are skeptical that any other authority out there knows or can be believed either. Civic engagement is built on trust and vision and constructive accomplishment. Yet those are what America seems to have precious little of in public life today. Emerging adults' opting out of public life and focusing on more immediately rewarding activities is not a completely irrational life strategy.

Even so, we think it would be simplistic to declare emerging adults' disengagement from public life merely to be the result of a combination of age effects and a reasonable assessment of the dismal prospects for change in the public square. Other factors also encourage emerging adults' disconnect from civic life and public affairs. The following pages explore some that we think are among the most important.

Moral confusion and disorientation. Committing oneself to participate in civic life, community affairs, political activism, or even charitable giving requires some vision for what is genuinely good in life. Engaging the public world entails working out with others the ideals that are ultimately normative and moral. What does a good personal life look like? What does a good society look like? What does a good government look like? What are the best ways to achieve those? Answers to such questions, and the belief that their answers really do matter, are usually what animate the most constructive participation in public life. But—as we saw in chapter 1—very many emerging adults today lack the basic intellectual and ethical tools for deciding what is genuinely morally right and wrong or what is really good for individuals and society. Almost none have been taught how both to hold real moral convictions and to live peaceably in a world of moral pluralism. It is not even clear that the larger culture that might have socialized them and into which they are being socialized itself has any idea how to teach those or what substantively it would teach if it tried. Most of what emerging adults have seen in public life had involved either disagreement and conflict, including "culture wars," or strategies of conflict avoidance and denial.

So, generally lacking clear moral convictions themselves, and having typically been socialized not to engage in conflict but rather to avoid it, few emerging adults feel equipped to participate confidently and constructively in public, civic, or political life. Better, they think, to steer clear of it altogether.

The correlation between morality and political interest among emerging adults is not mere speculation but reveals itself in significant associations in our empirical data. In fact, those who grew up believing in the existence of real moral right and wrong are more likely as emerging adults to be interested in politics. Six years before we interviewed our sample of emerging adults, we conducted a telephone survey with them. One of the survey questions asked if they believed in absolute rights and wrongs or if they instead believed that morality is relative. Among the emerging adults we interviewed in 2008, those who had answered on that survey that morality was *not* relative, that they believed there exist absolute rights and wrongs, were also significantly more likely to be among the genuinely political and marginally political emerging adult types. The distrustful and disempowered emerging adults were as likely to agree as disagree that morality is relative. And the politically apathetic and uninformed emerging adults we interviewed were highly likely to have agreed that morality is relative. Then, two years after the first survey, we asked the question again in a follow-up survey. And once again, analyzing those data, we found a significant association between believing that morality is relative and being apathetic, uninformed, distrustful, and disempowered when it comes to political engagement. It is instead those who believe in absolute morality who are more likely to be interested in participating in civic and political life. Moral vision is thus not irrelevant to democratic well-being.

Mass consumer materialism. A second factor that we think helps to explain emerging adults' disengagement from civic and political involvement is their larger investment in mass consumer materialism, as observed in chapter 2. Both politics and the economic market are spheres within the larger realm of public life, broadly conceived. But they operate by two quite different logics. One is about authority exercised for the common good; the other is about making exchanges that satisfy individuals' self-interest. One involves finding common ground in values, morals, and purposes in order to achieve collective benefits; the other is about finding matches between buyers' and sellers' self-interests that make their exchanges rational. One relies on the visible hand of government, the other on the invisible hand of market mechanisms (although, to be sure, the government plays a central role in defining and regulating markets). Normally, both coexist in the same society and are needed to support each other. But in recent decades in the United States, we think, the force of the market has increasingly spilled over into other realms of life, including civic and political life. The logic and practices of the market are increasingly taking over noneconomic domains of life. Most to the point here, the market's focus on mass consumer materialism has itself been consuming increasing amounts of young adults' interests and devotions. Very many of the emerging adults we interviewed—as we noted in chapter 2—dedicate major portions of their educational, work, career, and leisure lives to securing their positions as consumers of material goods, experiences, and services. For that is what primarily defines a genuinely good life for them. What is important is not civic life but shopping, not good political decision making but smart consumer choices, not a more fully realized common good but higher consumer satisfaction, not enhancing public life but increasing purchasing power. That is a simple fact of life among nearly all emerging adults, which has been borne out by solid surveys conducted among young adults over many decades.[9]

But the issue here is not merely the allocation of emerging adults' time and attention. More profoundly at issue are their very visions of what a human self and society *are* and ought to look like. The ideology and practice of mass consumerism reshapes people—their fundamental visions of who and what they are—not into active citizens but acquisitive consumers. Society itself is transformed not into a rich network of various sorts of communities and social institutions that together comprise a civil society that promotes human flourishing, but rather a national mega-supermarket of endless products and services where shoppers (having been "empowered" by their incomes) seek human fulfillment through mass consumption. In such redefined human and social realities, things like community life, civic participation, and political engagement become extraneous, almost meaningless. They are reduced to the places where the rules of the market, wealth distribution, and product safety can be considered. In the end, there is no such thing as a *common*wealth, a public square, a common good. All that exists are income-earning workers, commodity producers, service suppliers, markets, regulators, and sites for satiating consumption.

What disappears with the cultural takeover of mass consumerism are shared social identities, organic communities of solidarity, the civic virtues of duty and responsibility, and the learned processes of public deliberation, consensus building, and conflict resolution. What takes their place instead are individual-preference formation, acquisitive materialism, entertainment, and the sating of desires—not to mention resource depletion and environmental destruction. Things such as political debates between candidates during election campaigns are turned into managed, prepackaged charades. People come to exercise their sham, quasi-political "freedom of choice" in the form of expressing consumer freedom by selecting one product brand instead of another, texting or telephoning in their vote on which sports team gave the week's best performance or who should win on a reality-TV talent show. On occasion, political issues and world affairs might have to be considered because they may actually affect the world of consumption, as noted, for instance, by this emerging adults' observation: "I don't think that we should be mass consuming things that are coming out of China right now, because of the way our economy's going. Because what we're doing is we're supporting their economy while our economy's going down the tubes and no one's doing anything for us." Otherwise, the institutions that comprise what is most sacred in America—the economy—have few if any larger moral responsibilities in society, since they serve what is ultimately powerful. Consider, for instance, this emerging adult's answer to our question of whether corporations have any moral responsibilities, such as to help the less fortunate of the world: "No, a corporation's responsibility is to take care of the stakeholders."

Is it any wonder, then, that when emerging adults talk about living a good life, they rarely focus on what they might want to contribute to the world beyond their immediate friends and family? Instead, they mostly talk about "what I would like to *have*."[10] Possession, owning stuff, defines the good for emerging adults—for it fosters consumption, which is (supposedly) fulfilling, which then leads to more acquisition, in an endless cycle. Or is it any wonder, when it comes to thinking about personal goods and identities, that emerging adults talk about consumerism as personally beneficial because of the way it helps define individual autonomy and identity, as this one expressed: "I think consuming material things is good, because it helps people to set themselves apart from each other. Individually, like to stand out, not stand out, but make each other unique, different." Another emerging adult—in answer to our question about things she must have to make her happy—explained to us that owning the right possessions, like her own house, will enable her to avoid social interactions with other people that would make her uncomfortable:

> Me? My own home. I don't see me living in an apartment. I'm not saying anything's wrong with it, but I've lived in a house all my life. And even just going and visiting people in an apartment and seeing the difference. Like, in my house, if I'm mad at you or I wanna watch TV somewhere else, I'll go upstairs. I don't have to hear you. I don't have to see you. I don't have to bump into you going to the bathroom. But if I was in an apartment, I could hear you in the other room. I just think I would get frustrated if I, like, even tried to have a relationship in an apartment, I think it would put more strain on it.

Is it any wonder, further, that we again find a statistically significant correlation among the emerging adults we interviewed between enthusiasm for mass consumerism and lack of interest in political participation? We did—the more emerging adults are into consumerism, the less they are into politics and civic engagement.[11] Meanwhile, the effects that the mass consumer way of life are having on the environment and the larger culture are not something to worry about. As one told us, "I guess I don't really think about it as far as its effects on society. [. . .] I don't really think about long-term effects on society and mass production and mass consumption." Another stated it even more frankly: "I'm not going to live long enough to see it, so I don't care." That kind of view occupies the opposite end of the moral universe from the view needed to encourage and justify engagement in public, civic, political life. Mass consumerist culture thus is not irrelevant to the health of democratic culture.

Individualistic relativism. A third factor related to the two just examined is the very strong individualistic relativism that also undercuts emerging adults' civic and political engagement. A number of aspects of this individualistic relativism merit consideration in some depth here. The first is the simple fact that nearly all American emerging adults are, in fact, *highly individualistic*. One, for instance, told us, when considering the needs of other people:

> I really like this idea of self-responsibility and only caring about oneself. When some people sometimes feel that other people are relying on them, maybe they are, maybe they're not. Or that they don't have control over themselves because someone else has control over them, I don't know. I just really believe it's a self-responsibility. Yeah, people make mistakes, you need to accept that. But I don't think that we should be concerned with other people, unless they ask for help.

Another told us:

> I want people to understand that everybody is in charge of their life. Like, everyone is in charge of their own life, and nobody has to tell them what to do. I just wish everybody worldwide could realize that. I know it's not gonna happen. But it'd be nice, because, sure, there'd be a lot of people who would take that and do maybe atrocious things with it, like try and kill people, and be, "Well I don't care, it's my life." But at the same time, there's gonna be other people who would put them down. I don't know. I just think people would be better off if they weren't so trusting of each other. Not that trust is a bad thing, but just trying to figure things out for themselves, and not just eating up everything they're told.

This kind of individualistic outlook was summed up succinctly by another emerging adult who said, "I think your self is most important in making a decision." What was real and valuable for almost all emerging adults, then, was the freedom of individuals to live as autonomous actors without others taking care of them or getting in their way.

A second key aspect of individualistic relativism is the assumption by most emerging adults that *everybody's different*. If in reality people in the world have complex combinations of similarities and differences, emerging adults in the United States today tend mostly to see the differences. Conversations with them clearly reveal their great sensitivity to the core belief that "everybody's different," as they frequently say. Nearly any question asked of them about any norm, experience, rule of thumb, expectation, or belief is very likely to get an answer beginning with the phrase "Well, everybody's different, but for me . . ." Although nobody expresses the underlying viewpoint in so many words, they seem to believe that humans share very little in common with each other, that you can't count on any common features or interests across people that binds them together or gives them a basis on which to work out disagreements. And the differences emphasized are not merely cross-cultural dissimilarities between, say, Americans and Tibetans. The alleged differences actually reach down to individual personalities. Any given person has his or her own unique (if transient) beliefs, tastes, feelings, thoughts, desires, and expectations. Nobody can presume to impose on or perhaps even fully understand those of another. Literally every individual is different. This, it seems, is not merely basic American individualism. It is individualism given heavy doses of multiculturalism and pumped up by the postmodern insistence on disjuncture and *différance*. Few emerging adults have actually read postmodernist theory, of course, but its effects seem to have trickled down to the popular prereflective consciousness of emerging adults nonetheless. So in interviews we heard them saying things like, "I think the last few years have made me more aware of [how] what's right for me may be wrong for someone else or what's wrong for me may be okay for somebody else. I think it's made me more aware of other people's feelings about things." And to the question about how much material stuff people should own, another replied, "That's a personal choice. I don't know, I guess that's personal for everybody." When it comes to participation in the civic, political, and public realms, the view that "everybody's different" exerts a strong debilitating effect. It makes it impossible to identify what is socially shared, to discern any common good, or to consider how the public might need to pull together to achieve common goals. The natural implication of "everybody's different" is that each individual should simply go their own way and not get in others' ways.

It is hardly surprising, in light of much of what we have seen, that according to emerging adults, the absolute authority underwriting every person's beliefs or actions is simply his or her own sovereign self. Anybody can think or do whatever he or she wants. Of course, what a person chooses to think or do may have bad consequences for that person. But *everything is ultimately up to each individual to decide for himself or herself*. The most one should ever do toward influencing another person is to ask him or her to consider what one thinks. Nobody is bound to any course of action by virtue of belonging to a group or because of a common good. Individuals are autonomous agents who have to deal with each other, of course, but they do so entirely as self-directing choosers. The words "duty," "responsibility," and "obligation" feel somehow vaguely coercive or puritanical. That somebody "should" do something is about as far as many emerging adults are comfortable saying. You can't make anybody do anything, so don't even try to influence them. Stick to what you "feel" is right. Tell others what you think, if they ask you. But respect the fact that everything is finally the other person's own call. Thus, one emerging adult said about the source of her own moral beliefs: "I think mostly myself. Some from religion, I guess, some from parents. But, I think for me to actually pick my views, I mean, it has to come from me." When asked what it is that makes anything right or wrong, another replied, "I think it's your own personal belief system. I don't think it's anything like social norms or like that. I think it's just what you think, it's dependent on each person and their own beliefs and what they think is right or wrong." Thus, as applied to the issue of whether people have any responsibilities related to material wealth and possessions, for instance, another said:

> If someone works for their three billion dollars that they own, it's rightfully their three billion dollars. They should be able to buy whatever they want. Yeah, I think they should at least help some people out, but it's their money, they can do what they want. If they want to go out and get 40 different cars, whatever, that is [fine].

Once again, very little in this outlook justifies or encourages civic participation or political engagement. Society is not about citizens exercising responsibilities to decide collectively for the common good. It is about individuals deciding whatever they want for themselves and hopefully not having anyone else get in the way.

This approach is reinforced by a certain larger problem of knowledge that most emerging adults feel, namely, that is that it is hard for emerging adults *to see an objective reality beyond the individual self.* The majority of emerging adults can express very well how people are shaped and bound by their personal experiences. But most have great difficulty grasping the idea that a reality that is objective to their own awareness or construction of it may exist that could have a significant bearing on their lives. In philosophical terms, most emerging adults are functionally (meaning how they actually think and act, regardless of the theories they hold) "soft ontological antirealists," "epistemological skeptics," and "perspectivalists"—although few are aware of those terms. They seem to presuppose that they are imprisoned in their own subjective selves, limited to their biased interpretations of their own sense perceptions, unable to know the real truth of anything beyond themselves. They are doubtful that an identifiable, objective, shared reality might exist for all people that can serve as a reliable reference point for rational deliberation and argument. So, for example, when we interviewers tried to get respondents to talk about whether what they take to be substantive moral beliefs reflect some objective or universal quality or standard, or are relative human inventions, many—if not most—could not understand what we interviewers were trying to get at. They had difficulty seeing the possible distinction between objective moral truth and relative human invention. This is not because they are dumb. It seems rather that they simply cannot, for whatever reason, believe in—or sometimes even conceive of—a given, objective truth, fact, reality, or nature of the world that is independent of their subjective experience and in relation to which they and others might learn or be persuaded to change. Although none would put it in exactly this way, what emerging adults take to be reality ultimately seems to consist of a multitude of subjective and ultimately autonomous experiences. People are thus trying to communicate with each other simply in order to be able to get along and enjoy life as they see fit. Beyond that, anything truly objectively shared or common or real seems impossible to access. Again, such an outlook does little to foster civic participation or political involvement.

Furthermore, the background assumption of the majority of emerging adults is that when it comes to *helping others* in any way—including perhaps pursuing a more just social order through public engagement or political activism—that is an *optional, personal choice*. When asked whether people generally have a responsibility or obligation to help other people, only a minority of the emerging adults interviewed said that people do have a real responsibility to help others. The majority of the emerging adults we interviewed stated the opposite—that nobody has any natural or general responsibility or obligation to help other people. In an expression of the extreme individualism noted above that characterizes emerging adult culture more broadly, most of those interviewed said that it is nice if people help others, but that nobody has to. Taking care of other people in need is an individual's choice. If you want to do it, good. If you don't, that's up to you. You don't have to. Nobody can blame people who won't help others. They are not doing anything wrong, very many emerging adults said, if they ignore other people in need. Even when pressed—What about victims of natural disaster or political oppression? What about helpless people who are not responsible for their poverty or disabilities?—they replied: if someone wants to help, then good for that person, but nobody has to. Some simply declared without batting an eye, "That's not my problem." Others said, "I wish people would help others, but they really have no duty to do that at all. It's up to them, their opinion." Yet another, when discussing where obligations to help others begin and end, said, "It's all relative to the one person and what he or she wants to do."

Any notion of the shared responsibilities of a common humanity, a transcendent call to protect the life and dignity of one's neighbor, or a moral responsibility to seek the common good—which might motivate civic involvement, political engagement, volunteering, or even financial giving—was almost entirely absent among emerging adults. In the end, each individual does what he or she wants, and nobody has any moral leverage to persuade or compel him or her to do otherwise.[12] In this thin cultural soil, very little in the way of participation in civic or political life ever grows.

Technological submersion in interpersonal relationships in private settings. Finally, emerging adults' evident lack of optimism, and even fatalism at times, about their potential to influence the larger social and political world, and their associated withdrawal from public life, seem closely related to the fact that most of them are almost completely submerged in interpersonal relationships in their private worlds. Few emerging adults are involved in community organizations or other social change–oriented groups or movements. Not many care to know much of substance about political issues and world events. Few are intellectually engaged in any of the major cultural and ethical debates and challenges facing U.S. society. Almost none have any vision of a common good. Citizenship is not a word in their vocabularies. Some even said they were not planning on voting in the 2008 presidential election. The extent of public disengagement among the vast majority of emerging adults is astonishing. *On the other hand*, they are definitely extremely "socially engaged" in quite a different way: they are deeply invested in social life beyond their immediate selves through their interpersonal relationships. And they pursue these private-sphere emotional and relational investments with fervent devotion.

Much of the lives of emerging adults appears to be centered on creating and maintaining personal relationships of varying degrees of closeness. What makes emerging adults most happy in life are their good relationships with family, friends, and interesting associates. By comparison, as we have seen, the larger public world, civic life, and the political realm seem to them to be alien and impenetrable. Few emerging adults have hobbies, participate in community groups or other organized activities, or are even devoted to working long hours for the sake of careers. Instead, they are absorbed with friends and family. Most emerging adults would rather spend large amounts of time merely "hanging out" in private settings with various intimates and acquaintances, for instance, than being part of clubs or interest groups, not to mention political parties or social movements. Thus, the apparent move of Americans away from civic participation in public life and toward the enjoyment of "lifestyle enclaves"—previously noted by various cultural observers[13]—may for today's emerging adults be progressing yet further toward the nearly total submersion of self into fluidly constructed, private networks of technologically managed intimates and associates.

This strongly relational way of engaging their "larger" worlds clearly appears—as the phrase "technologically managed" above suggests—closely connected to the technologies of communication that preoccupy their lives. Even during the interviews, many emerging adults repeatedly checked and sometimes answered their cell phones. Some sent text messages between interview questions. Others set their cell phones out on tables to be closely monitored. Yet others expressed real interest in the latest cell phones and other communication devices that some of the interviewers owned. In short, emerging adults are keen on gadgets that facilitate their interpersonal communications. And managing personal relationships turns out for many to be not a distinct task reserved for routinely scheduled times of the day or week but rather a ubiquitous, constant activity. Myriad friends and family members are always available at their fingertips, through cell phones, texting, IMing, blogging, and e-mailing. Many emerging adults routinely text-message friends while in class and on the job. They e-mail from the bus. They blog late at night to share with peers every detail of their days' feelings and experiences. They check Facebook while doing homework, "just to check in with friends" and "to see what's going on with other people." The instant feedback and stimulation from friends and family about every choice and action they make and every emotion they feel seems to be very satisfying to them, sometimes perhaps addictive. Yet all of these relationship-managing activities and private communication distractions seem to make it difficult for emerging adults to pursue tasks that require full concentration or patient dedication. Instead, they have to multitask. More to the point of this chapter, these relationship-oriented activities appear to fill up, however problematically, the void left by their lack of civic participation in fostering the shared goods of public life.[14] Emerging adults simply do not have the interest or time for civic participation or political involvement, since they are too busy either hanging out or calling or texting their friends—who, after all, are much more immediately manageable and rewarding.

Conclusion

The idea that today's emerging adults are as a generation leading a new wave of renewed civic-mindedness and political involvement is sheer fiction. The fact that anyone ever believed that idea simply tells us how flimsy the empirical evidence that so many journalistic media stories are based upon is and how unaccountable to empirical reality high-profile journalism can be. And that itself—in light of all that has been said in this chapter and chapter 2 about mass consumerism—reflects the extent to which so much journalism, including news reporting, does not actually provide reliable, substantive information in the service of responsible democratic citizenship but rather entertainment for the masses. The reporting of such alleged political trends examined in this chapter consists in fact of essentially human interest stories based on the thinnest of anecdotal evidence—sometimes even merely journalists' own personal dreams and agendas. But whatever any popular cultural or political observers have had to say about the political interests of emerging adults, we—without joy—can set the record straight here: almost all emerging adults today are either apathetic, uninformed, distrustful, disempowered, or, at most only marginally interested when it comes to politics and public life. Both that fact itself and the reasons for it speak poorly of the condition of our larger culture and society.

Conclusion

There is only one cure for the malady that afflicts our culture, and that is to speak the truth about it. Once we can bring ourselves to do that, it will be time to worry about "constructive solutions," "practical proposals," and "social alternatives" for our young—discussions of which, so long as they are so absurdly premature, serve only to distract our attention from the truth about ourselves.

—Christopher Lasch

In the summer of 2008, we and a team of trained interviewer-researchers fanned out across the United States to interview 230 18- to 23-year-old emerging adults representing every region, social class, race, ethnicity, religion, educational situation, and family background in the country. Most of these we had interviewed twice before when they were younger. Much of what we heard in our interviews with these emerging adults was intriguing and encouraging. Many emerging adults, we learned, are leading interesting, promising, and sometimes impressive lives. At the same time, a lot of what we heard from them was also troubling, and sometimes disturbing and depressing. The first book to come out of this research focused especially on the religious lives of emerging adults.[1] But when that book was written and published, it was clear to us that there was much more of a story to tell than the first book disclosed, and more about emerging adults beyond their religious lives that needed to be reported and considered. That story became this book.

Building on previous studies of emerging adults by other scholars,[2] we have shown that the passage of American youth moving from the teenage years toward full adulthood today is often confusing, troubled, and sometimes dangerous. Many who make this passage find themselves disoriented, wounded, and sometimes damaged along the way. In the popular imagination, these early adult years are filled with youthful fun and freedom enjoyed in the prime of life. For some, this image is true. The actual reality for many, however, is instead one of personal struggle, confusion, anxiety, hurt, frustration, and grief. Some emerging adults of course sail through these years unscathed. But many suffer wounds in body and soul, in their relationships, and in their chances for leading good lives. Some, especially those with financial resources, manage to recover and move forward with hope. Others remain damaged for life. In our research, we have personally met and learned firsthand about the lives of all of these kinds of emerging adults.

The common confusions, troubles, and dangers of this emerging adult passage toward full adulthood are not limited to poorer, less responsible, or less educated youth. They are found in a variety of forms in the practices and institutions of the cultural worlds of emerging adults representing all strata and subcultures of American society. That is because the challenges and dangers of emerging adulthood are built into the very structure of that passage itself. In short, the long transition from the teenage years to full adulthood in America has a dark side that is not often talked about or portrayed by mainstream media. Some cultural activists and even academic scholars seem eager to celebrate and promote what we consider to be troubling aspects of emerging adult life. We are far less sanguine.

Getting It Wrong: Projection, Nostalgia, Idealization, Condemnation

Part of our motivation for writing this book is our concern that too many American adults—parents, teachers, professors, coaches, college administrators, pastors, and others—do not seem to adequately understand the fact of emerging adulthood and its larger implications. Some adults, particularly some baby boomers, seem to want to project back onto 18- to 23-year-olds today the kind of assumptions and experiences that characterized their own lives during the same period of their lives. For some, this takes on a nostalgic air. But this approach implies that nothing has changed in the world, that young people today are simply repeating what was relevant in the 1960s and '70s. That is wrong. It is a different world today. To be in one's twenties today is not the same experience as it was decades ago. To think otherwise is to self-impose a blurred vision that cannot recognize real life as it is experienced today and so cannot take emerging adults fully seriously.

Other American adults we observe seem more interested in projecting their ideals and hopes for what they think young people today *should* be like than in actually understanding what emerging adults today actually *are* like. Rather than taking contemporary emerging adult life seriously, for what it actually is, these adults appear to prefer instead to use emerging adults as a kind of blank screen onto which to project images of their own desires and ideals. One version of this tendency is to claim that "young adults today" are deeply committed to social justice, passionately engaged in political activism, actively volunteering in their local communities, devoting themselves to building a greener, more peaceful and just world. Almost nothing could be further from the truth, at least when it comes to 18- to 23-year-olds considered at a national level as a group. Of course there is a very small minority of emerging adults who are like this. And when they get together in campus groups or other meetings, one can with some wishful thinking convince oneself that they represent some kind of national trend. But that reflects what sociologists call a "highly skewed sampling bias." In fact those passionate, activist youth do not at all represent the vast majority of their peers, as we saw above.

Another version of this tendency to project ideal images onto emerging adults focuses not on their alleged political passion and activism but instead on the fun, the glamour, the excitement of young adult life. "These are the best years of your life!" some people announce. "Aren't all of the opportunities, the freedom, the romance, the parties, the learning, the travel, and the adventure exciting?" Some of these people are just naive, perhaps trying vicariously to live lives they themselves never got to enjoy. That may be understandable, but even that is not entirely harmless. Others are more strategic and self-interested, constructing and projecting images of a lifestyle they want emerging adults to emulate so they can make money from selling the products and services it takes to live that kind of projected lifestyle. These are the marketers, advertisers, salespeople, and service providers who make their living by compelling emerging adults to desire their wares.

It can all sound so nice, so fun, so sexy. But the truth we must report is that underneath all of that for many is a dark underbelly of disappointment, grief, confusion, sometimes addiction. Many emerging adults have discovered the hard way, for example, that the sexual revolution turns out not to be all it was cracked up to be. Many emerging adults cannot get away from intoxicating habits that help them cope with the difficulties and boredom of life and the world. Many cannot imagine what leading a truly good life might look like other than achieving financial security, having a nice suburban family, and buying lots of material possessions. Many emerging adults cannot explain in simple terms what is morally good and why but instead teeter on the edge of moral relativism. There is lots of fun, plenty of freedom, and many opportunities in emerging adulthood. But that is only part of the story. The darker side also needs to be reckoned with.

Yet another approach that we think simplifies and often misunderstands the lives of emerging adults is that of the doom-and-gloom crowd. These people are not nostalgic, optimistic, or naive. Instead, they see in contemporary emerging adult culture signs of the apocalypse. One version sees a particularly degenerate generation of "kids today" leading America down the path to cultural destruction. Another version sees emerging adults as the end of Christianity in America. Other renderings of such alarmist stories are out there. They are not without some basis in fact, as this book has shown. Yet in our view, such semihysterical distress signals and jeremiads are often more about promoting the agenda of some particular interest—such as right-wing politics or a religious program—than about actually understanding and responding with care to the complex reality of emerging adult life and culture today.

Emerging adults are not just statistics or stories with which to make some exaggerated or ideological point. They are real, complicated people, not much different, except in their relative immaturity and inexperience, from the rest of American adults. Furthermore, whatever problems exist in emerging adult life today are, as we have argued throughout this book, not exclusively emerging adult problems. The emerging adult phase of the American life course certainly facilitates and accentuates many of them. But all emerging adult problems are ultimately American problems. They reflect the faults and failures of the mainstream institutions and values of the American way of life *in which most doom-and-gloomers are also deeply implicated.* To single out emerging adults as the source of troubles or the main symptom of what ails us is too convenient, too simplistic, too self-serving a view.

Getting It Right: The Sociological Imagination

If nothing else, we hope that this book disabuses people of any of these misguided and unhelpful views they may hold about emerging adults. Emerging adulthood as a phase in the American life course and emerging adults as human beings must be taken seriously, on their own terms, for the actual realities of their real lives as they play out in the world. Projections, nostalgia, idealizations, and condemnations cannot be the first order of business. The first step must be to gauge reality itself as best as we can. We need to approach that reality on its own terms, with care and readiness to connect to its human face. We must try to describe it as well as we can in its full complexity. That is what we have attempted in this book.

What we saw and heard in our interviews and have tried to show here is that many emerging adult lives are complex, fraught with difficulty, and often beset with big problems, serious confusions, and misplaced values and devotions. Some of that has to do with a lack of elementary reasoning abilities for sorting out basic moral questions. Some of it is about being harmed by sexual involvements that do not turn out the way emerging adults had been led to expect.

Other problems have to do with holding extremely shallow notions of what a good life could be, in which mass consumerism and material possessions define an extremely limited horizon of vision. Some of the concern is about the significant role of intoxication in emerging adult life, not a role that centers on community and celebration but rather on stress, anxiety, boredom, and temporary relief. Part of it too is a deep detachment or alienation from personal involvement in civic, communal, and political life, which seems to reflect a kind of despair about the prospects for change and a grim outlook for the future.

Does this mean emerging adults are terrible people? No. Does it mean the world will fall apart tomorrow? No. Does it mean all is not well among emerging adults, that there is cause for serious concern? We think so.

Adequately understanding and explaining what we have observed in this book requires that we use our *sociological imaginations*.[3] We need to apply to emerging adulthood today the particular sociological viewpoint that teaches us to ask certain kinds of questions and looks for specific types of answers— ones that have to do with the power of the social world to influence individuals. The sociological imagination, as we said, is a particular way of seeing and thinking that takes the influence of cultural and social life very seriously, in order to understand and explain the world, our lives, and the lives of others more fully.

Such a perspective helps us to see that the experiences and outcomes of individual emerging adult lives are powerfully shaped by the trends, forces, and powers of larger social institutions and cultural meaning systems. Again, focusing on individual psychology or personalities is not enough. Understanding and explaining people sociologically means using a "social logic" or *socio-logic* that expands our range of vision for what makes the world work as it does. Such a socio-logic increases our power to better comprehend life and the world around us. That is the promise of the sociological imagination, the payoff of adopting such a view that we hope we have demonstrated in this book.

How? We have sought in the previous chapters to better understand the lives of 18- to 23-year-old Americans. We have *described* their lives, but also sought to *understand* and *explain* their lives sociologically, by viewing them in the larger context of American culture and society. Specifically, we have argued that the outlooks and actions of 18- to 23-year-old Americans concerning morality, sex, consumerism, alcohol and drugs, and civic and political engagement must be understood and explained in terms of the larger social institutions and forces that help to generate and promote them.

For starters, we examined the powerful influence of the objective life-course phase known as "emerging adulthood" on the personal expectations, beliefs, and behaviors of those we studied. We also explored the relationship between America's pervasive mass consumer economic system and the way 18- to 23-year-olds think and act when it comes to a variety of seemingly unrelated matters. In addition, we considered how many other social institutions, cultural trends, and technological developments—such as mass public schooling, the digital communications revolution, colleges and universities, sociocultural pluralism, the mass media, political gridlock, socioeconomic inequality, the sexual revolution, and postmodernism—shape the lives of 18- to 23-year-olds in ways they often seem not to enter their awareness.

Our goal has been to help readers grasp the many connections between these (usually seemingly unrelated) social and cultural forces and key aspects of the personal, often private lives of 18- to 23-year-olds. If we have succeeded, then that sociological imagination should help readers understand and explain their world, their own lives, and the lives of others much better than any simple view focused on individual psychology or personality could ever do.

Cultural Soul Searching

We think that the troubles we have discovered in emerging adult life and with the help of the sociological imagination provide an opportunity for some broader soul searching about our larger cultural commitments and institutional practices. When something seems wrong, it is often good to step back and ponder what it may tell us about the bigger picture. We do not pretend to have it all figured out, and we certainly are not prophets or reformers. But we do have some ideas to contribute to what we hope will be larger public discussions about the matter.

The obvious place to begin is, of course, with the structural fact of emerging adulthood itself. Emerging adults are not whatever they are because they have chosen as individuals certain ideas and values and lifestyles out of the air. Most of what they are devoted to and what they experience is powerfully shaped by the central facts about emerging adulthood as an institutionally structured reality of American life today. Emerging adulthood is at heart about postponing settling down into real adulthood. It is about possibilities, options, and openness. In its pure form it is about spending a long period unmarried, without children, and not settled into a real career or residence. Emerging adulthood as a social fact means not making commitments, not putting down roots, not setting a definite course for the long term. It is about experimenting, exploring, experiencing, preparing, anticipating, having fun, and hopefully not screwing things up too badly in the meantime. Emerging adulthood entails few significant obligations, relatively little accountability to others, and (for those with the means) plenty of interesting detours and escape hatches. It is a time of limbo, of transition, of being neither a teen nor a real adult. Emerging adults can be unsure, can change their minds, can give things a shot, and can try something else if it doesn't work out. Again, this reality is driven by personal choices but also by social-structural forces that make those choices seem sensible for many emerging adults.

All of that creates a broad social context in which what we have observed about emerging adult life makes lots of sense. The moral aimlessness, the sexual troubles, the materialistic consumerism, the intoxicated living, the lack of interest in civic and political life—it all fits well with the essence of emerging adulthood. The experiences and outlooks of the people involved, as we have described it in previous chapters, are thus less about their specific individual qualities or personalities than about the particular social-structural systems through which they are passing. The same people at the same ages living in the same places in, say, 1830, or living today in Bolivia or Botswana, would obviously be living very different lives.

So the core explanation for what we have observed in this book goes back to the structural facts of emerging adulthood. The life-course phase through which these young adults are living is structured by a certain configuration of interlocking institutions, flows of sustaining resources, technologies of communication and bodily control, information and image streams, and cultural standards and expectations that mold individuals to look, think, speak, act, and aspire in very particular ways. In many senses, we think emerging adulthood offers many valuable possibilities and human goods. But it also provides a macro-structural context that generates the kind of problems and troubles we have reported in this book.

Stated differently, understanding the matters examined in this book requires placing them in the context of historical changes that have transformed the lives of youth over many decades. Social and cultural changes over that time period have generated a genuinely new phase in the American life course. This new life phase involves a stretching out of the time it takes to move from the teenage years into full adulthood, a complication of the number and directions of the paths that youth take toward adulthood, and a softening up, if not dissolution, of many established categories, norms, boundaries, and standards that previously helped to regulate and guide the transition of youth into full adulthood.

That passage has become longer, more confusing, and less directed by clear cultural and institutional instructions and boundaries. It definitely has some positive features. But it is also marked by a lot of ambiguity, murkiness, fluidity, and uncertainty. It involves characteristic behaviors and practices that often make life difficult and painful. This is in part what leads to its sometimes confusing, troubled, and dangerous character for those who pass through it. So if we wish to understand and explain some of the problematic features of emerging adult life, we are saying, we need to focus on the objective cultural, institutional, and structural characteristics of this life-course phase that shape the lives of those who pass through it, not simply on the individual choices and behaviors of young people.

Besides the macro fact of emerging adulthood as a life-course phase, we have also repeatedly stressed in the previous chapters the institutionally rooted nature of many of these problems operating at a more middle-range level. Poor moral reasoning comes significantly from poor teaching of thinking skills in schools, families, religious communities, sports teams, and other youth-socializing settings. Damaging sexual experiences have connections to things like the way colleges and universities are run and the lifestyle scripts disseminated by advertising and the mass media. Mass consumer materialism is of course deeply rooted in the structure of the American capitalist economy and the advertising industry. Intoxicating habits have much to do with the financial motives of the alcohol industry ("Drink Responsibly" ads notwithstanding) and the structures of college life, among other things. And disconnection from civic, communal, and political life surely has something to do with the many real dysfunctions of American politics and the lure of private, mass consumerist, media-stimulated lifestyles. Such troubles and problems are generated and often driven by basic social institutions, like schools, families, industries, religious organizations, and so on.

Not only that, but the institutions in which many emerging adult troubles are rooted are often structurally interlocked with each other. The routine practices of schools, for example, are linked to the demographic and religious pluralism of populations, to judicial interpretations of the Constitution, to imperatives linked to government funding, and to the gate-keeping standards of higher education. The nature of life on college and university campuses, particularly in the evening after classes end, cannot be understood apart from the advertising interests of the alcohol industry, the institutional secularization of higher education, and the narratives and images of collegiate life comedically portrayed for decades by Hollywood, for example.

The problematic sexual practices of emerging adults are not intelligible apart from knowledge about things like the centrality of alcohol in social life, the structural isolation from older adults of emerging adult residential life, the ideologies of many college campus health centers,[4] the interests of business firms that manufacture birth control technologies,[5] and the continuing societal tendency of men dominating women in various ways. We could elaborate, but we hope the point has been made. Nearly everything that helps to define the character of emerging adult life is institutionally and culturally interconnected in a big, complex social web to many other things that are also defining of emerging adulthood. That makes the entire system extremely powerful and resilient.

A point just mentioned but not discussed much in this book deserves greater elaboration. One of the striking social features of emerging adulthood is how structurally disconnected most emerging adults are from older adults (as well as from younger teens and children). This disconnect from full adults was clear to us already when we studied these same youth as teenagers.[6] It became even more obvious when they became emerging adults. Most of the meaningful, routine relationships that most emerging adults have are with other emerging adults. Emerging adults most often live with other emerging adults, hang out with other emerging adults, go to school with other emerging adults, party with other emerging adults, engage in sports and recreational activities with other emerging adults, have romantic relationships with other emerging adults, and so on. True, most emerging adults do have older adults for bosses or professors. But their relationships with them are almost always restricted, functional, and performance oriented. And those adults usually disappear when class or work is over. Those are not their important relationships.

Most emerging adults also have positive relationships with their parents, relationships that most value and spend time and effort to maintain. But most of those family relationships have also been renegotiated to selectively keep parents in the dark or at a distance about many of the important things going on in emerging adults' lives. Parental relationships may remain important in many ways, but they usually do not form the fabric of the daily interactions or consume the hours of time spent together that other emerging adult relationships do. This means that, structurally, most emerging adults live this crucial decade of life surrounded mostly by their peers—people of the same age and in the same boat—who have no more experience, insight, wisdom, perspective, or balance than they do. It is sociologically a very odd way to help young people come of age, to learn how to be responsible, capable, mature adults.

This relative social isolation in age-bounded social networks has, for simple sociological reasons, major potential consequences, many of them negative. It limits what kind of advice or information an emerging adult might have at hand, what kind of oversight or accountability may be possible, what kind of obligations and responsibilities they might feel. It constrains exposure to potential older adult role models, mentors, and friends. It facilitates a narrow view of reality seen through the perspective of the emerging adult social position, validated and reinforced by the dominant others in the constrained social network. It obstructs a more natural process of integration into the social circles and practices of the fully adult world. Surrounding emerging adults mostly with a lot of other emerging adults is like putting a bunch of novice tennis players together on the court and expecting them to emerge later with advanced skills and experience. There are too few others around to teach, to model, to advise, to exemplify, to question, to challenge. There are mostly only more of the same emerging adults who are struggling through all the same life issues, problems, uncertainties, and messes.

In the end, many emerging adults often have at hand nobody wiser with whom to work through their moral confusions, nobody on the other side of emerging adulthood who can temper their expectations, nobody to invite them to the neighborhood association or a political rally. In short, the structural position of many emerging adults results in the relatively immature socializing the relatively immature, the morally blind leading the morally blind, and so on. Of course, spending time with friends and peers of the same age is a good thing. But it is not good when it constitutes most or all significant daily relationships. So we are talking here about issues of balance and diversity. It may be comfortable and fun for emerging adults to spend most or nearly all of their personal lives with other emerging adults. But sociologically we believe there is a real cost.

Stepping back a bit farther for an even wider view, the observations of this book, if they are of any concern at all, must raise questions about American individualism. Individualism is of course as American as mom and apple pie. American culture will always be individualistic. That is despite the fact that American society is made up of massive corporations, mass education, big government, oligarchic media, a globalized military, big agribusiness, massive formal bureaucracies, cookie-cutter neighborhoods, public regulations and red tape, and standardized national media programming. Yet America's cultural individualism seems somehow to survive all of that. No matter how the institutional features and typical life experience in America contradict the ideals of rugged individualism, that ideal prevails and dominates the cultural imagination.[7] We have seen powerful strands of that individualism in emerging adult accounts of their moral reasoning, sexual experiences, and relations to the public world of civic life and politics. Some of the problems and troubles of emerging adults can be traced back to the influence of this stark individualism.

Yet there are ironies in American individualism. Having freed people from the formative influences and obligations of town, church, extended family, and conventional morality, American individualism has exposed those people to the more powerful influences and manipulations of mass consumer capitalism. Stripped down to a mere autonomous individuality, people stand naked before the onslaught of commercial media, all-pervasive advertising, shopping malls, big-box stores, credit-card buying, and the dominant narrative of a materially defined vision of the good life. In this, one form of external authority has been displaced by another, much more insidious and controlling external authority—all done in the name of individual self-determination.

Consider, however, as a thought experiment, a different world. Imagine one in which young adults knew their limits and looked to more experienced adults for teaching and wisdom. Think of a society where structures of social life fostered real community, which integrated people of different ages in a variety of settings. Imagine a culture that was always aware of the bodily, moral, and material limits of human beings and of the earth. Think about a people who believed in balancing personal interests and profits with fostering the common good. Consider a nation that understood its well-being as dependent on the recognition and honoring of human interdependence, participation, and generosity. Would emerging adults still have problems? Certainly. Would those problems be as troubling as those we have reported in this book? We suspect not.

We think American individualism is out of sync with many socially structured realities of American society and important aspects of human nature. We therefore believe that it often serves as a source of harm to human well-being. If so, we should question the cultural power of radical individualism and expectations of individual autonomy. Of course, other aspects of American society—such as our subdivision neighborhood structures, consumer shopping, political liberalism,[8] and the centrality of the private automobile in American life—foster and reinforce the idea of individualism. So, again, it is not simply a matter of somehow getting the right ideas into our heads. But how people think is one important starting point for working on intentional institutional change. American culture will always be individualistic. But perhaps our culture could be somewhat less extreme and unrealistic in that individualism. We think that would be good for all people, including emerging adults.

One way to think about cultures is to ask about the scope or limits of their horizons.[9] By horizons we mean the furthest visions of what is believed to be real and therefore what ought to be prized and pursued. The horizons of some cultures have been the achievement of human equality, prosperity, and solidarity through the abolition of private property and triumph of Communism. The horizons of other cultures have been to live in harmony with the spirit of nature and Mother Earth. The horizons of yet other cultures have been to conquer and subdue the known world for the glory of the emperor, the Great City, and the gods. Clearly, some cultural horizons can promote what is good, just, and humane; while others promote exploitation and destruction.

So what is the horizon of mainstream American culture today? In America's current "cultural ontology," what is taken to be ultimately real and what therefore ought to be prized and sought after? Could it be that the triumph of liberal democratic capitalism has erased from the common American imagination any higher, transcendent horizon? Might it be true that the farthest boundary of sight that youth today can envision as real and being worth pursuit is entirely imminent, purely material, and completely mundane? Some emerging adults still believe in humanity or progress or God or development or something else transcendent. But we came away from our 230 interviews with emerging adults thinking that, for most, their horizon is disappointingly parochial. Get a good job, become financially secure, have a nice family, buy what you want, enjoy a few of the finer things in life, avoid the troubles of the world, retire with ease. That's it. Nothing much bigger, higher, more meaningful, more transcendent, more shared, more difficult.[10]

That is not a bad life, exactly. But neither, we think, is it terribly inspiring, ambitious, or great. And neither, we believe, will it be terribly fulfilling or enriching in the long run. Good human societies have always been built on the very human belief that there's got to be something better than this. We fear that the horizons of emerging adults today instead follow more closely the outlook of the 1988 song "Birth, School, Work, Death" by The Godfathers.[11] Given what we know about the stirrings and aspirations of the human spirit, we do not think that such an outlook can be sustained forever and does not bode well for what might come after in reaction.

In short, we think there are bigger issues of cultural vision, historical meaning, and social purpose implicated in the troubling symptoms of emerging adult life that we report. It may be tempting to assess the darker side of emerging adulthood in a simple public-health framework, or as so many trackable statistics that tell us trends in social problems to deploy various and sundry programs and policies to remedy. Those are perhaps some useful ways to view the matter. But to only be able to think in those terms may miss the forest for the trees. Such a technocratic mentality itself may be part of the very problem we are concerned is at fault here.

Ultimately we come back to core existential questions. What are humans? Do they have any purpose? If so, what is it? What is good in life and the world? How do we make sense of suffering, tragedy, evil, and death? Are history and the world going somewhere meaningful, or is it all just random chance? Our point is not to push particular answers to these questions. Our point is that human beings and cultures recurrently, inescapably ask and answer these questions one way or another. For better or worse, people and cultures recurrently find themselves drawn to answers that reflect horizons that are higher, bigger, more transcendent, or more meaningful than the prosaic, immanent, natural, mundane world.

Humanity can live for some time on mere bodily comfort and material security. But over time that does not seem to satisfy the human spirit. Such a limited horizon cannot last. Either material security gives way or the human spirit seeks to push beyond it. If so, then the standard cultural horizons of most emerging adults today, and thus of the culture that has raised them, cannot be said to reflect a high point of the human imagination and aspirations. Maybe the case is quite the opposite. If so, we think that deserves reflection and discussion, sooner rather than later.

Perhaps we should put the matter even more strongly. Perhaps it is not too stark to say that we as a society are *failing* our youth in crucial ways. If our analysis in this book is correct, then it may not be too strong to suggest that we are failing to equip teenagers and emerging adults with the basic tools for good moral reasoning. We are failing to teach them how to deal constructively with moral, cultural, and ideological differences. We are failing to teach them to think about what is good for people and in life. We are failing to equip our youth with the ideas, tools, and practices to know how to negotiate their romantic and sexual lives in healthy, nondestructive ways that prepare them to achieve the happy, functional marriages and families that most of them say they want in future years. We are failing to teach our youth about life purposes and goals that matter more than the accumulation of material possessions and material comfort and security. We are failing to challenge the too-common need to be intoxicated, the apparent inability to live a good, fun life without being under the influence of alcohol or drugs. And we are failing to teach our youth the importance of civic engagement and political participation, how to be active citizens of their communities and nation, how to think about and live for the common good. On all of these matters, if our analysis is correct, the adult world is simply abdicating its responsibilities.

Moreover, if our analysis is correct, we in the older adult world are failing youth and emerging adults in these crucial ways *because our own adult world is itself also failing* in those same ways. It is not that the world of mainstream American adults has something great to teach but is simply teaching it badly. That would also be a problem, but at least a remediable one. Rather, we suspect that the adult world is teaching its youth all too well. But what it has to teach too often fails to convey what any good society needs to pass on to its children. In short, if our sociological analysis in this book is correct, the problem is not simply that youth are bad students or that adults are poor teachers. It is that American culture itself seems to be depleted of some important cultural resources that it would pass on to youth if it had them—and yet not just for "moral" but also for identifiable institutional reasons, as repeatedly noted above. In which case, not only emerging adulthood, but American culture itself also has a dark side as well.

At the same time, we must insist that this is not the doom-and-gloom perspective described above. Our primary concern is to rethink aspects of American life and culture that would hopefully improve the well-being of emerging adults and other Americans. Thinking about that, rather than denouncing the moral decline of American culture, is our central concern. And in that we are not pushing any one ideological, political, or religious agenda. Our critique in this book has in fact drawn on concerns and analyses of both the left and the right. And it has raised issues that in various ways should concern both religious and nonreligious Americans.

We hope that readers from different political, religious, and moral perspectives are able to get together to consider such common concerns and talk civilly and constructively about the issues raised in this book. We wish to be able to keep their eyes focused on the very human, flesh-and-blood, sometimes life-and-death character of the matters at hand as they relate to real emerging adults, and hope they can avoid descending into sectarian ideological and political disputes that can separate them, despite their common concerns. Succeeding in having such conversations would itself represent a significant step in the right direction of demonstrating to emerging adults that it is possible to engage across differences without descending into conflict and war, that there is hope for the future of civic life in America, that it is possible to step back and set one's sights on higher, more worthwhile goals entailed in the common good.

What Is To Be Done?

It is not the normal business of sociologists to prescribe normative responses to the social realities they study. It is better, we generally think, to simply describe and explain the social world to and for others, and then to let various kinds of readers figure out what, if anything, they want to do about it. We are inclined to take that approach here as well. The problems we have raised in this book do not have easy answers, if indeed they have any, and in any case it is not clear that sociologists are the right people to figure out what the answers might be. To the extent that these are public problems, they require public discussions and responses to address them. And the responses appropriate in different social settings and communities will vary depending in part on the cultural and moral particulars of those settings and communities. There will be no one-size-fits-all response. So, we decline the opportunity to spell out a plan for what to do about emerging adult and American problems.

Nevertheless, at least some readers will wish to think through possible responses to the matters raised in this book, and we are willing to lay out a bit more thinking in response. First, we think it helpful to distinguish macrosocial institutions and forces from microsocial settings. We do not think anyone has much capacity to intentionally promote changes at the *macro level* that will much alter the character of emerging adulthood. Nobody is in a position to transform mass consumer capitalism, the globalizing economy, liberal individualism, and other macro-social factors that give form and content to emerging adulthood. Mobilized social and political movements in theory could have some effect, but we do not see signs of their forming and do not have a vision for what exactly they would look like. So, we do not have answers or solutions to offer that address the macro-social sources of the problems in emerging adult life. They seem to be a fact of life that must be understood, appreciated, criticized, and coped with. Having made the case for the deep cultural and institutional causes of emerging adulthood itself and its particular features highlighted in this book, we would be foolish to suggest that we or anyone has handy answers or solutions with which to affect helpful changes.

In theory, certain *middle-level* institutional reforms are conceivable that could ameliorate some of the problems discussed in this book. Given the personal, relational, and economic costs of alcohol abuse among teenagers and emerging adults, for example, the alcohol industry could be better regulated in, say, its marketing strategies to minors—just as the tobacco industry has become more highly regulated since the 1990s. We should be able to do much better on that front than asking for the voluntary, semiserious admonishments to "drink responsibly" offered in token by those who reap big profits from youth not drinking responsibly and in the context of advertisements that otherwise promote irresponsible drinking. Furthermore, American colleges and universities could shift slightly to strike a better balance between the *in-loco-parentis* model of institutional responsibility for student life outside of classrooms of former days and the "that's none of our business, so do as you please as long as it doesn't lead to lawsuits" approach that seems to be the modus operandi of many colleges and universities today. There is no reason why colleges and universities could not play a more proactive role in promoting and enforcing more responsible, healthy, and respectful lifestyles among their students than they do. Some universities already do this and do it well, we think. Insofar as colleges and universities themselves are morally accountable to the families of their students and to the social order that sustains them with resources, they could be asked to do more to foster better practices and outcomes.

For a third example, secondary schools could offer required classes in basic moral reasoning, which would not promote any one particular moral commitment but which would expose students to the issues, problems, and challenges involved and provide them with some intellectual tools for addressing them. Given the state of mass primary and secondary education in the United States today, that hope may be quixotic. Our point is simply that in theory it is possible. In the end such things flow from widespread social concerns and commitments that justify the devotion of resources to accomplish goals. Finally, as a fourth example, leaders in the American political system could somehow find ways to make politics and public debate more civil, less acrimonious, and more functional. That itself is a huge challenge that may or may not be possible. But we believe that any effective moves toward reform in that direction would have the effect of encouraging youth to be more hopeful about civic, public, and political life and involvement in it.

The closer most people get to the micro level of social life—the world of friendships, families, neighborhoods, local schools, voluntary associations, religious congregations, and so on—the more control and influence they can exert in those settings. Macro-social changes may seem impossibly out of reach and middle-level social changes quite difficult to affect. But that does not mean that everyone is helpless when it comes to micro-level practices and influences. People usually do have some limited but meaningful control over the choices they make that shape their lives, even when those choices are framed and constrained by larger social structures and forces. And those choices can make significant differences when it comes to the issues we have examined in this book.

Families, for example, can be intentional about their values, commitments, and lifestyles in ways that can have significant effects on their members. Not every American household, for instance, *must* watch television a great deal of the time. It is actually possible to find recreational activities besides going to the shopping mall. Often families can choose, for example, to eat more meals together than they typically do. Heads of families can in fact decide to practice and model for children generosity in the form of greater charitable and religious financial giving, volunteering, giving blood, and so on. Such choices are within the hands of families.

Similarly, adult friends and relatives of teenagers can intentionally stay in touch with them as they move into their twenties to continue their relationships into emerging adulthood. We know sociologically that emerging adults benefit from relational ties to mature adults outside of their age group. Whether emerging adults recognize it or not, they definitely need models, mentors, and conversation partners with older, more experienced adults who care for and about them—adults other than their parents. The less emerging adults are isolated from older, more mature adults, by being integrated into social worlds other than those created and populated by emerging adults, the better it is for those emerging adults. Yet those who care for and about emerging adults cannot rely on them to make this happen. Older friends, relatives, and mentors need to take the initiative to sustain and strengthen relationships and spend time with emerging adults.

Religious communities can play a role in all of this. Many emerging adults once belonged to communities of faith in younger years, where they presumably enjoyed the benefits of community, instruction in their faith, and moral teaching. Many religious congregations in fact devote significant resources to children and teenagers, yet unfortunately seem to passively accept that their ties to youth will be lost after the high school years. But this need not happen. There is no reason why churches, synagogues, temples, mosques, and other centers of local religious life cannot more proactively sustain old ties and build new ones to local emerging adults, both those in college and those not in college. Success in this would require thoughtful planning, intentionality, investment, and sustained effort. But we suspect that many religious communities could do a much better job at connecting with emerging adults and supporting them than many currently seem to be doing. And this would presumably be good both for the religious communities and the emerging adults involved.

Similarly, nonreligious voluntary and nonprofit organizations could do a better job of connecting to and attracting the involvement of 18- to 29-year-olds. We know that older adults are normally more likely to become civically involved in these kinds of local organizations. So it may seem easier for them to focus on older adults who are easier to recruit. But part of their own missions and social benefits could be reconceived as better relating to emerging adults and integrating them into their work. Again, success would require planning, intentionality, investment, and sustained effort, but it would also benefit both the voluntary and nonprofit organizations and the emerging adults involved.

Despite the overdetermining influence of very many macrosocial, cultural, and institutional forces that converge to create emerging adulthood itself as a phase in the American life course and to shape its character in the ways described above, people and groups at the local level of social life are not entirely helpless in responding to those forces. Emerging adulthood and all it entails is certainly not a matter of absolutely freely chosen, undetermined individual preference. It is a socially structured fact. Even so, it can be negotiated and navigated differently by emerging adults and those around them at the micro level, depending on the nature of their beliefs, commitments, relationships, and practices.

While micro-level alternatives or resistance to the mainstream will not directly change the mainstream anytime soon, they still can make a significant difference in the lives of real people and groups, and at the very least can avoid contributing to the social reproduction of problematic features of mainstream emerging adulthood. We would be naive to bring to the power of emerging adult life and culture what sociologists call an individualistic voluntarism that assumes that each person can live however they choose. But we would also be wrong to accept a kind of sociological determinism that assumes that people have little or no choice, in the midst of the social and cultural influences and forces that impinge upon them, about how to live their lives. We need in our understanding to balance and see the interaction of what sociologists call "structure and agency." Seeing the interplay between the two is what the sociological imagination is all about.

Having said all of this, however, we wish to close by returning to and re-emphasizing the idea of Christopher Lasch highlighted in the epigraph at the start of this conclusion: "There is only one cure for the malady that afflicts our culture, and that is to speak the truth about it. Once we can bring ourselves to do that, it will be time to worry about 'constructive solutions,' 'practical proposals,' and 'social alternatives' for our young—discussions of which, so long as they are so absurdly premature, serve only to distract our attention from the truth about ourselves."[12] That is, before anyone works on solutions, proposals, and alternative, it is necessary first to see, understand, and acknowledge the full truth about the problems of our larger culture and society that reveal themselves in the lives of so many emerging adults.

Until we grasp and accept the challenges and difficulties involved, proposed solutions and alternatives will likely be superficial and fruitless. The premature activism they would set into motion might make some people feel better about themselves and the world, but they will not likely effect actual substantial change. More important than immediately solving the problems examined in this book—as if they could be immediately solved—is owning up to the actual magnitude of the larger social and cultural troubles those problem point to and the mainstream institutions that they implicate. That itself is a major challenge. The purpose of this book is to shed some light on what we think are some helpful steps toward that end.

NOTES

Introduction

1. Thanks to Chris Eberle, Skip Smith, Sean Kelsey, Keith Meador, and Mark Regnerus for reading and providing feedback on sections of the earlier manuscript of this book.

2. That good has been documented by other observers, particularly by the leading scholar of emerging adulthood, Jeffrey Arnett; see Jeffrey Arnett, *Emerging Adulthood: The Winding Road from the Late Teens through the Twenties* (New York: Oxford University Press, 2004); Jeffrey Arnett and Jennifer Tanner, eds., *Emerging Adults in America: Coming of Age in the 21st Century* (Washington, DC: American Psychological Association, 2006); Jeffrey Arnett, *Adolescence and Emerging Adulthood: A Cultural Approach* (Upper Saddle River, NJ: Prentice Hall, 2009). A recent portrayal of emerging adult life that strikes us as altogether too rosy and optimistic is Richard Settersten and Barbara Ray, *Not Quite Adults: Why 20-Somethings Are Choosing a Slower Path to Adulthood, and Why It's Good for Everyone* (New York: Bantam Books, 2010).

3. We did not invent the idea of the sociological imagination. The term was originally coined by the Columbia University sociologist C. Wright Mills (1916–62) and developed in his book *The Sociological Imagination*, published in 1959 but still fresh and important today. Mills summarized the sociological imagination as "the intersection of biography and history," observing that,

> neither the life of an individual nor the history of a society can be understood without understanding both. Yet people do not usually define the troubles they endure in terms of historical change and institutional contradiction.... What they need ... is ... the sociological imagination.... The sociological imagination enables us to grasp history and biography and the relations between the two within a society. That is its task and its promise.

By this Mills meant that people need to develop the ability to see that our individual biographies are profoundly shaped by our social, cultural, and institutional environments—that our "personal" and "private" experiences are embedded within and profoundly shaped by our place in history and society. That is the

general perspective that underwrites all sociological analysis and explanation.
See C. Wright Mills, *The Sociological Imagination* (New York: Oxford University
Press, 2000), 3–24.

4. Max Weber, *The Methodology of the Social Sciences*, Edward Shils and Henry Finch,
eds. (New York: Free Press, 1949).

5. Gariel Abend, "Two Main Problems in the Sociology of Morality," *Theory and
Society* 37 (2008): 87–125. Note that Abend endorses a modified Weberian view,
not the Durkheimian approach adopted here.

6. Robert N. Bellah, Richard Madsen, William M. Sullivan, Ann Swidler, and Steven
M. Tipton, *Habits of the Heart: Individualism and Commitment in American Life*
(Berkeley: University of California Press, 1985); Robert Bellah, "The Ethical
Aims of Social Inquiry," in *Social Science as Moral Inquiry*, ed. N. Hann, Robert N.
Bellah, Paul Rabinow, and William M. Sullivan (New York: Columbia University
Press, 1983), 360–81; Philip Selznick, *The Moral Commonwealth* (Berkeley: Uni-
versity of California Press, 1992); Amitai Etzioni, *The Active Society* (New York:
Free Press, 1968); Amitai Etzioni, *The New Golden Rule: Community and Morality
in a Democratic Society* (New York: Basic Books, 1996); see Alan Wolfe, *Whose
Keeper? Social Science and Moral Obligation* (Berkeley: University of California
Press, 1989).

7. For a more detailed exposition of the approach to sociology and "the good" that
informs this book, see Christian Smith, *What Is a Person?: Rethinking Humanity,
Social Life, and the Moral Good from the Person Up* (Chicago: University of Chicago Press, 2010), especially 384–490.

8. Guttmacher Institute, *U.S. Teenage Pregnancies, Births, and Abortions: National and
State Trends and Trends by Race and Ethnicity* (http://www.guttmacher.org/pubs/
USTPtrends.pdf).

9. National Center for Education Statistics, *Digest of Education Statistics: 2009*, U.S.
Department of Education (http://nces.ed.gov/programs/digest/d09/), specifically tables 202 and 331, available at http://nces.ed.gov/programs/digest/d09/
tables/dt09_202.asp and http://nces.ed.gov/programs/digest/d09/tables/
dt09_331.asp.

10. Maria Krysan, 2008, "Data Update to *Racial Attitudes in America*," an update and
website to complement Howard Schuman, Charlotte Steeh, Lawrence Bobo,
and Maria Krysan, *Racial Attitudes in America: Trends and Interpretations*, rev. ed.
(Cambridge, MA: Harvard University Press, 1997), http://www.igpa.uillinois.
edu/programs/racial-attitudes/. Tyrone Forman, "Beyond Prejudice? Young
Whites' Racial Attitudes in Post–Civil Rights America, 1976–2000," paper presented at 17th International Sociological Association World Congress of Sociology, Gothenburg, Sweden, July 11–17, 2010.

11. See Joe McIlhaney and Freda Bush, *Hooked: New Science on How Casual Sex Is
Affecting Our Children* (Chicago: Northfield, 2008).

12. The alternative possibility is that our observations of emerging adult culture
reflect instead what scholars call a "cohort effect." In that case, older adults would
not share the problems of emerging adulthood. Something unique about the
troubled character of the culture of the rising cohort of emerging adults would
then be newly introduced into American culture by that rising generation. Our
view is that, while particular elements of today's generation of emerging adults
may be accentuating certain aspects of our broader American culture in new ways

that are influencing the larger culture, emerging adults stand in strong continuity with the assumptions, values, goals, and morality of the broader culture to which they belong.

13. At the same time, however, we want to restate: this book is not merely a simple conservative bemoaning of the moral degeneration of liberal society, not simply a new version of "slouching towards Gomorrah." As individuals, we authors do of course have our own social and political views. But none of us is consistently liberal or conservative in our outlooks. The analysis that follows, in fact, ascribes blame as much to some conservative sacred cows as it does to liberal idols. More importantly, our story is driven not by a concern to promote some political or social ideology or agenda. We are driven rather by a real concern for the personal well-being of young Americans whose lives are now being influenced and will continue to be, often for the worse, by problematic aspects of contemporary emerging adult life that we describe in this book. And we are concerned for the condition of American culture more broadly, a culture that is problematic we think for both conservative and liberal reasons.

14. Jeffrey Arnett, "Emerging Adulthood: Understanding the New Way of Coming of Age," in *Emerging Adults in America: Coming of Age in the 21st Century*, ed. Jeffrey Arnett and Jennifer Tanner (Washington, DC: American Psychological Association, 2006), 5.

15. Some of the statistics about emerging adulthood today are not historically unique. For example, young Americans in the nineteenth and very early twentieth centuries, when society was more rural and agricultural, also married later in life than they did in the 1950s. But changes in the larger culture and social order in late-twentieth-century America make the experience of emerging adulthood today very different from the young adulthood of a century ago. Today's unprecedented freedom and mobility, availability of lifestyle options, and greater influence of secular culture make the years between 18 and 30 less orderly and in various ways more risky for most.

16. Robert Schoeni and Karen Ross, "Material Assistance from Families during the Transition to Adulthood," in *On the Frontiers of Adulthood*, ed. Richard Settersten, Frank Furstenberg, and Rubén Rumbaut (Chicago: University of Chicago Press, 2005), 396–416.

17. Jeffrey Arnett, *Emerging Adulthood: The Winding Road from the Late Teens through the Twenties* (New York: Oxford University Press, 2004).

18. Jean Twenge, *Generation Me: Why Today's Young Americans Are More Confident, Assertive, Entitled—and More Miserable Than Ever Before* (New York: Free Press, 2006); Richard Kadison and Theresa DiGeronimo, *College of the Overwhelmed: The Campus Mental Health Crisis and What to Do About It* (San Francisco: Jossey-Bass, 2004).

19. Our study, the National Study of Youth and Religion (NSYR), is funded for a fourth wave of data collection in 2013, which should produce empirical answers to the question about the religious and spiritual lives of 24- to 29-year-olds.

20. For detailed information about the research methodology used in the first wave of the NSYR, see Christian Smith and Melinda Lundquist Denton, *Methodological Design and Procedures for the National Survey of Youth and Religion (NSYR)* (Chapel Hill, NC: National Study of Youth and Religion, 2003); and Christian Smith, with Melinda Lundquist Denton, *Soul Searching: The*

Religious and Spiritual Lives of American Teenagers (New York: Oxford University Press, 2005), 272–310. On the research methodology used in the second wave of NSYR, see Christian Smith, Lisa Pearce, and Melinda Lundquist Denton, *Methodological Design and Procedures for the National Study of Youth and Religion (NSYR) Longitudinal Telephone Survey (Waves 1 & 2)* (Chapel Hill, NC: National Study of Youth and Religion, 2006). On the third wave, see Christian Smith, Lisa Pearce, and Melinda Lundquist Denton, *National Study of Youth and Religion Telephone Survey Codebook Introduction and Methods (Waves 1, 2 & 3)* (Chapel Hill, NC: National Study of Youth and Religion, 2008). Much but not all of the analysis of the data to date has focused on the religious and spiritual lives of youth, even though most of the data collected is not about religion. For example, Melinda Lundquist Denton and Christian Smith published the book *Soul Searching: The Religious and Spiritual Lives of American Teenagers* in 2005 (New York: Oxford University Press), based on what we learned from that first wave of data collected. Lisa Pearce and Melinda Denton published a book based on the second wave of data collected, entitled *A Faith of Their Own: Stability and Change in the Religiosity of America's Adolescents* (New York: Oxford University Press, 2010). And Christian Smith, along with Patricia Snell, published in a book in 2009 entitled *Souls in Transition: The Religious and Spiritual Lives of Emerging Adults* (New York: Oxford University Press), based on findings from the third wave of data. For a full list of the many other books, articles, and reports based on NSYR data, see the project website: http://www.youthandreligion.org/. The NSYR, however, contains immense amounts of data not about religion, and this book is an NSYR-based report not focused on religion but on the character of emerging adulthood more generally. After writing *Souls in Transition*, it was clear that there was much more that needed to be told about the world of emerging adults, which gave rise to this book.

21. Others are welcome to analyze more closely the social locations of the views we examine here, as well as other cultural outlooks, providing more nuanced and structural understandings of the different kinds of outlooks raised by our analysis. For our present purposes, however, we stay focused on the dominant themes of the big picture.

22. This is not mere speculation. In setting up our third wave of interviews, we encountered some cases where emerging adults who had done interviews with us previously as teenagers did not want to do personal interviews a third time, and their reluctance seemed clearly to have to do with not wanting to talk about certain personal matters. Upon inspection of their three waves of survey answers to questions about sex and partying, it was clear that in the preceding years they had gotten into things that were viewed as bad in their religious and family (e.g., conservative evangelical) backgrounds. It was obvious on the phone that they were uncomfortable with the idea of more interviews.

23. Of our original first-wave sample, at least 14 respondents were unable to complete the subsequent third-wave survey because they were deceased (that number could be higher, since the dispositions of some other incomplete cases are unknown). We are unable to determine the exact cause of death in most of those cases, but we do know from our survey-respondent tracking efforts that not all of these cases were natural and military deaths. In addition, 27 of our first-wave cases

were institutionalized and thus unable to complete subsequent surveys, and two were incapacitated in some other way.

Chapter 1

Epigraph: Charles Taylor, *Sources of the Self* (Cambridge, MA: Harvard University Press, 1989), 27–28, 41. We could have just as well quoted Michael Polanyi: "Sociology [has] developed a program for explaining human affairs without making distinctions between good and evil. Our true convictions [are] being left without theoretical foundation.... Our morally neutral account of all human affairs has caused our youth, and our educated people in general, to regard all moral professions as mere deceptions—or at best as self-deceptions. For once we induce ourselves to regard all established rules of moral conduct as mere conventions, we must come to suspect our own moral motives, and thus our best impulses are silenced and driven underground.... In other words, we also have been busily engaged in laying the groundwork for nihilism." Michael Polanyi, *Meaning* (Chicago: University of Chicago Press, 1975), 22, 23. We might also have quoted Pascal: "True nature having been lost, everything becomes natural. In the same way, the true good having been lost, everything becomes their true good"; or, "Those who lead disordered lives say to those who lead ordered ones that it is they who stray from nature, and believe themselves to follow it; like those on board ship think people on shore are moving away.... We need a fixed point to judge it. The harbor judges those on board a ship. But where will we find a fixed harbor in morals?" Blaise Pascal, *Pensées and Other Writings* (New York: Oxford University Press, 2008), 7, 132. And we might also have quoted Wendell Berry: "It must be asked if we can remove cultural value from one part of our lives without destroying it also in other parts." Wendell Berry, "The Use of Energy," in *The Art of the Commonplace: Agrarian Essays of Wendell Berry* (Washington, DC: Shoemaker and Hoard, 2002), 288.

1. Moral issues, perspectives, and stories could have and often did come up during any part of our interviews, but the following questions are those we asked in the interview section specifically about morality:

> Imagine a distant relative died and left you $100,000. What would you do with the money? Why? Is there anything else you might do with it?
>
> How do you normally decide or know what is good and bad, right and wrong in life? In general, is it easy or hard for you to decide between right and wrong? Has deciding between right and wrong gotten easier or harder over the past 2 years? Why?
>
> Can you tell me about a specific situation you've been in recently where you were unsure of what was right and wrong? How did you decide what to do? Why that?
>
> What about doing right instead of wrong? How easy or hard is it for you to actually do what you know is right?
>
> What do you think it is that makes something right or wrong? [Example probe for "consequences": What kinds of consequences would make something wrong?] [Example probe for "feelings": What kinds of feelings do you mean? Where do these feelings come from, in your view?] [ONLY if stuck] Is it rules or laws? Consequences? How it feels? God's will? Something else?
>
> Some people say that there really are no final rights and wrongs in life, that everything is relative, that morality is simply what people make it for themselves or their culture. Do you agree or disagree? Why?

From where have you acquired your moral views? Where do they come from?

Have your views about right and wrong changed over the past three years, or not? Why? In what ways?

Some people say that the world is always changing and we should adjust our views of what is morally right and to reflect those changes. What do you think of that view?

Some people believe that it is sometimes okay to break moral rules if it works to your advantage and you can get away with it. What do you think about that? [IF THINKS WRONG] Why exactly is that wrong?

Do you think people have any moral obligation to help others or not? [If yes] Can you give me some examples of ways we are obligated to help others? Why? What if someone just wasn't interested in helping others? Would that be a problem or no? Why? Are there certain situations in which an obligation to others ends? Why or why not? Are there any types of people or groups of people who you believe are more or less deserving of help?

Whether we like to admit it or not, we all look down on some people or feel like we're better than some people at least some of the time. At the times in your life when you've felt this way, what kinds of people did you have these thoughts about? Why? [IF UNCLEAR] What do these people have in common, do you think?

Now, are there any kinds of people you really look up to? What kind of people would you like to be more like? Why? [IF UNCLEAR] What do these people have in common?

If you could change one thing about the world today, what would it be? Why?

I want to follow-up on a question we asked in our survey that you completed. You may recall that we asked: "If you were unsure of what was right or wrong in a particular situation, how would you decide what to do? Would you most likely . . .

1. do what would make you feel happy,
2. do what would help you to get ahead,
3. follow the advice of a parent or teacher, or other adult you respect, or
4. do what you think God or the scripture tells you is right?"

So my question here is: What is your answer to that question and why? Why do you choose that answer instead of the others? [Probe] Is there anything wrong with the answers you did not choose?

These questions were posed and discussed in a highly conversational style.
2. A lot, though not all, of these we actually removed from the quotes in this chapter, simply to help make them comprehensible.
3. We realize that speaking of "truth" in such a context is itself contentious, but for a defense of our meaning here, see Christian Smith, *What Is a Person?: Reconsidering Humanity, Social Life, and the Moral Good from the Person Up* (Chicago: University of Chicago Press, 2010), especially 119–219.

4. By "moral relativism" we mean the descriptive belief that moral standards are culturally defined—that the truth or falsity of moral claims and judgments is not
universal or objective but instead relative to the particular historical and cultural
beliefs, views, traditions, and practices of particular groups of people, which leads
to the normative belief that everyone ought to tolerate all of the moral beliefs and
belief-justified behaviors of others, even when they are very different from our
own cultural or moral standards, since no universal or objective moral standard
exists by which to judge their beliefs and behaviors.

5. That is, they mostly unquestioningly presuppose that most things about the sociocultural world are not fixed or given facts of nature but rather human constructions
invented through shared social definitions and practices that are historically contingent, changeable, and particular. It apparently has not required emerging adults
attending multiple anthropology, sociology, and postmodern humanities classes
for most of them to have arrived at this view. For many, it appears that the sheer
impact of the realization of the particularity of the conditions in which they were
raised drives them to assume this de facto social constructionism. When they were
younger, like anyone else, their personally experienced reality was, for them, simply reality. Now that they have grown older, have met some different people, and
maybe have seen some of the world, they seem keenly aware that they were raised
in a very particular way that is different from the way others were raised. Sociology
and anthropology show that human cultures are indeed significantly socially constructed and vary in certain ways across time and space. That awareness by most
emerging adults presses them—for better or worse—to relativize their own perspectives. For instance, they repeatedly frame and qualify their views on life with
statements such as "Well, at least for how I was raised I feel that . . ." and "For other
people it's different, but for me I tend to think that . . ." For example, one emerging
adult observed, "Being raised in a certain culture you have certain norms for what
are moral. I guess for me there is a certain way to act based on my culture. But if
someone else is coming with a different perspective, they would maybe have a different outcome, based on what they believe." Often these are not intentionally
expressed statements of feelings replacing thought or opinions replacing beliefs
but rather unconscious habits of speech reflecting larger cultural norms.

  To whatever degree it is intentional, however, the phrase "I feel that" has
frequently replaced the phrases "I think that," "I believe that," and "I would argue
that"—a shift in language use that expresses an essentially subjectivistic and
"emotivistic" approach to moral reasoning and rational argument; see Alasdair
MacIntyre, *After Virtue: A Study in Moral Theory* (Notre Dame, IN: Notre Dame
University Press, 1984). Consider, for instance, this emerging adult's use of "feel"
12 times in seven sentences: "Morality is how I feel too, because in my heart, I
could feel it. You could feel what's right or wrong in your heart as well as your
mind. Most of the time, I always felt, I feel it in my heart and it makes it easier for
me to morally decide what's right and wrong. Because if I feel about doing something, I'm going to feel it in my heart, and if it feels good, then I'm going to do it.
But if it doesn't feel good, I'm going to know, because then I'm going to be nervous
and I'm going to be tensed, and it's not going to feel good. It's not going to feel
right. So it's like I got that feeling as well as thinking." One of the apparent effects of
this culturally relativistic view and the continual self-relativizing to which it leads
is speech in which claims are not staked, rational arguments are not developed,

differences are not engaged, nature (that is, the natural world, the reality beyond what humans construct) is not referenced, and universals are not recognized. Rather, differences in viewpoints and ways of life—including religious ones—are mostly acknowledged, respected, and then set aside as incommensurate and off limits for evaluation.

6. To be sure, however, other emerging adults disagree in firmer terms. For example: "I don't think morality is relative and the fact that most people today think it's relative is, I think, one of the reasons our society is on such a downward spiral. In television, in the movies, and even in art, and I'm really liberal when it comes to art, but I don't think morality is relative. We make it relative to make ourselves feel better in a way." And: "I would definitely say that morals are more even fluid now than they were ten years ago. You have to watch TV to know that, maybe it's not good, but people are more and more okay with more things. Think of promiscuity and that kind of thing, that is just everywhere now. That you never would've seen ten, fifteen, twenty years ago. That just wasn't the way that it worked. But people don't see it as morally wrong now because it's socially accepted, no matter how I feel about it or each individual or a religion or however, but it's accepted. So obviously morals change over time, and now they're fluid, they are things that change because of experience, because of situation, because of just an individual person."

7. Thanks to Chris Eberle, our ever-helpful philosopher at the U.S. Naval Academy, for pointing out this problem and these distinctions, as well as offering some of the language we use here, including the label "reluctant moral agnostics and skeptics."

8. To be specific, it is possible as a moral realist to believe, for instance, in universally binding moral standards that are applied in all situations (such as "It is never morally permissible for anyone to steal anything from another person"). It is also possible to be a moral realist and believe in universally binding moral standards that apply to only *some* circumstances or situations ("It is never permissible for anyone to steal anything from another person, unless that other person intends to use the item to commit a grave evil, which the stealing will prevent"). It is also possible to be a moral realist and believe in some *non*universally binding standards that apply in *all* circumstances ("Nearly all people [certain kinds of government and military spies being an exception] should not steal anything from another person"). And it is possible to believe as a moral realist in certain *non*universally binding standards that apply in only *some* circumstances ("No student in this college may, as long as they are enrolled, steal anything from a fellow student, unless that stealing is part of an official ice-breaker game played during new-student orientation, the rules of which sanction stealing certain objects").

9. Consider, for instance, this case related by an emerging adult in a discussion about moral dilemmas:

> Recently on a job, at work, I was working for the first time on overtime, and we had a patient we found lying on the floor, and we lifted the patient up, put her on the bed, and elevated her feet because we couldn't get her blood pressure. We called for the medics. I know that the medics are supposed to try to run the line to give her fluids. [But] the [medic] guy made up [i.e., fabricated] a blood pressure, because me and my partner tried, and neither one of us got one. He's been on the job for, like, five or six years. We knew he made it up, and then he wanted us to take her out. Mind you, every time we tried to tip the lady up, she's fighting to lay back

down. So already, a light bulb goes off, like, she's comfortable down there, it's easier for her to breathe. But on my job, he's a higher medical authority, so I have to listen to him. Basically, to make a long story short, when we got to the staircase, the lady went into cardiac arrest. So the whole time the job was going on, I knew that that wasn't the right thing to do, but I didn't know what to say because they were higher medical authority, and I'm supposed to listen to them, because their knowledge is beyond ours. That's the idea, anyway. [And how do you decide what to do in that situation?] I did as per what the guy tells us to do. Basically, they have control of the scene. So I did as he asked me to. [You followed protocol?] Yeah.

In this instance, this emerging adult was at least aware of a moral truth that was distinct from the imperative to follow a superior's orders. Yet it still operates as a cautionary tale of the dangers of defining morality per se by the content of positive law and by obedience to regulations and rules.

10. For example: "Whether morals are relative is a hard one to say, because I'm not the type of person to say my religion is right, this is how it should be, but at the same time, that's what I follow. I think different religions in different parts of the country have different ways of living. I don't consider them right, but I can't say that their religion or belief is wrong, but I don't think you can really change morals. I think . . . wow, that's a hard question. I think there's right and wrong, I don't think you can change them." Also, concerning where right or wrong come from: "I don't know. I guess it's kind of a mixture between religion and society. Society has their own views of what's right or wrong as far as their morals, what most people believe in. And religion is the same way, you go by the Bible as far as what all is in the Bible. [What about the fact that people in society think different about morality and religion?] It's an opinion, opinion." Another spoke about how to discern eternal and changing moral truths:

> I think it is spoken tricky kind of. Yeah, I think the world is always changing, and I think your beliefs and stuff should remain the same. You should just find a more modern way to keep that same belief true. If you believe like doing wrong to others is wrong, you have to find what's wrong these days. I think about this a lot because my religion that my family was raised is like really dated now. So the belief is the same, and then the things involved are different. It plays out differently. The names of things change, the objects involved change, the people change, but the idea is still the same and it plays out kind of the same way.

One last example: "I think you have to eventually answer to yourself and answer to God, but I mean, that's your decision to do that, kind of cheat on yourself in the end."

11. Consider three examples of how emerging adults combine multiple approaches and criteria, including religious, to moral issues. First: "Just my own, my two beliefs that you have to treat people as you'd like to be treated and leave the world a better place than you found it. So long as the religion abides by those two rules, then it's cool with me." Second:

> Oh, man. I definitely learn by cause and effect, and trial and error. But a lot of my ethical and moral decisions, I feel like had come from a compilation

of what I've learned in my life and from what I've just developed as my personal beliefs. You know, often times like if I'm really stuck on something, I'll pray about it, or I definitely talk to friends about you know like, "Oh! You know I'm in this situation, what do you think I should do? Do you think I should go this way or that way?" Because I really enjoy hearing what other people say they would do because I feel like a personal decision, while it's personal, is better off if you have some sort of basis on where it would—how it effects the people around you and how they would go about fixing whatever problem it is or you know, doing whatever it is that needs to be done.

Third:

Probably three main things I do [to make moral decisions]. The first thing I'd probably do just naturally is think about it reflectively. Just like, what do I think, what do I feel about this? Is it a logical choice kind of thing? But I'd probably consult, alongside that I'd probably then just consult the spiritual beliefs. Is this religiously, does this have impact? Is this against what I believe? And the third one is probably just consult friends, and peers, and adults. Since I do have a close relationship with my parents I usually ask them a lot of questions, and I just like to just hear a lot of points of view. Unfortunately, I did this when I was deciding to go or not go to grad school, and about every other person had a different opinion. So at the end of it, half of the people I consulted said to go, and half of them said not to.

Also, consider this somewhat post-Christian case:

How I decide moral issues is a tough question. I would say intuition. But I think it's a lot more than that. I think a lot of it has to do with the way I was raised by my parents, as much as I'd like to think I'm different from my parents. I know that I'm really similar to my parents and I go on a lot of what my parents raised me, what was right and wrong and treating other people with respect and all those sorts of things. Basically being a kind person. I think my parents beat that into me pretty well and I think I would feel weird doing otherwise. I would say I still draw a lot on my experience with this religious group of friends and I would still consider myself more of a secular Christian and at least in terms of social justice, following Christian teachings, like putting others before yourself, I think that's still something that's pretty important to me even if I might not believe the religious part of it, I still believe in the secular part of doing good.

12. For more on that theme, see Christian Smith, with Patricia Snell, *Souls in Transition: The Religious and Spiritual Lives of Emerging Adults* (New York: Oxford University Press, 2009).
13. That increase is most likely explained by the opportunity in long, in-depth, personal interviews, in which rapport with interviewers develops, for respondents to ponder various circumstances and options and as a result realize scenarios in

which they might in fact violate moral standards—in contrast to the social-desirability bias often operating during surveys with anonymous survey interviewers asking closed-ended questions.

14. These answer categories are rooted theoretically in the four types of languages (republicanism, biblical, expressive individualism, and utilitarian individualism) offered in Robert N. Bellah, Richard Madsen, William M. Sullivan, Ann Swidler, and Steven M. Tipton, *Habits of the Heart: Individualism and Commitment in American Life* (Berkeley: University of California Press, 1985); this question has been profitably used in numerous other surveys. (The answers provided were randomly rotated to avoid an answer-order bias.)

15. Remember, however, that the categories here are not mutually exclusive, such that an emerging adult can talk in the interview about moral instinct, doing what would make them happy, the influence of a guilty conscience, and relying on authorities.

16. For thoughtful sociological reflections on the significance of this observation, see Stephen Vaisey, "Motivation and Justification: A Dual-Process Model of Culture in Action," *American Journal of Sociology* 114, no. 6 (2009): 1675–1715; Stephen Vaisey, "Socrates, Skinner, and Aristotle: Three Ways of Thinking about Culture in Action," *Sociological Forum* 23, no. 3(2008): 603–13.

17. By which we mean something like a set of principles, laws, and/or natural tendencies—including moral facts or laws that certain things are right or wrong, good or bad—that are inherent in the given order of nature or the structures of reality, as opposed to being created by human beings, and are therefore universally valid.

18. For our respondents, the context of this question was unmistakably a discussion of morality. The questions asked just prior to this moral-dilemmas question were: "How do you normally decide or know what is good and bad, right and wrong in life? In general, is it easy or hard for you to decide between right and wrong? Has deciding between right and wrong gotten easier or harder over the past 2 years? Why?" We therefore do not think that the majority of emerging adults' inability to engage the matter of moral dilemmas, seen below, is the result of overly ambiguous questions.

19. A 2002 *U.S. News & World Report* article cited a Zogby International survey of 401 randomly selected U.S. college seniors, which was commissioned by the National Association of Scholars. Seventy-three percent of the surveyed students said that when their college professors taught about ethical issues, the usual message was that uniform standards of right and wrong don't exist, and that "what is right and wrong depends on differences in individual values and cultural diversity." The sample is small, but the findings do not seem unlikely. John Leo, "Professors Who See No Evil," *U.S. News and World Report*, July 22, 2002, 14.

20. Flannery O'Connor, *The Habit of Being: Letters* (New York: Farrar, Straus, and Giroux, 1979), 100.

21. Marx's original remark is: "The ruling ideas are the ideas of the ruling class," or, in a more literal translation, "The ideas of the ruling class are in every epoch the ruling ideas." Karl Marx, "The German Ideology," in *The Marx-Engels Reader*, ed. Robert Tucker (New York: Norton, 1978), 172. We think social life is more complicated than Marx believed, and that cultural ideologies are more powerful than the logics of class relations—hence our emphasis here on social institutions.

22. Just like we ourselves in this chapter are not pushing particular positions on substantive moral issues but are rather calling for better thinking about how to sort out moral issues.

23. For a counter argument, see Christian Smith, *Moral, Believing Animals: Human Personhood and Culture* (New York: Oxford University Press, 2003).

24. Wendell Berry, "Sex, Economy, Freedom, and Community," in *The Art of the Commonplace: Agrarian Essays of Wendell Berry* (Washington, DC: Shoemaker and Hoard, 2002), 181. Berry continues: "In order to survive, a plurality of true communities would require not egalitarianism and tolerance but knowledge, an understanding of the necessity of local differences, and respect. Respect, I think, always implies imagination—the ability to see one another, across our individual differences, as living souls."

25. Charles Taylor, *Sources of the Self* (Cambridge, MA: Harvard University Press, 1989), 90.

Chapter 2

Epigraph: Blaise Pascal, *Pensées and Other Writings* (New York: Oxford University Press, 2008), 10.

1. Judith Lichtenberg, "Consuming Because Others Consume," *Social Theory and Practice* 22 (1996): 273–97. This article helps explain why emerging adults may feel the *need* to consume such items, because in a world where they have become ubiquitous, it is a real disadvantage not to have them. Human "needs" in consumption are thus defined not by objective need but by what people around them consume.

2. Martha Nussbaum, *Not For Profit: Why Democracy Needs the Humanities* (Princeton, NJ: Princeton University Press, 2010); Nussbaum, *Cultivating Humanity: A Classical Defense of Reform in Liberal Education* (Cambridge, MA: Harvard University Press, 1998); Louis Menand, *The Marketplace of Ideas: Reform and Resistance in the American University* (New York: Norton, 2010).

3. Not earning a college degree, however, has the drastic consequence of low wages for the vast majority of those who do not attend college, raising the larger question of a livable minimum wage, which we cannot of course pursue here.

4. This case was among only 16 out of the 230 emerging adults (6.96 percent) we interviewed who mentioned at any time during their interview the importance, value, or goal of learning contentment in life—otherwise, the idea of wanting to be content was absent from our interviews.

5. See Zygmunt Bauman, *Does Ethics Have a Chance in a World of Consumers?* (Cambridge, MA: Harvard University Press, 2008).

6. See, for example, Eric Greenberg and Carl Weber, *Generation We: How Millennial Youth are Taking Over America and Changing the World Forever* (Emeryville, CA: Pachatusen, 2008); Morley Winograd and Michael Hais, *Millennial Makeover: MySpace, YouTube, and the Future of American Politics* (New Brunswick, NJ: Rutgers University Press, 2008); Neil Howe and William Strauss, *Millennials Rising: The Next Great Generation* (New York: Vintage, 2000); Roger Bissessar, *Spirit of Youth: Empowering a New Generation* (Bloomington, IN: Trafford, 2006); Joseph Vogel, *The Obama Movement: Why Barak Obama Speaks to America's Youth* (Bloomington, IN: iUniverse, 2007); John Bartlett, *The Future Is Ours: A Handbook for Student Activists in the 21st Century* (New York: Holt, 1996); Melvin Delgado and

Lee Staples, *Youth-Led Community Organizing* (New York: Oxford University Press, 2007); Barry Checkoway and Lorraine Gutierrez, eds., *Youth Participation and Community Change* (New York: Routledge, 2006); Leoisa Ardizonne, *Getting My Word Out: Voices of Urban Youth Activists* (Albany: State University of New York Press, 2007).

Chapter 3

Epigraph: Christopher Lasch, "What's Wrong with the Right?" *Tikkun* 1 (1987): 26. We might have also quoted Wendell Berry: "It should tell us something that in healthy societies drug use is celebrative, convivial, and occasional, whereas among us it is lonely, shameful, and addictive. We need drugs, apparently, because we have lost each other." Wendell Berry, *The Art of the Commonplace* (Washington, DC: Shoemaker and Hoard, 2002), 61.

1. For example, raising the legal drinking age to 21, along with the influence of other cultural and political movements against drunk driving, have helped to significantly reduce the number of traffic accidents and fatalities in the United States since the 1970s; see http://www.nih.gov/about/researchresultsforthepublic/AlcoholRelatedTrafficDeaths.pdf.

2. It is actually possible, if not likely, that heavy drinkers cooperate with social research telephone surveys at lower rates, meaning that the incidence in the actual population is higher than these reported numbers.

3. Binge drinking is here defined by the National Institute of Health standard of consuming five or more alcoholic drinks (for males; four for females) on one occasion. The exact question wording was: "How many times, if at all, over the past two weeks have you drunk at least [If female: '4'] [If male: '5'] drinks in the same night? ('One drink is a 12-ounce bottle or can of beer; a 4-ounce glass of wine; a 12-ounce bottle or can of wine cooler; or a 1.25-ounce shot of liquor, either straight or in a mixed drink.')"

4. These statistics on 18- to 25-year-olds come not from the NSYR but from Substance Abuse and Mental Health Services Administration, Office of Applied Studies, *Results from the 2007 National Survey on Drug Use and Health: National Findings* (Rockville, MD: Department of Health and Human Services, NSDUH Series H-34, DHHS Publication NO. SMA 08-4343, September 2008), http://oas.samhsa.gov/NSDUH/2k7NSDUH/2k7results.cfm#2.3.

5. Ibid. This increase is not surprising, since many emerging adults have reached the age of legal drinking and smoking and are in structural positions that make alcohol and drugs highly available (being in college, living on their own, etc.).

6. As defined by their own self-report.

7. See the description below, under "Partiers," of one interviewee who was badly beaten up at a college party.

8. R. Hingson, T. Heeren, M. Winter, and H. Wechsler, "Magnitude of Alcohol-Related Mortality and Morbidity among U.S. College Students Ages 18–24: Changes from 1998 to 2001," *Annual Review of Public Health* 26 (2005): 259–79; L. Johnson, P. O'Mally, J. Bachman, and J. Schulenberg, *Monitoring the Future National Survey Results on Drug Use, 1975–2007* (Bethesda, MD: National Institute of Health, National Institute on Drug Abuse, 2008, Publication No. 08-6418A), 26; D. Dawson, B. Grant, F. Stinson, and P. Chou, "Another Look at Heavy Episodic Drinking and Alcohol Use Disorders among College and Non-College Youth," *Journal for the Study of Alcohol* 65, no. 4 (2004): 477–88; U.S. Department

of Health and Human Services, *What Colleges Need to Know Now: An Update on College Drinking Research* (Bethesda, MD: National Institute of Health, National Institute of Alcohol Abuse and Alcoholism, November 2007, Publication No. 07-5010). Related findings from these studies include the following: about one in four college students reports negative academic consequences of drinking alcohol, such as missing class, falling behind in work, doing poorly on exams and papers, and earning low grades; more than one in ten college students report that they have vandalized property while under the influence of alcohol; self-reports show that 31 percent of college students meet the criteria for a diagnosis of alcohol abuse and 6 percent for a diagnosis of alcohol dependence in the previous 12 months; about one in twenty four-year college students become involved with the police or campus security as a result of their drinking alcohol; alcohol is involved in 36 percent of traffic deaths among 16- to 20-year-olds. Again, binge drinking here is defined by the National Institute of Health standard of consuming five or more alcoholic drinks for males, or four for females, on one occasion, though studies show that many students consume more than five drinks at one time— see, for example, Aaron White, Courtney Kraus, and Harry Swartzwelder, "Many College Freshmen Drink at Levels Far Beyond the Binge Threshold," *Alcoholism: Clinical and Experimental Research* 30, no. 6 (2006): 1006–10.

9. See George Dowdall, *College Drinking: Reframing a Social Problem* (Westport, CT: Praeger, 2009); and Mark Hickson III and Julian Roebuck, *Deviance and Crime in Colleges and Universities: What Goes on in the Halls of Ivy* (Springfield, IL: Charles Thomas, 2009).

10. *Ninth Special Report to the U.S. Congress on Alcohol and Health from the Secretary of Health and Human Services* (Rockville, MD: USDHHS, Public Health Service, Alcohol, Drug Abuse and Mental Health Administration, National Institute on Alcohol Abuse and Alcoholism, June 1997); Laura Kann, Charles W. Warren, William A. Harris, Janet L. Collins, Barbara I. Williams, James G. Ross, and Lloyd J. Kolbe, "Youth Risk Behavior Surveillance—United States, 1995," *Morbidity and Mortality Weekly Report Surveillance Summaries* 45, no. SS-4 (September 27, 1996): 1–84.

11. David Nutt, Leslie King, Lawrence Phillips, on behalf of the Independent Scientific Committee on Drugs, "Drug Harms in the UK: A Multicriteria Decision Analysis," *Lancet* 376 (2010): 1558–65, doi:10.1016/S0140-6736(08)61345-8.

12. http://www.monitoringthefuture.org/data/05data/pr05t13.pdf.

13. The 46 nonusers we interviewed gave these types of reasons (with the number citing the reason in parentheses) for why they don't imbibe, inhale, or inject: feelings of personal responsibility and concern about future aspirations (17), health concerns (14), religious reasons (13), just "not interested" (13), having seen damage caused by another's substance abuse (9), not wanting to get in trouble or break the law (5), social networks discourage it (4), general moral objections (3).

14. Two more such testimonies:

> Before we started going to church my dad actually was an alcoholic. Him and my mom lived together but they didn't really get along. We've seen them totally change into parents that just raised us and loved us. So not alcohol, because I knew, I've seen what my dad went through. My mom and dad both smoked and I'd say I seen what they went through, and pot, drugs, and I've seen what my uncle has turned himself into.

And: "My family actually has a history of being alcoholics, so I've always been thankful that we've had the rule not to drink, because I don't want to become an alcoholic. And my sister also used drugs, and that just scared us a lot."

15. This also fits well our thesis at the end of this chapter about the connection between intoxication, addictions, and the addictive quality of America's mass-consumerist economy and society.

16. Their current frequency of alcohol use is: weekly (6 out of 53 occasional users), 2–3 times a month (16), monthly (5), and less than monthly (16). The age of first alcohol or pot use for social users are middle school (3), high school (10), after high school but before age 21 (13), and age 21 and older (5). Two are addicted to tobacco, seven smoke cigarettes occasionally, and one used to smoke but quit. Their professed reasons for drinking and sometimes smoking pot are to be social and have fun (12), to participate in rare celebrations (8), and simply to exercise their choice (5). Reasons they cite for limiting alcohol and drugs are responsibilities they have (13), health (11), not finding it that fun or interesting (6), seeing a family member or friend abuse drugs or alcohol (3), and the problem of being underage (1).

17. The full quote: "I think, like, you know, we're at college, so it's fun, college is great, but then also like, at some point you have to figure out a job and stuff like that, so just balancing fun with not screwing up your entire life because you had too much fun."

18. Two more social substance user quotes:

> I didn't start drinking actually, well I started drinking when I was joining our fraternity, and that was just because everyone else was and I didn't want to seem like a huge [outcast]. Half the time I drank a couple sips and usually emptied it as I was walking when people weren't looking. I drink just because it is more of a social thing, and everyone else is. Not because I'm trying to fit in, I've never gotten drunk, you know."

And, "I wouldn't say I started drinking. I think that kind of implies that I am out of control. I drink just to hang out with my friends. The first time was a summer or two ago, everyone came back after their first year in college and we had like a party, that was the first time really."

19. In theory there could be a category between occasional users and partiers representing emerging adults who drink or do drugs more than occasionally but who are not really partiers. Examples would be those who have a glass of wine or a beer nearly every day with dinner but who are not into the party scene. It turns out, however, that among the 18- to 23-year-olds we interviewed, there are almost none of this more-than-occasionally-but-not-partying type. We suspect the numbers of this type will increase as these younger emerging adults age into their middle and late 20s. But there are very few at age 18–23.

20. Typical stories ran like this: "I didn't have much to do, school was not going well in certain places so then I had time off, a lot more time to get myself in trouble." And "It goes all the way back to high school where you have to learn things for yourself and do things that are anti the system, and everyone says, 'Don't smoke, don't smoke,' so [we decided] let's smoke, is what it stems from."

21. The problem, however, is that the partying itself often turns out to be boring, which is why it seems never to be fulfilling or particularly worth recounting in interviews.

22. That is, grab, punch or squeeze someone's genitals from behind in a nonsexual manner.

23. Barrett Seaman, *Binge: What Your College Student Won't Tell You—Campus Life in an Age of Disconnection and Excess* (Hoboken, NJ: Wiley, 2005); Richard Kadison and Theresa DiGeronimo, *College of the Overwhelmed: The Campus Mental Health Crisis and What to Do About It* (San Francisco: Jossey-Bass, 2004). Also see Anne Matthews, *Bright College Years: Inside the American Campus Today* (Chicago: University of Chicago Press, 1997); Rebekah Nathan, *My Freshman Year: What a Professor Learned by Becoming a Student* (New York: Penguin, 2005).

24. In addition, this view is sociologically and economically naive, insofar as partying often involves various opportunity costs, health consequences, and negative relational and sexual experiences that one cannot simply make disappear when one is ready to settle down later.

25. Emerging adults we interviewed who had moved beyond the partying phase (recovering partiers, discussed below) also said that they thought the same way at the time, but later recognized they were wrong—that they were in fact out of control.

26. More of her story is worth recounting:

> Somehow it happened where she had done it and then she was trying to convince me, in which I didn't fall for it at first, I was like, no, I'm not doing it, it's bad, it's bad. I think it took her a year to convince me. And then I didn't do anything else. And honestly, when you live here, there is just nothing to do. This may be the most boring place ever. I mean there's only so many times you can go to the mall. And you have nothing to do, so it got to a point where we were just sitting in her room on her bed, being like, what do you wanna do? I don't know, what do you wanna do? I don't know. And that's what you do it. That's why I laugh when I see these commercials that are anti drugs [that don't really understand]. When you're doing it is when it's ten o'clock at night and you really have nothing to do, nothing to do, and you're bored out of your mind, and you flip through every channel and it's all crap. That's when people do it.

27. Along similar lines:

> I feel like marijuana is just a phase that, you do it. There were some points when I was smoking every day, but it's a four-year phase and the effects just wear off or you mature, and I don't really get a kick out of it anymore. I kind of enjoyed being an idiot. But now, as I got older and older, I was like, why am I making myself more unintelligent? It takes away from the lifestyle I am trying to live, an active, healthy lifestyle. I used to smoke with a group of friends, and you know, when you smoke pot, you're an idiot. I will admit that the body high you get from marijuana, it does relax your muscles and makes you feel good and more relaxed, but what it does to my mind, it makes me lazy and it carries over from when I'm not high. I can't afford to use that time being lazy.

28. Marijuana is not as addictive as many other drugs but does have some addictive potential—though marijuana withdrawal symptoms are not necessarily any more difficult than those of nicotine. Our use of "addict" here is also somewhat

metaphorical, affirmed by many of those we labeled "addicts" who talk about marijuana as something they are addicted to. Official sources report that

> long-term marijuana abuse can lead to addiction; that is, compulsive drug seeking and abuse despite its known harmful effects upon social functioning in the context of family, school, work, and recreational activities. Long-term marijuana abusers trying to quit report irritability, sleeplessness, decreased appetite, anxiety, and drug craving, all of which make it difficult to quit. These withdrawal symptoms begin within about 1 day following abstinence, peak at 2–3 days, and subside within 1 or 2 weeks following drug cessation.

http://drugabuse.gov/infofacts/marijuana.html#anchor. See A. J. Budney, R. G. Vandrey, T. R. Hughes, J. D. Thostenson, Z. Bursac, "Comparison of Cannabis and Tobacco Withdrawal: Severity and Contribution to Relapse," *Journal of Substance Abuse Treatment* 35, no. 4(2008): 362–68. For relevant neurochemistry studies, see F. Rodríguez de Fonseca, M. R. A Carrera, M. Navarro, G. F. Koob, and F. Weiss, "Activation of Corticotropin-Releasing Factor in the Limbic System During Cannabinoid Withdrawal," *Science* 276, no. 5321 (1997): 2050–54; and M. Diana, M. Melis, A. L. Muntoni, and G. L. Gessa, "Mesolimbic Dopaminergic Decline after Cannabinoid Withdrawal," *Proceedings of the National Academy of Science* 95, no. 17 (1998):10269–73.

29. However, see A. Eftekhari, A. Turner, and M. E. Larimer, "Anger Expression, Coping, and Substance Use in Adolescent Offenders," *Addictive Behaviors* 29, no. 5 (July 2004): 1001–8; and P. J. Fite, C. R. Colder, J. E. Lochman, and K. C. Wells, "Pathways from Proactive and Reactive Aggression to Substance Use," *Psychology of Addictive Behaviors* 21, no. 3 (September 2007): 355–64.

30. Here pot is compared favorably to alcohol:

> I'm a social drinker. You'll never find me sitting at home alone having a drink by myself, unless something happened where I'm stressed. Alcohol is a really strong drug. If you don't think it is, make somebody do seven shots in an hour and see how different their personality is, how they're acting. It's just not for me. It makes bad parts of me come out sometimes, it makes me too emotional.

31. For a case study of an emerging adult we interviewed, whom we call "Raymond," who is more addicted to alcohol than drugs, see Christian Smith, with Patricia Snell, *Souls in Transition: The Religious and Spiritual Lives of Emerging Adults* (New York: Oxford University Press, 2009), 188–93.

32. The most inspiring case to us is one young woman we call "Andrea," described in Smith and Snell, *Souls in Transition*, 169–73. Another is "Joy," described in ibid., 181–86, and five years before, prior to her having recovered from her addictions, in Christian Smith with Melinda Denton, *Soul Searching: The Religious and Spiritual Lives of American Teenagers* (New York: Oxford University Press, 2005), 10–17.

33. In a discussion about traumatic experiences in life:

> My dad being an alcoholic was kind of rough because we had a little relationship problem back then. The alcoholism was hard, because he and I

had always gotten along and then all of a sudden.... You never wanna see your parents with a weakness. They're always supposed to be the stronger people, so for him to have the weakness, to be my father, the male figure, that was really confusing. Like almost switching roles to where you have to play parent now, and you have to say, "Listen, you can't be doing this, you need to get help," stuff like that. I actually had to go through his house while he was in rehab and get all the liquor bottles and throw them out, and things like that. It was pretty, he had it pretty bad, but he, he's a Vietnam veteran, so I think it just, I guess it had been building all of these years, and finally he just snapped, so. And my ex-boyfriend passing away was one of them. I was really sad about him, because I thought that we could've worked at a later time. When we were together, it was not a good time. So when I heard about his dying, I shouldn't say I expected it, because you never expect that, but he was a very crazy kind of person. He didn't have the bike while I was with him, but when I found out he had the motorcycle, I was almost kinda waiting. You never expect to get that phone call, but you almost, I kinda knew it was probably gonna happen. And unfortunately, it was a little bit worse than I thought it was gonna be, so that was hard. Those were really two really hard points.

34. For a discussion of the very common theme of having no regrets among emerging adults, see Smith and Snell, *Souls in Transition*, 41–42.
35. Taken at face value, this statement suggests a belief in an eternal dualism of good and evil, which is odd, since the religious context of all of these events is the Bible-belt South, and dualism is neither orthodox Christian theology nor characteristic of Southern fundamentalism or evangelicalism of the sort with which she seems to be associated. The statement becomes somewhat clearer below in light of her grandmother's interpretation of events, namely, that it was God, not Satan, in the back seat, and that God's message was not a metaphysical claim about an eternal dualism of good and evil but rather the confrontational existential message that her life was heading in the direction of death, evil, and Satan's domain of hell.
36. This last sentence, whose meaning is not apparent to us, we have left verbatim, since it seems to convey some of the confusion, perhaps even trauma, of the experience she recounts.
37. Whether this was truly God as Satan or a hallucination, or both, we of course have no way of knowing, although we are told that frequent use of meth increases hallucinations. Then again, people's accounts of God meeting and speaking to them include a wide variety of means and situations (see William James, *The Varieties of Religious Experience* (New York: Library of America, 2009).
38. Her baby's father was the former boyfriend who started her on meth. Although she was "clean" when she bore her daughter, because she thought she was not ready to be a responsible mother, she made what she described as a gut-wrenching but right decision—which she is very proud of—to put her daughter up for adoption, who was placed with a family seeking a baby, and with whom she enjoys open visitation rights.
39. See Smith and Snell, *Souls in Transition*.
40. "The utter servility of the masses comes out of their preference for a bovine existence; still, their view obtains consideration from the fact that many of those who are in positions of power share the tastes of Sardanapalus [an Assyrian king of

legendary sensuality]." Aristotle, *The Nicomachean Ethics* (New York: Penguin Books, 1953), 8.

41. Which make temazepam, a strong hypnotic benzodiazepine.
42. United Nations Office on Drugs and Crime, *2005 World Drug Report*, vol. 1, *Analysis* (Vienna: United Nations Office on Drugs and Crime, 2005), available at www.unodc.org/pdf/WDR_2005/volume_1_web.pdf.
43. http://www.whitehousedrugpolicy.gov/publications/factsht/drugdata/index. html; http://www.npr.org/templates/story/story.php?storyId=127937271.
44. http://oas.samhsa.gov/nsduh/2k5nsduh/2k5Results.htm; "Youth Risk Behavior Surveillance—United States, 2005," http://www.cdc.gov/mmwr/preview/mmwrhtml/ss5505a1.htm.
45. United States Department of Justice, National Drug Intelligence Center, *National Drug Threat Assessment 2010* (available at http://www.justice.gov/ndic/pubs38/38661/).
46. Advertising Age Database, "Marketer Trees 2010," *Advertising Age*, http://adage. com/marketertrees2010/?agency=42; Center on Alcohol Marketing and Youth, *Alcohol Advertising and Youth* (Washington, DC: Center on Alcohol Marketing and Youth, November 2003), http://camy.org/factsheets/index.php?FactsheetID=1.
47. Anheuser-Busch 2009 Corporate Financial Report, http://www.ab-inbev.com/pdf/Financial_Report_2009.pdf. Check strictly advertising costs with *Advertising Age*. Also see resources at http://www.marininstitute.org/anheuser-busch/index.htm/.
48. Paul J. Chung, Craig F. Garfield, Marc N. Elliott, Joshua Ostroff, Craig Ross, David H. Jernigan, Katherine D. Vestal, and Mark A. Schuster. "Association between Adolescent Viewership and Alcohol Advertising on Cable Television," *American Journal of Public Health* 100, no. 3 (2010): 555–62; Maria Luisa Alainz, "Alcohol Availability and Target Advertising in Racial/Ethnic Minority Communities," *Alcohol Health & Research World*. 22, no. 4 (1998): 286–89; Diana P. Hackbarth, Barbara Silvestri, and William Cosper, "Tobacco and Alcohol Billboards in 50 Chicago Neighborhoods: Market Segmentation to Sell Dangerous Products to the Poor," *Journal of Public Health Policy* 16, no. 2 (1995): 213–30.
49. Robert Thompson, as quoted in Kate MacArthur, "Lite of the Party: Miller Ties in with 'Animal House,'" *Advertising Age*, August 18, 2003, 6.
50. IEG, "Miller's New Sponsorship Approach: Enough Is Enough," *IEG Sponsorship Report*, October 17, 2005, available at http://www.sponsorship.com/IEGSR/2005/10/17/Miller-s-New-Sponsorship-Approach-Enough-Is-Enoug.aspx.
51. This story is told marvelously by Roland Marchand, *Advertising the American Dream: Making Way for Modernity, 1920–1940* (Berkeley: University of California Press, 1985). Also see Pamela Walker Laird, 1998, *Advertising Progress: American Business and the Rise of Consumer Marketing* (Baltimore: Johns Hopkins University Press); Jackson Lears, *Fables of Abundance: A Cultural History of Advertising in America* (New York: Basic Books, 1994); William Leach, *Land of Desire: Merchants, Power, and the Rise of a New American Culture* (New York: Vintage, 1993); T. J. Jackson Lears, "From Salvation to Self-Realization: Advertising and the Therapeutic Roots of the Consumer Culture, 1880–1930," in *The Culture of Consumption*, ed. Richard Wightman Fox and T. J. Jackson Lears (New York: Pantheon, 1983), 3–38.
52. Quoted in Richard S. Tedlow, "The Struggle for Dominance in the Automobile Market: The Early Years of Ford and General Motors," *Business and Economic History*, second series, 17 (1988): 49–62.

53. Daniel Bell, *The Cultural Contradictions of Capitalism* (New York: Basic Books, 1976), 65–70.
54. Christopher Lasch, "What's Wrong with the Right?" *Tikkun* 1 (1987): 26.
55. Lasch's critique of so-called conservatives is relentless and, we think, devastating, albeit dated:

> Conservatives sense a link between television and drugs, but they do not grasp the nature of this connection any more than they grasp the important fact about news: that it represents another form of advertising, not liberal propaganda. Propaganda in the ordinary sense of the term plays a less and less important part in a consumer society, where people greet all official pronouncements with suspicion. Mass media themselves contribute to the prevailing skepticism; one of their main effects is to undermine trust in authority, devalue heroism and charismatic leadership, and reduce everything to the same dimensions. Conservatism appeals to a pervasive and legitimate desire in contemporary society for order, continuity, responsibility, and discipline; but it contains nothing with which to satisfy these desires. It pays lip service to "traditional values," but the policies with which it is associated promise more change, more innovation, more growth, more technology, more weapons, more addictive drugs. Instead of confronting the forces in modern life that make for disorder, it proposes merely to make Americans feel good about themselves. Ostensibly rigorous and realistic, contemporary conservatism is an ideology of denial. Its slogan is the slogan of Alfred E. Neumann: "What? Me worry?" . . . Conservatives stress the importance of religion, but their religion is the familiar American blend of flag waving and personal morality. It centers on the trivial issues of swearing, neatness, gambling, sportsmanship, sexual hygiene, and school prayers. Adherents of the new religious right correctly reject the separation of politics and religion, but they bring no spiritual insights to politics. They campaign for political reforms designed to discourage homosexuality and pornography, say, but they have nothing to tell us about the connection between pornography and the larger consumerist structure of addiction maintenance. . . . Conservatives complain that television mocks "free enterprise" and presents businessmen as "greedy, malevolent, and corrupt," like J. R. Ewing [of the then-popular television show *Dallas*]. To see anti-capitalist propaganda in a program like Dallas, however, requires a suspension not merely of critical judgment but of ordinary faculties of observation. Images of luxury, romance, and excitement dominate such programs, as they dominate the advertisements that surround and engulf them. Dallas is itself an advertisement for the good life, like almost everything on television. . . . Relentless "improvement" of the product and upgrading of consumer tastes are the heart of mass merchandising, and these imperatives are built into the mass media at every level. Even the reporting of news has to be understood not as propaganda for any particular ideology, liberal or conservative, but as propaganda for commodities, for the replacement of things by commodities, use values by exchange values, and events by images. The very concept of news celebrates newness. The value of news, like

that of any other commodity, consists primarily of its novelty, only secondarily of its informational value.

Ibid., 26–27.

56. See Collin Campbell, *The Romantic Ethic and the Spirit of Modern Consumerism* (London: Blackwell, 1987), 1–96.

57. While physiological and cultural addictions are not identical, we do not use the former as simply a metaphor for the latter. Neuroscience has taught us in recent decades that there is not a hard line separating the chemical effects of alcohol and drugs on people and the neurological effects of behavioral stimuli, including experiences of shopping, consuming commodities, and so on. All neural processes interact with environmental conditions to affect brain processes. And all human interactions with the world beyond the self are processed through neurological processes. See Erik du Plessis, *The Branded Mind: What Neuroscience Really Tells Us About the Puzzle of the Brain and the Brand* (London: Kogan Page, 2011); April Benson, *I Shop Therefore I Am: Compulsive Buying and the Search for Self* (Lanham, MD: Aronson, 2000); Leon Zurawicki, *Neuromarketing: Exploring the Brain of the Consumer* (New York: Springer, 2010); April Benson, *To Buy or Not to Buy: Why We Overshop and How to Stop* (Durban, South Africa: Trumpeter, 2008); A. K. Pradeep, *The Buying Brain* (Hoboken, NJ: Wiley, 2010).

58. Eugene Halton, *The Great Brain Suck* (Chicago: University of Chicago Press, 2008).

Chapter 4

Epigraph: Wendell Berry, "The Body and the Earth," in *The Unsettling of America* (San Francisco: Sierra Club Books, 1996), 105. I might also have quoted, "There is a paradox in all this, and it is as cruel as it is obvious: as the emphasis on individual liberty has increased, the liberty and power of most individuals has declined." Wendell Berry, 2002 [1992], "Sex, Economy, Freedom, and Community," in *The Art of the Commonplace: Agrarian Essays of Wendell Berry* (Washington, DC: Shoemaker and Hoard), 163.

1. For one side, see, for instance, Jessica Valenti, *The Purity Myth: How America's Obsession with Virginity Is Hurting Young Women* (Berkeley, CA: Seal Press, 2009); Robert Muchembled, *Orgasm and the West: A History of Pleasure from the 16th Century to the Present* (Cambridge, UK: Polity, 2008); Judith Levine, *Harmful to Minors: The Perils of Protecting Children from Sex* (Cambridge, MA: De Capo, 2003); Dagmar Herzog, *Sex in Crisis: The New Sexual Revolution and The Future of American Politics* (New York: Basic Books, 2008). For the other side, see, for example, Sharna Olfman, ed., *The Sexualization of Childhood* (Santa Barbara, CA: Praeger, 2008); M. Gigi Durham, *The Lolita Effect: The Media Sexualization of Young Girls and What We Can Do about It* (New York: Overlook, 2008); Diane Levin and Jean Kilbourne, *So Sexy So Soon: The New Sexualization of Childhood and What Parents Can Do to Protect Their Kids* (New York: Ballentine, 2008); Patrice Opplinger, *Girls Gone Skank: The Sexualization of Girls in American Culture* (Jefferson, NC: McFarland, 2008); Carmine Sarracino and Kevin Scott, *The Porning of America: The Rise of Porn Culture, What It Means, and Where We Go from Here* (Boston: Beacon, 2008); Robert Jensen, *Getting Off: Pornography and the End of Masculinity* (Cambridge, MA: South End, 2007). More nuanced accounts include Deborah Tolman, *Dilemmas of Desire: Teenage Girls Talk about Sexuality* (Cambridge, MA: Harvard University Press, 2005); Laura Carpenter, *Virginity*

Lost: An Intimate Portrait of First Sexual Experiences (New York: New York University Press, 2005).

2. Note up front that the study did not examine same-sex relationships, though discussion of them might have come up in interviews.

3. Paula Kamen, *Her Way: Young Women Remake the Sexual Revolution* (New York: New York University Press, 2000); Amber Madison, *Hooking Up: A Girl's All-Out Guide to Sex and Sexuality* (Amherst, NY: Prometheus Books, 2006); Howard Schiffer, *How to Be the Best Lover: A Guide for Teenage Boys* (Santa Barbara, CA: Heartful Loving, 2004); Jessica Rozler, Andrea Lavinthal, and Cindy Luu, *The Hookup Handbook: A Single Girl's Guide to Living It Up* (New York: Simon Spotlight Entertainment, 2005); Alexa Sherman and Nicole Tocantins, *The Happy Hook Up: A Single Girl's Guide to Casual Sex* (New York: Ten Speed, 2004); Sharon Thomson, *Going All the Way: Teenage Girls' Tales of Sex, Romance, and Pregnancy* (New York: Hill & Wang, 1996); Heather Corrina, *S.E.X.: The All-You-Need-to-Know Progressive Sexuality Guide to Get You Through High School and College* (Cambridge, MA: De Capo, 2007); Lauryne Wright, *On a Revolution: My Estrus Escapades in the Sexual '70s* (Bloomington, IN: iUniverse, 2006); Sharon Thompson, "Putting a Big Thing into a Little Hole: Teenage Girls' Accounts of Sexual Initiation," *Journal of Sex Research* 27 (1990): 341–61; Barbara Risman and Pepper Schwartz, "After the Sexual Revolution: Gender Politics in Teen Dating," *Contexts* 1, no. 1 (2002): 16–24. Also see Elizabeth Armstrong, Laura Hamilton, and Paula England, "Is Hooking Up Bad for Young Women?" *Contexts* 9, no. 3 (2010): 22–27.

4. See Kathleen Bogle, *Hooking Up: Sex, Dating, and Relationships on Campus* (New York: New York University Press, 2008); Donna Freitas, *Sex and the Soul: Juggling Sexuality, Spirituality, Romance, and Religion on America's College Campuses* (New York: Oxford University Press, 2008); Norval Glen and Elizabeth Marquardt, *Hooking Up, Hanging Out, and Hoping for Mr. Right: College Women on Dating and Mating Today* (New York: Institute for American Values, 2001); Laura Sessions Stepp, *Unhooked: How Young Women Pursue Sex, Delay Love, and Lose at Both* (New York: Riverhead Books, 2007); Michael Kimmel, *Guyland: The Perilous World Where Boys Become Men* (New York: HarperCollins, 2008), 169–241; Kylie Harrell, "Recreational Hookups, or Emotional Hang-Ups? *Herald-Sun* (Durham, NC), August 17, 2008, F1-F3; also see *Unprotected: A Campus Psychiatrist Reveals How Political Correctness in Her Profession Endangers Every Student* (New York: Sentinel, 2006).

5. Couples that cohabit before marrying are more, not less, likely to end up divorced. See Elizabeth Thompson and Ugo Collela, "Cohabitation and Marital Stability: Quality or Commitment?" *Journal of Marriage and the Family* 54 (1992): 259–68; Lee Lillard, Michael Brien, and Linda Waite, "Pre-marital Cohabitation and Subsequent Marital Dissolution: Is It Self-Selection?" *Demography* 32 (1995): 437–58; in addition, cohabiting relationships are more likely than marital ones to involve higher levels of violent conflicts, general unhappiness, sexual unhappiness, sexual infidelity, and wealth accumulation—see Linda Waite and Maggie Gallagher, *The Case for Marriage: Why Married People are Happier, Healthier, and Better Off Financially* (New York: Broadway Books, 2000).

6. Such as anxiety, guilt, or self-esteem issues related to earlier sexual experiences, continued real or imaginary bonds or contacts with former sexual partners that unhelpfully intrude into or otherwise affect commitments to subsequent relationships, and possibly sexually transmitted infections.

7. Jessica Valenti, *He's a Stud, She's a Slut, and 49 Other Double Standards Every Woman Should Know* (Berkeley, CA: Seal, 2008).

8. To be sure, the survey did not ask specifically what these emerging adults had regrets about; in some cases, they could be regrets not that they had sex or that they had it with certain people, but that they did not have sex when they had the chance to do so.

9. Sonya B. Gamble, Lilo Strauss, Wilda Parker, Douglas Cook, Suzanne Zane, and Saeed Hamdan, *Abortion Surveillance—United States, 2005* (Washington, DC: National Center for Chronic Disease Prevention and Health Promotion Division of Reproductive Health, 2005), table 4; http://www.cdc.gov/mmwr/preview/ mmwrhtml/ss5713a1.htm#tab4.

10. H. Weinstock, S. Berman, and W. Cates, Jr., 2004, "Sexually Transmitted Diseases among American Youth: Incidence and Prevalence Estimates," *Perspectives on Sexual and Reproductive Health* 36 (2000): 6–10; American Social Health Association, *Sexually Transmitted Diseases in America: How Many Cases and at What Cost?* (Research Triangle Park, NC: American Social Health Association, 1998); http://www.cdc.gov/std/stats07/trends.htm; http://www.cdc.gov/nchhstp/ newsroom/. Also see Jill Grimes, *Seductive Delusions: How Everyday People Catch STDs* (Baltimore: Johns Hopkins University Press, 2008).

11. Bonnie Fisher, Francis Cullen, and Michael Turner, *The Sexual Victimization of College Women* (Washington, DC: U.S. Department of Justice, National Institute of Justice, Bureau of Justice Statistics, December 2000, Publication No. 182369); Lawrence Greenfield, *Sex Offenses and Offenders: An Analysis of Data on Rape and Sexual Assault* (Washington, DC: U.S. Department of Justice, National Institute of Justice, Bureau of Justice Statistics, 1997); Brian P. Marx, Cindy Nichols-Anderson, Terri Messman-Moore, Robert Miranda, Jr., and Chebon Porter, "Alcohol Consumption Outcomes Expectancies and Victimization Status among Female College Students," *Journal of Applied Psychology* 30, no. 5 (2000): 1056–70; K. Basile, J. Chen, M. Lynberg, and L. Saltzman, "Prevalence and Characteristics of Sexual Violence Victimization," *Violence and Victims* 22, no. 4 (2007): 437–48; Patricia Tjaden and Nancy Thoennes, *Extent, Nature, and Consequences of Rape Victimization: Findings from the National Violence against Women Survey* (Washington, DC: National Institute of Justice, 2006). These studies show that women who were raped as adolescents (between ages 12 and 17) tended to be raped by intimate partners and acquaintances; those raped as adults (after their 18th birthday) tended to be raped by intimate partners. Twenty-two percent of women ages 18–29 were raped in their lifetime at the time of the survey.

12. Two other cases reported to us that were not date rape are these:

> I was a victim of attempted rape by someone really close to my family, a really old man, and my family didn't help at all. I was told not to talk about it, literally told to not bring it up: "You are not going to talk about it." To hide it. But you can't hide something like that, and it really hurts. That went on for three or four years. [. . .] I finally went to counseling, which gave me strength to talk to my family about it, because they were still around this person, and it was awful. I mean, then they had to believe me. And then I actually saw him. It was so bad, I mean it was really bad. I actually saw him last fall, he was at one of my parents' parties, and my family for the first time actually took care of me and told him to leave me alone.

And:

> I believe in the death penalty, though I'm not a violent person, but one of my really good friends, when I was in ninth grade, she was a victim of rape. Just completely random, I mean still, a junior in high school. And her total view of men is now so warped. No one should ever have done that to her, and that kind of thing. He was out for good behavior in three to five years. I had a huge problem with that, 'cause it's a proven statistic that eight in ten [rapists] rape again. He's already ruined who knows how many lives. Hers for sure. She's gonna be in pain forever because of that.

13. This young woman was working at the time of our interview at the same summer camp as the boyfriend who had dumped her. "It's still difficult, to see him around and get used to not having him there," she confessed. "We were really good friends before so it's like there's this big hole."

    We asked her, as a pretty conservative religious believer, how much similar physical involvements and sex go on in her strict denominational college. "A lot of stuff happens, despite," she says. "Most people in my circle of friends would feel guilty about it, hoping they could change, but it feels like they would be judged for it if they talked about it. So mostly it's just under the surface and nobody talks about it. People are ashamed. How much sex people actually have, I don't know, because people don't talk about it."

14. Statistical analysis of NSYR data shows that among unmarried emerging adults age 18–23, those who have never had sex are statistically significantly happier with their lives—not less happy—than those who have had sex, although the difference is not substantively large (the difference between the mean life satisfaction scale score of the virgins and those who have had sex but not recently is 26 percent of one standard deviation).

15. Mireya Navarro, "The Very Long Legs of 'Girls Gone Wild,'" *New York Times*, April 4, 2004, section 9, 1; Vickie Mayer, "Soft-Core in TV Time: The Political Economy of a 'Cultural Trend,'" *Critical Studies in Media Communication* 22, no. 4 (2005): 302–20; V. E. Jones, "Thong and Dance Skin is in as a Promotional Tool for Female Pop Stars, but it's Unclear if this Approach will Ultimately be Liberating or Limiting," *Boston Globe*, August 26, 2003, E1; Karen Pitcher, "The Staging of Agency in *Girls Gone Wild*," *Critical Studies in Media Communication* 23, no. 3 (2006): 200–218; Ariel Levy, *Female Chauvinist Pigs: Women and the Rise of Raunch Culture* (New York: Free Press, 2005).

16. Milton Diamond, "Pornography, Public Acceptance, and Sex Related Crime: A Review," *International Journal of Law and Psychiatry* 32 (2009): 304–14 (see specifically section 2, "Availability and Consumer Interest," which starts on p. 305).

17. It is in response to such experiences that more recent movements toward personal modesty and sexual chastity have arisen. See, for example, Dawn Eden, *The Thrill of the Chaste: Finding Fulfillment While Keeping Your Clothes On* (Nashville, TN: Nelson, 2006); Wendy Shalit, *The Good Girl Revolution: Young Rebels with Self-Esteem and High Standards* (New York: Ballantine, 2008); Shalit, *A Return to Modesty: Discovering the Lost Virtue* (New York: Touchstone, 2000); Laura Sessions Stepp, *Unhooked: How Young Women Pursue Sex, Delay Love, and Lose at Both* (New York: Riverhead Books, 2007); Lauren Winner, *Real Sex: The Naked Truth*

about Chastity (Grand Rapids, MI: Brazos, 2006). Also see Myron Magnet, ed., *Modern Sex: Liberation and Its Discontents* (Chicago: Dee, 2001).

18. We realize that many liberals and progressives will think our story here is too bleak, suggesting that the problem is not with sex per se but with other problems and baggage that people bring to their romantic and sex lives. Alex is a good example of that. We understand. But we find the argument tenuous. It may be technically true, but it is also largely irrelevant. Of course other people's problems can cause major troubles when it comes to their sexual involvements. But the fact is, many people *do and will* have other problems. And sexual relationships are a major arena in which those problems can and often do wreak particular havoc, in ways that many people often cannot anticipate or control. That is why we think romance and sex, as powerful as they are, need to be engaged in wisely to limit such troubles. The idea that it is the *other* problems emerging adults bring to sex and nothing about sex itself that is the real trouble sounds suspiciously like the conservative "argument" against gun control, that guns don't kill people; people do. The correct liberal response to that, of course, is: Actually, *people* kill people *with guns*, and, in most situations in which people are killed by guns, would *not* have killed other people *had they not had guns in their hands*. Likewise, pornography may not be Alex's ultimate problem, but its easy availability makes his problem worse than it has to be. Perhaps there is nothing to be done about that. But at the very least we ought to honestly face the fact that the current sexual regime in emerging adult culture has a darker side that involves much confusion, pain, and regret. Then again, perhaps there is something to be done.

Chapter 5

Epigraph: Wendell Berry, *The Unsettling of America: Culture and Agriculture* (San Francisco: Sierra Club Books, 1977), 111.

1. For example, Damien Cave, "Generation O Gets its Hopes Up," *New York Times*, November 7, 2008, http://www.nytimes.com/2008/11/09/fashion/09boomers.html. This chapter draws upon some of the material previously published by Patricia Snell, "Emerging Adult Civic Disengagement: A Longitudinal Analysis of Moral Values in Explaining Interest in Political Involvement," *Journal of Adolescent Research* 25, no. 2 (2010): 258–87; and by Christian Smith, with Patricia Snell, *Souls in Transition: The Religious and Spiritual Lives of Young Adults* (New York: Oxford University Press, 2009). We wish to thank four Notre Dame undergraduate students who helped with the organization of quotes for this chapter: Jessica Technow, Molly Kring, Matt Fanous, and Scott Hurley.

2. C. Zukin, S. Keeter, M. Andolina, K. Jenkins, Delli Carpini, and X. Michael, *A New Engagement? Political Participation, Civic Life, and the Changing American Citizen* (New York: Oxford University Press, 2006).

3. E.g., A. W. Astin, S. A. Parrott, W. S. Korn, and L. J. Sax. *The American Freshman: 30 Year Trends, 1966–1996* (Los Angeles: Higher Education Research Institute, 1997); Robert Putnam, *Bowling Alone: The Collapse and Revival of American Community* (New York: Simon and Schuster, 2000).

4. At times we wondered—though could not know for sure—whether such expressions of mild regret about not knowing more about politics was an artifact of our having interviewed most of these same youth twice before, when we also asked about politics and civic engagement, thus making them realize by asking again in

the latest interview that they had become no more politically interested or engaged than they were before.

5. Again, however, to maintain a fair balance, we must remember that, while most respondents held very modest and sometimes no expectations about positive social or political changes that they could help to bring about, a very small minority—less than 5 percent—voiced a dissenting opinion. Some emerging adults believe that in fact they "can make a difference." They see opportunities for having an impact on society for the better and believe they are obliged to take on those challenges. They strive for economic and educational opportunity, grassroots urban renewal, racial justice, the end of human trafficking, and other causes through creative communication, community organizing, and social-movement activism. They view anything less as a selfish indifference that is morally intolerable. One, for example, stated, "I think politics is good. I think people should be involved in their own world, rather than sitting back and complaining about issues, they should become more involved in politics. They should vote. If they're dissatisfied, they should run for an office. People should involve themselves in politics."

6. See Peggy Giordano, "Relationships in Adolescence," *Annual Review of Sociology* 29 (2003): 257–81.

7. Existing research findings suggest the following factors to be important. Some explanations for civic disengagement that focus on behaviors and practices examine the relationship between political participation and factors such as family relationships, social ties, extracurricular activities, voluntary association participation, and religious service attendance. Elizabeth S. Smith, for example, finds evidence that close familial relationships early in life facilitate civic engagement for adolescents and emerging adults later on. Smith, "The Effects of Investments in the Social Capital of Youth on Political and Civic Behavior in Young Adulthood: A Longitudinal Analysis," *Political Psychology* 20, no. 3 (1999): 553–80. She also finds that having extensive social connections beyond the family early on results in greater political participation later. The importance of social network ties and social connections is also well supported in the political involvement literature more generally. See Robert M. Fishman, *Democracy's Voices: Social Ties and the Quality of Public Life in Spain* (Ithaca, NY: Cornell University Press, 2004). Many researchers believe that emerging adult civic engagement rests primarily on being asked by your friends or social connections to become involved in politics. See D. E. Campbell, "Acts of Faith: Churches and Political Engagement," *Political Behavior* 26, no. 2 (2004): 155–80. According to these researchers, the lack of emerging adult civic engagement is due to a lack of family, friendship, and social connections that support and introduce involvement in the political system. The role of social connections in political involvement also relates to perhaps one of the most well-studied explanations for civic engagement: participation in voluntary associations. This explanation shares a history of thought traced back to Tocqueville, who argued that participation in voluntary associations was crucial for a healthy democracy; see Alexis de Tocqueville, *Democracy in America*, ed. I. Kramnick (New York: Penguin, 2003). The best-known modern continuation of this line of thinking is the argument that organizational involvement leads to increased political participation; see Sidney Verba, K. Schlozman, and H. Brady, *Voice and Equality: Civic Voluntarism in American Politics* (Cambridge, MA: Harvard University Press, 1995); Robert Putnam, R. Leonardi, and R. Nanetti,

Making Democracy Work: Civic Traditions in Modern Italy (Princeton, NJ: Princeton University Press, 1993); M. Hanks, "Youth, Voluntary Associations and Political Socialization," *Social Forces* 60 (1981): 211–23. An extension of voluntary association–involvement explanations are studies that find community service in particular is important in enhancing civic engagement because helping those in need leads to a more general concern for social issues, leading to political participation; see E. Metz, J. McLellan, and J. Youniss, "Types of Voluntary Service and Adolescents' Civic Development," *Journal of Adolescent Research* 18, no. 2 (2003): 188–203. Integrally connected to behavior-and-practices explanations are civic-engagement studies that consider the connection between political involvement and religious-service attendance. Similar to voluntary-association literature, these studies explore religious-service attendance as an organizational behavior causing a greater willingness to become involved more generally, including in political activities. Religious participation leads to political participation, similarly to the way other forms of voluntary association participation are found to influence civic engagement, see E. S. Smith, "The Effects of Investments in the Social Capital of Youth on Political and Civic Behavior in Young Adulthood: A Longitudinal Analysis," *Political Psychology* 20, no. 3 (1999): 553–80. Researchers generally say that religious-service attendance is on a slow decline among young and emerging adults (Smith and Snell, *Souls in Transition*; W. M. Rahn and J. E. Transue, "Social Trust and Value Change: The Decline of Social Capital in American Youth, 1976–1995," *Political Psychology* 19, no. 3 (1998): 545–65). Another related behavior-and-practices explanation for civic engagement, specifically tailored to the activities of adolescents, is participation in extracurricular activities, which, outside of the regular school day in early adolescence, predicts later political involvement; see E. S. Smith, "Effects of Investments." Extracurricular activity participation increases prosocial activities such as volunteering and voting; see J. F. Zaff, K. A. Moore, A. R. Papillo, and S. Williams, "Implications of Extracurricular Activity Participation during Adolescence on Positive Outcomes," *Journal of Adolescent Research* 18, no. 6, (2003): 599–630. Research finds a connection between extracurricular activities early in life and adult voluntary and political participation; see Verba et al., *Voice and Equality*; D. A. McFarland and J. T. Reuben, "Bowling Young: How Youth Voluntary Associations Influence Adult Political Participation," *American Sociological Review* 71, no. 3 (2006): 401–25. The basic conclusion then is that youth who are less likely to participate in extracurricular activities are also less likely to be civically engaged; see K. A. Rasinski, S. J. Ingels, D. A. Rock, J. M. Pollack, and S. Wu, *America's High School Sophomores: A Ten Year Comparison* (Washington, DC: Government Printing Office, 1993). Though it is less frequently studied, some social scientists also research the role of beliefs and convictions in forming interest in civic participation. This area is less explored within the civic-engagement literature, perhaps due to the difficulties in knowing whether or not beliefs and convictions can be accepted as accurate information; see W. A. Gamson, *Talking Politics* (New York: Cambridge University Press, 1992). Social scientists who study beliefs and convictions find that a central set of them tend to relate to civic participation. Trust and hope versus distrust and pessimism, materialism versus idealism, individualism versus collectivism, and moral commitments have been identified as important elements in understanding political participation. Youth who believe they can trust in others and society also tend to be those who volunteer and participate in political activities; see D. C.

Kelly, "In Preparation for Adulthood: Exploring Civic Participation and Social Trust among Young Minorities," *Youth and Society* 40 (2009): 526–40. Interpersonal trust, individualized attributions of responsibility, and a belief in the value of religion also predict civic engagement; see D. S. Crystal and M. DeBell, "Sources of Civic Orientation among American Youth: Trust, Religious Valuation, and Attributions of Responsibility," *Political Psychology* 23, no. 1 (2002): 113–32. An interest in political activity clearly relies to some extent on a belief both that others within society can be trusted and that positive change can result from civic engagement. Thus, trust and hope are an important element influencing political interest. Nevertheless, a high school student survey from 1976 to 1995 indicated not that trust was declining so much as materialism was increasing (Rahn and Transue, "Social Trust and Value Change"). Emerging adults tend to have high hopes for themselves and their own futures while remaining highly pessimistic about the broader social world; see J. J. Arnett, "High Hopes in a Grim World: Emerging Adults' Views of Their Futures and 'Generation X'," *Youth and Society* 31, no. 3 (2000): 267–86. Bellah and colleagues, for example, followed a Tocquevillian line of thought in exploring the extent to which Americans express interest in participating in collective activities, finding that the majority of Americans have a highly individualized focus, which is seen to be a result of the intense focus on materialism. The nature of focusing on material goods causes people to first seek wealth and then express their identities via their material purchases. This inherently draws people toward focusing on themselves rather than being interested in joining with others to work together on ideals that by nature of being beyond themselves are more abstract and not as materialist-specified; see Robert N. Bellah, Richard Madsen, William M. Sullivan, Ann Swidler, and Steven M. Tipton, *Habits of the Heart: Individualism and Commitment in American Life* (Berkeley: University of California Press, 1985). Morality has also become more inwardly focused over time; see G. Bovasso, J. Jacobs, and S. Rettig, "Changes in Moral Values Over Three Decades, 1958–1988," *Youth and Society* 22, no. 4 (1991): 468–81; and this individualistic focus is more intense among young adults; see L. Jensen, "Habits of the Heart Revisited: Autonomy, Community, and Divinity in Adults' Moral Language," *Qualitative Sociology* 18, no. 1 (1995): 71–86. Moral conviction is defined as believing that something can be right or wrong, moral or immoral; see L. J. Skitka and E. Mullen, "Understanding Judgments of Fairness in a Real-World Political Context: A Test of the Value Protection Model of Justice Reasoning," *Personality and Social Psychology Bulletin* 28 (2002): 1419–29. Moral convictions are often what people cite as their reason for becoming politically involved. In fact, moral convictions are cited more frequently than self-interested motives as the reason they believed they needed to act politically; see N. Teske, "Beyond Altruism: Identity-Construction as Moral Motive in Political Explanation," *Political Psychology* 18, no. 1 (1997): 71–91. Moral motivation results in differences in political involvement; see Peter Muhlberger, "Moral Reasoning Effects on Political Participation," *Political Psychology* 21, no. 4 (2000): 667–95, and voting behavior is linked to moral convictions (Skitka and Bauman, "Moral Conviction And Political Engagement"). Moral convictions were found to be linked to a belief in respect for humanity which led people to participate in community-oriented behaviors; see J. Youniss and M. Yates, "Youth Service and Moral-Civic Identity: A Case for Everyday Morality," *Educational Psychology Review* 11, no. 4 (1999): 361–76. Moral reasoning and an understanding of the political domain are capabilities that are held in tandem; see E. Lonky, J. M. Reihman, and R. C. Serlin, "Political Values and Moral Judgment in Adolescence," *Youth and Society* 12 (1981): 423–41. Both stem from principled thinking skills in which people are able to discern what they believe on a particular topic and make a choice between options. The materialism that is closely linked to this individualism is also said to fundamentally alter all spheres of social life in America, including political interests; see C. Derber, *The Wilding of America: How Greed and Violence Are Eroding Our Nation's Character* (New York: St. Martin's, 1996). Increased television watching is often thought to be at the root of the increased materialism that undermines civic engagement (Putnam, *Bowling Alone*). At the very least, youth who spend a great deal of time watching television simply do not have as much time to be engaged meaningfully with other people and therefore do not have as much practice in interacting collectively as previous generations did. A highly individualized religion has also been found among emerging adults; see J. J. Arnett and L. A. Jensen, "A Congregation of One: Individualized Religious Beliefs among Emerging Adults," *Journal of Adolescent Research* 17, no. 5 (2002): 451–67. Therefore, even this seemingly collective-behavior-oriented practice of previous generations is altered to more personalized belief systems.

8. Tim Clydesdale, *The First Year Out: Understanding American Teens after High School* (Chicago: University of Chicago Press, 2007).

9. John Pryor, Sylvia Hurtado, Victor Saenz, Jose Santos, and William Korn, *The American Freshman: Forty Year Trends* (Los Angeles: Higher Education Research Institute, 2007).

10. Two more examples of emerging adults discussing their hoped-for lifestyles, as reminders: "I would like to own a lot of things. I would like to have houses all over, in multiple countries, and be well enough off to be able to do that"; and

> I'd like to have a house. I'd like to have, I'd like to be able to go on trips. I'd like to have enough money so that I can be generous and donate money and also be well enough off, I guess say wealthy, so that I can be able to travel and do things that I want to do, and involve my family. But also have a car that I like, or something like that. I guess some material objects.

11. Individualist materialism is statistically significantly related to political involvement. We divided emerging adults' responses to our consumerism questions into three categories: materialist, nonmaterialist, and anticonsumerist. Materialist responses were those in which the emerging adults stated that they saw no problem with consumerism, thought it was a good thing, and participated in mass consumption themselves; nonmaterialism responses were from emerging adults who stated that they themselves were not interested in focusing on consumption and thought that it was not a good decision for them to be heavily involved in materialism, though it is fine for others to do that if they choose; and antimaterialism denotes responses from the few emerging adults who think that consumerism is a problem in general and whose existence can have deleterious effects on people and society—they are emerging adults who explicitly stated that they themselves did not wish to participate in mass consumerism and also think there should be limits on the extent to which others can participate. Comparing these categories to the political types described above (genuinely

political, marginally political, disempowered, distrustful, uninformed, and apathetic) reveals a clear relationship: 80 percent of the anticonsumerists are political or semipolitical, and 66 percent of the nonmaterialists fall into one of the two politically involved categories. None of those in the disempowered or apathetic political categories fell within the anticonsumerist grouping. The disempowered were more likely than the other three forms of political disengagement run to be nonmaterialists, indicating that these emerging adults tend to see, understand, and care about political problems but do not believe they have enough efficacy to create change in the broader society. Only 14 percent of materialists fall into one of the two political categories, with only 1 percent falling into the fully political grouping. Ninety percent of those who are apathetic are materialist, and 86 percent of uninformed, 84 percent of distrustful, and 71 percent of disempowered are also materialist. This is in stark contrast to the fact that only 32 percent of semipolitical and 20 percent of political fall into the materialist grouping. Thus, having a materialistic attitude is significantly associated with political noninvolvement.

12. Again, to maintain balance, a few said that helping others was what God taught in the Bible—"Love your neighbor." More evoked the idea that sociologists call "generalized reciprocity"—that everyone benefits in a world in which each person helps specific others in need even when he or she will not be repaid directly by them, because somebody else will someday help that person when he or she is in need, so that in the end everybody gets help from somebody. Well, these kinds of emerging adults asked, if a person doesn't help other people, what are they going to do when they need help? But, to be clear, these views were a definite minority.

13. For example, Bellah et al., *Habits of the Heart*; Putnam, *Bowling Alone*; Richard Sennett, *The Fall of Public Man* (New York: Knopf, 1977).

14. We are indebted to Terri Clark, NSYR's project manager, who conducted numerous third-wave personal interviews, for her insight and some of the language used here to describe this theme of absorption into interpersonal relationships through communications gadgets at the expense of participation in public life. Also see Eugene Halton, *The Great Brain Suck* (Chicago: University of Chicago Press, 2008); David Mindich, *Tuned Out: Why Americans under 40 Don't Follow the News* (New York: Oxford University Press, 2005); Mark Bauerlein, *The Dumbest Generation: How the Digital Age Stupefies Young Americans and Jeopardizes Our Future* (New York: Tarcher, 2008). As this relates to religion, see two popular accounts: Christian Piatt and Amy Piatt, *MySpace to Sacred Space: God for a New Generation* (St. Louis, MO: Chalice, 2007); Mike Hayes, *Googling God: The Religious Landscape of People in Their Twenties and Thirties* (New York: Paulist Press, 2007).

Conclusion

Epigraph: Christopher Lasch, "Give Youth Cause to Believe in Tomorrow," *International Herald Tribune*, December 29, 1989, 7. We might just as well have quoted Blaise Pascal: "We run carelessly over the precipice after having put something in front of us to prevent us seeing it." Pascal, *Pensées and other Writings* (New York: Oxford University Press, 2008), 59.

1. Christian Smith, with Patricia Snell, *Souls in Transition: The Religious and Spiritual Lives of Emerging Adults* (New York: Oxford University Press, 2009).

2. Jeffrey Arnett, *Emerging Adulthood: The Winding Road from the Late Teens through the Twenties* (New York: Oxford University Press, 2004); Jeffrey Arnett and

Jennifer Tanner, eds., *Emerging Adults in America: Coming of Age in the 21st Century* (Washington, DC: American Psychological Association, 2005); Jeffrey Arnett, *Adolescence and Emerging Adulthood: A Cultural Approach* (Upper Saddle River, NJ: Prentice Hall, 2009); Smith and Snell, *Souls in Transition*. Also see Jean Twenge, *Generation Me: Why Today's Young Americans Are More Confident, Assertive, Entitled—and More Miserable Than Ever Before* (New York: Free Press, 2006).

3. Again, we refer readers here to the sociologist C. Wright Mills, particularly his 1959 book *The Sociological Imagination* (New York: Oxford University Press).

4. *Unprotected: A Campus Psychiatrist Reveals How Political Correctness in Her Profession Endangers Every Student* (New York: Sentinel, 2006); Richard Kadison and Theresa DiGeronimo, *College of the Overwhelmed: The Campus Mental Health Crisis and What to Do About It* (San Francisco: Jossey-Bass, 2004).

5. To be clear, we are not suggesting that manufacturers of birth-control technologies intend to promote problematic emerging adult sexual behaviors, or that birth control cannot be used for good, but rather that such outcomes are among the unintended consequences of those firms' activities and are real in their consequences despite being unintended.

6. Christian Smith, with Melinda Denton, *Soul Searching: The Religious and Spiritual Lives of American Teenagers* (New York: Oxford University Press, 2005).

7. Robert N. Bellah, Richard Madsen, William M. Sullivan, Ann Swidler, and Steven M. Tipton, *Habits of the Heart: Individualism and Commitment in American Life* (Berkeley: University of California Press, 1985).

8. By "political liberalism" here we do not mean the specific ideology of the U.S. Democratic Party in the twentieth and early twenty-first centuries but rather the broadly individualistic political and social philosophy descended from thinkers like John Locke, John Stuart Mill, and Thomas Hill Green, down to Milton Friedman and John Rawls, emphasizing individual autonomy, egalitarianism, personal liberty and self-determination, private property, free markets, multiparty democracy, civil liberties, toleration, contracts, universal enfranchisement, minimizing of coercion and external constraints in life, consent, and rule of law—which can then either take the form of "classical liberalism" ("conservatism" in U.S. politics) or "social liberalism" ("liberalism" in U.S. politics).

9. Here we follow Charles Taylor's discussion of "horizons" in his 1989 book *Sources of the Self* (Cambridge, MA: Harvard University Press), 17–19, 27–29.

10. If we were Old Testament prophets, we might say that all nations reap what they sow, that what we have seen of emerging adult life warns us that America is reaping the fruit of having worshipped the idol of individualistic autonomy, and that since this idol is nothing more than the making of our human hands, and not the true God, it has failed us, is failing us, and will fail us as long as we worship it (prophetic sentences, of course, have to be very long). But we are not religious prophets. We are mere sociologists. So we claim no such thing.

11. The Godfathers, "Birth, School, Work, Death," Epic 34-07725. Full lyrics available online, including at http://www.songlyrics.com/the-godfathers/birth-school-work-death-lyrics/. Not, of course, that birth, school, work, and even a death are themselves bad—the question here has rather to do with the larger contours of cultural horizons.

12. Lasch, "Give Youth Cause."

INDEX